SAMI

MAINSTREAM / SPORT

SAMI HYYPIÄ

FROM VOIKKAA TO THE PREMIERSHIP

SAMI HYYPIÄ WITH OLLO HAKALA

MAINSTREAM
PUBLISHING

EDINBURGH AND LONDON

First published by Tommi Publishers, 2002

Translated from the Finnish language by Mika Elovaara

First published in Great Britain in 2002 by
MAINSTREAM PUBLISHING (EDINBURGH) LTD
7 Albany Street
Edinburgh EH1 3UG

ISBN 1 84018 768 9

This edition, 2003

A catalogue record for this book is available from the British Library

Typeset in Apollo and Avant Garde

Printed in Great Britain by
Cox & Wyman Ltd

Contents

Acknowledgements

THE IDEA FOR SAMI HYYPIÄ'S BIOGRAPHY ORIGINATED IN SPRING 2001 when Ilpo Laurila, Sami's good friend from years back, said to me: 'Sami is worth a book.' What could I say to that? By the twenty-first century, Sami had become the brightest star of Finnish football, and I knew him well enough for writing his biography to feel like a tremendous challenge. Ilpo Laurila's support has been crucial for this book from its inception.

During the spring, we talked about the book on occasion, but Sami's final approval for the project in the summer gave us the green light we had been waiting for. Then I started extensive background work with which I was helped by numerous people. The open-minded attitude of Sami's parents, Irma and Jouko Hyypiä, towards this project was particularly important, and I am truly grateful for the pleasant conversation we had as well as you offering your home archives for my use. Thank you both so much.

This book has been created out of love for football, which is a team sport. As an old full-back myself, I needed the help of a striker, and without the irreplaceable Timo Walden, PR officer of the Finnish national team and walking encyclopedia of football, I wouldn't have finished this book. It seems that Timo knows every Finn working in football – and a good number of foreigners involved with the game, too. Thank you, Timo.

When we started to think about the photography for the book, there was only one option. Juha Tamminen's football pictures are simply the best there are, and his archives have an increasing amount of pictures of Sami, whose copyrights we acquired with much ease. However, choosing the photographs was difficult because there were no poor shots. Thank you, Juha, and I hope you like our selection.

Many people have offered their help for this book in the form of interviews, background information and valuable comments. You all know who you are, and I am truly grateful for your help.

In conclusion, I would like to thank Sami himself. From the beginning, the intention was that Sami's own voice should be heard throughout these pages. This is a story about Sami Hyypiä, not an official historical review or chronicle. Sami never tired of telling me about his past and answering my endless questions – sometimes he even pushed me to work. Finally, I got to hear a surprising confession. Sami told me he is even bigger than people generally think, and he is actually a respectable 196 cm tall, three centimetres more than the 'official' records state.

Not all Sami's stories made it between these covers – but 'whereof man cannot speak thereof man must be silent'. Sami, you made a difficult job easy for me – thank you for that. You truly are worth a book.

Olli Hakala

1

The Dream Comes True

IN MAY 1999 THE FINNISH FOOTBALL WORLD HEARD SOME NEWS, THE significance of which could be immediately understood only by a few. Sami Hyypiä, the reliable centre-back of the Finnish national team, and the Dutch Premier League side Willem II had signed a four-year contract with Liverpool FC in the English Premiership. While the transfer was of major interest internationally, in Finland the transfer of a Finnish player to one of the most legendary teams in English football was stunning.

For decades, the English League has been the most important football league in the world to Finnish football fans. The traditional Saturday-evening matches on TV have brought English football live into the living-rooms of Finland since the 1970s. And because of the national betting system structured around English Football League matches, Finnish football enthusiasts had become as familiar with the English teams and players as they were with their local clubs and footballers. Being the most successful team in England with 18 championship victories and having been particularly triumphant in the 1970s and 1980s, Liverpool FC have secured a place in many Finnish football fans' hearts along with a passion for English football. Now, with the signing of Sami Hyypiä, the Finnish fans of English football were about to see legends like Kevin Keegan, Kenny Dalglish, Alan Hansen, Ian Rush, John Barnes, Steve McManaman, Michael Owen and many others joined by one of our own.

Sami Hyypiä was by no means the first Finnish player to play at the highest level of English football. In the 1980s, Aki Lahtinen (Notts County) and Pertti Jantunen (Bristol City) played in the former First Division. In the 1990s, Mika-Matti (Mixu) Paatelainen played for the Bolton Wanderers team who were promoted to the Premiership in the mid-

9

SAMI HYYPIÄ

1990s. Mixu's visit to the Premiership with Bolton was short-lived, after which the Finnish football fans had to wait a few more years until the next Finnish player signed with a Premiership club. Then, in 1998, Chelsea FC signed Mikael Forssell, the young talent from HJK Helsinki, and one year later, Aston Villa signed Peter Enckelman, a promising goalkeeper from TPS Turku. Despite these pioneers of Finnish football, Sami Hyypiä was the first Finnish player in the Premiership who immediately became a regular first-team player in his club. Furthermore, in his first season with the Reds, Sami assumed an important role in the squad and wore the captain's armband of the legendary English club, making the Finnish Cinderella story complete.

Before Sami Hyypiä, the only Finnish player who had made it to the top level of international football was Jari Litmanen, perhaps the best Finnish football player ever. Litmanen's career at Ajax Amsterdam was filled with success – the 1995 Champions League title and third place in the vote for European Footballer of the Year in the same year being the icing on the cake.

Nevertheless, Sami Hyypiä's emergence as one of the key players in the current Liverpool FC side and team captain are major steps towards matching Litmanen's achievements. After all, Liverpool FC was ranked the world's best club team in October 2001. Although the move to Liverpool FC was a dream come true for Sami – the Reds were his favourite team as a young boy – he didn't expect any immediate glory as he entered the new club. At the time of the transfer he told the public that he was facing a once-in-a-lifetime opportunity at Liverpool and that he would first work to establish himself as a regular first-team player. Although he believed that the English style of play – hard but fair – would suit him perfectly, he also insisted that no success would come easy for him: the new job meant hard work.

LIVERPOOL FC'S RETURN TO THE TOP

Liverpool FC 1892–2002
Home stadium: Anfield Road
Nicknames: The Reds, Pool
Anthem: 'You'll Never Walk Alone'
Silverware: 18 League Championships, 6 FA Cup titles, 6 League Cup titles, 14 Charity Shield titles, 4 European Cup (current Champions League) titles, 3 UEFA Cup titles and 2 European Supercup titles

Liverpool FC is an institution with a strong fanbase around the world, including Finland. When Sami arrived at Liverpool in the summer of 1999, the club had a long, dry season behind them. Manchester United had dominated the English Premier League for the past few years while Liverpool FC had gone for a long period without a trophy. They won their last championship in the former First Division in 1990 and the FA Cup in 1992, and the last trophy the Reds won before their success in the 2000–01 campaign was the League Cup title in 1995.

Although Liverpool FC managed to win a few trophies in the 1990s, the downturn in the club's fortunes started in 1985. On the fateful evening of the 1985 European Cup final between Liverpool FC and the Italian side Juventus at the Heysel Stadium in Brussels, Belgium, all hell broke loose before the match and a riot between the English and Italian football fans resulted in a shocking death toll of 39. Blame fell to English football hooligans and, consequently, all English clubs were banned from European Cup competitions for five years. A few years after the Heysel tragedy, on 15 April 1989, Liverpool FC experienced another horrendous tragedy when 96 people were killed because too many people had been let into the Hillsborough Stadium to watch Liverpool FC and Nottingham Forest in an FA Cup semi-final match. The victims were mainly teenage fans, the youngest among them a ten-year-old boy. Understandably, the effect of these tragedies was felt at the club for years and the aura of success surrounding Liverpool was dimmed.

The quiet period at Liverpool FC lasted throughout the 1990s, leaving a mark on the lively people of this once-glorious port city. Liverpool looked like a run-down town whose honourable past was a heavy burden. As the new millennium approached, however, the worst was put behind in Liverpool and the city began to undergo a process of revitalisation, which refreshed the football team as well. Liverpool FC began their rise back to the top by hiring the Frenchman Gérard Houllier as the assistant to Roy Evans, the then manager, in 1998. In the autumn of that year, Houllier took sole responsibility for the first team when Roy Evans resigned. The systematic rebuilding process of a new championship team had started.

A weak defence was generally seen as the main reason for Liverpool FC's poor success in the 1990s. Therefore, it was no surprise when Houllier declared that rebuilding the club's defensive end would be his first and most important task as first-team manager. As we now know, Sami Hyypiä became an important part of this project. With Sami as a leader, the Reds' defence became a lot tighter during the first season of Houllier's reign, taking the side on a course towards success.

SAMI HYYPIÄ

As football is the heart of Liverpool, the new face of the team could be seen everywhere in town, and, generally, Sami has been considered one of the main architects in the new rise of Liverpool FC. Chris Bascombe, a football journalist at the *Liverpool Echo* and a reporter who follows every move of Liverpool FC carefully, does not hesitate in giving Sami his share in the Reds' recent success:

> Without a doubt, Sami is one of the best players Liverpool FC have ever signed. The Liverpool defence was terribly weak before Sami and a few other important players arrived. Throughout the 1990s, the club has had tremendous forwards like Robbie Fowler and Michael Owen, but in order to win trophies you need to have a solid defence. In that respect, I value Sami's input to Liverpool FC's recent success very highly – the Reds would probably not have come this far without him.

Sami's first year at Liverpool FC was far more successful than people in Finland had anticipated. The fact that Sami became the captain of the legendary team was more than could be reasonably expected from a newcomer. Additionally, Sami was selected Player of the Month in November and he was a candidate for Player of the Year at the end of the season – the people in Finland had been fed more than they could digest in one football season.

Winning the Player of the Month is an award that even some of the best players in the Premiership never achieve, yet this award did not gain much attention in Finland. The reason was that Finnish football fans had just recently grown used to the fact that Sami was actually playing first-team football at Liverpool FC, and when he was named the captain of the team, his selection as the Player of the Month seemed like a natural succession in Sami's blooming career.

In Sami's first season at Liverpool FC, the club finished fourth in the League, granting them a ticket to Europe in the form of entry to the UEFA Cup. At the outset of Sami's second season at Liverpool, the expectations set upon the club in general and Sami in particular had increased significantly. Many were predicting that Sami was just a shooting star who would revert back to average performance during his second year, but those sceptical predictions were far from the truth. The 2000–01 season was Liverpool FC's most successful season for a decade and, along with the club's success, Sami solidified his status among the elite defenders in the Premiership. Both Liverpool FC and Sami Hyypiä were on top.

THE UNKNOWN 'SAMMY HYPPIA'

After only two seasons in the Premiership, the respect Sami has gained in England is astounding considering that, at the beginning of his career at Liverpool FC, only a few local football experts knew him by name. When the first news of Sami's transfer to the Reds broke, the British media generally called the Finnish centre-back 'Sammy Hyppia'. Sami had avoided any shocking headlines in his home country, too, even though he had played three and a half years as a professional in Holland before his move to Liverpool. It now seems peculiar, but Sami never drew much attention while playing for the Finnish national team either, before he signed with Liverpool FC.

Finland was not short of doubtful football 'experts' when Sami signed with the Reds. People were dubious about Sami's ability to succeed in one of the toughest leagues in the world. During his years in Holland, only a few Finnish football fans had seen Sami play anywhere except in international matches. The majority of the Finnish football fans' interest was focused on skilful forwards such as Jari Litmanen and Joonas Kolkka. After all, goalscorers have always been more likely to make the headlines instead of the hardworking, persistent defenders.

Sammy Lee, a former midfielder of Liverpool FC in the club's golden years in the 1970s and '80s and current assistant coach, admits that he was among those not expecting much from Sami during his first year. Sammy Lee did not doubt Sami's abilities outright, he just wasn't totally aware of them and didn't expect him to become such a key player so soon. After coaching Sami for two years, Lee now says:

> I have to admit, honestly, that I knew very little about Sami before his arrival at Liverpool FC. However, when I first saw him play I asked myself why was it that I had never heard of him before. He is tremendously talented and he keeps on improving his game.
>
> Of course, new players and squad selections draw a lot of criticism, but that's part of the game. I think that already in his first season, Sami played more minutes than any other player at the club, and I don't think there are many doubts remaining about his quality.

Sammy Lee's opinion of 'Big Sami' as a player is flattering, but the legendary player also finds some room for improvement:

> First of all, he is very athletic and tall. He passes and heads the ball

well, and he also reads the game well and takes the role of a leader quite naturally. If I have to name one weakness in his game, perhaps it's low scoring. He doesn't score a lot of goals, but, then again, we hope for more goals from all our players, not only from Sami.

It is difficult to tell any colourful stories about Sami Hyypiä's playing career. He has never misbehaved on away trips or at training camps, and he has always focused on playing and other things essential to his career. Jyrki Heliskoski, a youth national team coach in Finland who has followed Sami's development since his teen years, explains that Sami does have a good sense of humour, but he is certainly not a joker:

> He has never been one to laugh just for the sake of laughing, and the joke must be quite a good one in order to make Sami laugh or even smile. If there is no catch in the joke or in a story, don't expect a smile just for sympathy. Sami is a really even-tempered lad.

Nevertheless, Sami is not a dull player or person, he just doesn't like to put himself forward without reason – his teammates notice him just fine anyway. Heliskoski adds: 'It's about personality and the example set by it. Sami never used to talk that much in the dressing-room, he didn't have to. But when he spoke, others would always listen. I would imagine it's about the same at Liverpool FC, too.'

Harri Kampman, Sami's coach at MyPa for four years, also talks about Sami as a peaceful and level-headed person who likes to avoid any additional attention. Perhaps this is also why people sometimes see Sami too much as a one-dimensional player. Kampman emphasises his view that Sami's abilities are not limited to defensive tasks on the field:

> First and foremost, Sami Hyypiä has his head screwed on right. He knows what he is good at and acts accordingly. At Liverpool FC, he would probably do even more if they let him. I remember when he was playing for MyPa and how he sometimes passed the ball from the back, then touched it again to our outside-half and made a sprint through the pitch to score a goal off the cross. People often forget how good he is in the offensive end.

Janne Kosunen, a Finnish football journalist who has followed the Finnish national team around the world, doesn't have any juicy stories about Sami either. He doesn't remember any incident where Sami has behaved in an unmannerly fashion after an international match, and even though he has now made a name for himself among the elite players in the world, there are no signs of arrogance in his conduct.

Sami hasn't particularly avoided publicity, but he has always wanted to keep his personal life private. There can be no question that the life of a professional football player is sometimes public, and Sami has never had any problems in playing his part in cooperating with the media. However, he has never let his private life appear in any paper, even though the tabloid press in England often hunts for any little scent of scandal in order to produce headlines of football players' wild lives. This is also why the players at Liverpool are protected from the downside of publicity in numerous ways, and all interviews, for example, have to be approved by club representatives. Knowing the media's thirst for shocking stories, you have to be careful with what you say: even a harmless joke or a slip of the tongue in the wrong place may produce sensational headlines and a few pages of scandalous writing in the tabloids. Dozens of journalists from Finland would also call Sami weekly, if they only could.

A few years back, the situation was completely different. Sami Hyypiä grew up as a footballer in peace and quiet, away from any shocking headlines and without much hype. He was never pushed forward, but he has achieved everything through his persistent nature and his immense desire to develop as a football player. The road to the top of the Premiership has required an enormous amount of work and tenacious training. The fruit of this effort is now known to the whole footballing world.

2

Voikkaa's Players of 1973

VOIKKAA, SAMI'S HOME TOWN OF A COUPLE OF THOUSAND PEOPLE, is a quarter of Kuusankoski, a town with a population of 20,000 in south-eastern Finland. Kuusankoski, a lively place famous for its paper mills, lies in the bend of the Kymijoki river, next to Kouvola, 55 km north from Kotka and 65 km south from Lahti. The road from the snowy training fields of Voikkaa to the top of the English Premier League seems impossibly long. Nevertheless, Sami has managed to make it all the way, even though his miniscule home town barely had enough young boys to form a football team.

Sami was born on 7 October 1973. Although he has lived almost all his life in Kuusankoski, his passport states Porvoo as his place of birth. Sami's parents, Jouko and Irma Hyypiä, lived in the small, historic town because of a work assignment, but returned to Voikkaa six months after Sami, their only child, was born.

For Sami's first few years, they lived in a high-rise apartment in the centre of Voikkaa, before moving to the small-house area of Mäentausta, where they still live today. Sami explains with a little grin:

> There has been some confusion over my birthplace. My passport says it's Porvoo, but I was actually born in the Helsinki Women's Clinic. So, in that sense, I'm a native of Helsinki. Yet people always think of me as a country boy, although I've never lived in the countryside, but in a very small town.

Life in Voikkaa is concentrated around the operation of the paper mill and football has been an outlet for the area. Since the 1970s, Kumu (The Din) and later in the '90s, FC Kuusankoski, were known as the powerhouses of local football, but Voikkaa had a source of pride of its own – the club called Voikkaan Pallo-Peikot (PaPe), founded in 1946. In its most successful years, PaPe's first team played in the former Finland division, i.e. the current Finnish First Division. Jouko Hyypiä, Sami's father, played for PaPe during his career, so the small-town side was a natural choice as Sami's first club as well. Adding to this the fact that Irma Hyypiä, Sami's mother, had also played football as a youngster, you could say that Sami's football genes were quite strong. Sami recalls his early encounters with his future profession: 'When I was a little kid, Mum used to take me to her matches. When she was playing, the subs looked after me on the bench.'

Even with such strong family ties to football, a career in football for a youth from Voikkaa did not seem like a matter of course. The small town did not always have enough players to form a youth team, but, fortunately for Sami, his age group was an exception. When football began to interest local boys competitively around the age of seven, the team was put together rapidly. Sami's father, Jouko, now a retired player himself, decided to coach the team.

From the very beginning, it became obvious that Sami's age group formed an exceptional team on PaPe's scale. It seemed that football was a unifying factor among all local boys born in 1973. The Voikkaa comprehensive school had two classes that particular age and, according to Jouko Hyypiä, each of the 16 boys in Sami's class participated in PaPe's training sessions at some point. The interest among the boys in the other class was slightly less passionate.

The number of players was a surprise itself, but even more surprising was the astounding quality of the players. In addition to Sami, two other talented players have made it to the top of Finnish football from that small-town team of players born in 1973: Mika Hernesniemi and Toni Huttunen. They both still play in the Finnish Premier League side MyPa, and Huttunen has also made a few appearances for the Finnish national team. Another player from PaPe's exceptional youth team who has made a reasonable career for himself in Finnish football is Janne Pahkala, who has played for KTP Kotka and FC Kuusankoski in the Finnish First Division. Considering that even the youth teams of bigger cities sometimes fail to produce players for the top level, it is truly a remarkable and fortunate coincidence that Voikkaa had a team with three future Premier League players.

Of course, chance does not turn anyone into a professional footballer, and even the best talent has to be refined and developed further by hard training, persistent work and personal commitment. When discussing his youth team, Sami also emphasises the importance of a good-spirited youth team for his own career. With the best friends playing for the same team, going to training was enjoyable. As Sami thinks back to his school years, he comments:

> It was important that I got to play in a familiar environment and with familiar lads. The enthusiasm may have weakened if I had had to travel elsewhere for training at such a young age. We all went to the same school and played all kinds of sports together. We played football in the school field during every recess, and sometimes we didn't make it to class in time. When the school bell rang, we still always played the game until the end and, of course, sometimes the game lasted a bit longer . . . the teachers never set any particular rules for stopping our play, but they always made some kind of a remark if we came to class late. We always did our homework, and I guess the teachers would have been harder on us if we didn't.
>
> In later years, too, when football took up a lot of time from school because of early training and away games, the teachers were very understanding, and they knew we would still do our schoolwork, too. Even though we sometimes missed classes, as long as we did our work, the teachers' attitude towards our careers was encouraging.

The boys' team spirit helped them both on and off the field. When they left comprehensive school, their teacher, Mr Ari Häkkinen, noted at the parents' evening before the last day of school that this age group was unique in its spirit, and that there would never be another one like it. One key element promoting this good team spirit was the victorious football team which won one championship after another in the regional tournaments for its age group. No other school had a team as unified and prepared and which was formed from players born in the same year. When Sami recalls his childhood memories, sport comes up in practically every one, but more as a shared passion than as serious competition.

For the boys in Sami's age group, playing sport was a natural and accessible way of spending their free time together. Everyone in Voikkaa lives so close to each other that everything is within a short trip away, including the school and the sports ground. Sami's home is only a few hundred metres from the school and the sporting ground, and as there is a skiing track that goes right next to the house, cross-country skiing was also a popular form of exercise for Sami as a youth.

In the winter, the children in the area populated the school sporting ground just as they did in the summer, except that in wintertime they played ice-hockey or skated just for fun. When they weren't playing any sport, Sami and his friends did the same sort of things as anyone else their age, spending their time with different games, building little huts in the forest, and so on. The beautiful, hilly landscape of the Voikkaa area provided a tremendous environment to grow up in. People lived primarily in small houses and the lifestyle was safe and easy-going.

The bend of the Kymijoki river separates Voikkaa from the rest of Kuusankoski. Voikkaa is a peaceful quarter whose inhabitants have a strong community spirit. Sometimes Voikkaa is even marked in the maps as a separate town from Kuusankoski. Sami has always been precise about his home town: in various footballing records, MyPa has often been named as his home club because the side from nearby Anjalankoski is the club where Sami played his first Finnish Premier League games, but Sami has untiringly corrected this false information whenever possible. Voikkaan Pallo-Peikot are and always will be his home club. Correspondingly, Sami Hyypiä's name will always remain visible in his home town, as the new, stately indoor football facility in Kuusankoski was named after him in the autumn of 2001.

FATHER AS A COACH

If having a talented and unified group of youth players born in the same year was a stroke of luck for PaPe and being part of the team was fortunate for Sami, having Jouko Hyypiä as the coach was also a tremendous asset for both the club and Sami. Jouko did his work with the boys with immense dedication and commitment, and he carried a large responsibility at the club as well. At the same time, he was the coach, the trainer, the kit manager, team physio and a reliable friend. Jouko coached Sami throughout his years in youth football, until he turned 16.

As for his own playing career, what troubled Jouko the most was the minimal amount of time he had spent on practising his skills. He had been an enthusiastic and active youth player, but as he reached adulthood, football had been left on the sidelines behind other interests. Interestingly, at the age of 22 he showed up at PaPe's first-team training as a result of a bet among friends and surprisingly made it to the playing squad immediately. Although he did his job on the field and actually played rather consistently, he also understood that improving his meagre skills considerably was too great a challenge for someone his age – the time for acquiring ball-handling skills had passed. Nevertheless, Jouko's talent was good enough for PaPe's first team, and he kept playing for ten years before retiring to coach Sami's youth team.

Mr Lennart Wangel, a long-time team secretary of the full Finnish squad and current event manager at the Finnish FA, who is also originally from Voikkaa, remembers Jouko Hyypiä as a quality centre-back who always stopped either the ball or the opponent, and sometimes both. At the time of Sami's birth, Wangel played a few years in the same team with 'Jokke'. The football players at Voikkaa always knew each other exceptionally well, and it was customary that the players' wives and girlfriends travelled with the team. It was always a family event when the PaPe bus took off for an away game.

As a coach, Jouko wanted to make sure that the players in his team wouldn't make the same mistakes he did: he planned his training so that there was always enough time to refine the players' passing and dribbling skills. You learn the foundation of ball control and kicking techniques at a young age, and Jouko's drills and methods seem to have found their mark with Sami and other players from his youth team. Sami obviously approved of his father's coaching methods, as he explains:

> I don't know, you can probably tell from my form that my training as a youth always focused on the technical side of the game. With my dad as the coach, the team never did much running or weight-lifting. After all, football is first about ball control – you can always develop your physical strength at a later age, too.

Under Jokke's guidance, his teams acquired the required level of strength and stamina in natural ways and without any unnecessary toil. Sami notes:

> We never did much with weights, not even when we were older. The first time I was on a team that had a regular weight training programme was at 17 when I played for Kumu's first team. Of course, almost everyone does a little something with weights as a young kid, for working out at a gym is one of those things that all young athletes do to a certain extent. However, I was never particularly keen on going to the gym, and I never felt that I should be either.
>
> I do remember how some lads were always bragging about how they could bench press 70 kg, but things like that were never that

important to me. The stories everyone was telling about the weights they could lift were wild and fun to listen to, but I never felt that I had fallen behind as far as strength goes. Even now, I probably couldn't bench press 70 kg, and yet I don't feel weaker than anyone else.

Even though Sami's youth team was powerful and had enough players for a solid team, Sami got to try his talent with older players in the early years of his career as PaPe's other youth teams were often short of players. Playing with older boys was very important for Sami's development because his own youth team were hardly challenged by the other teams in the 1973 age group. At that time, the regional championships at Kymenlaakso were played in two groups – the north and the south – and PaPe dominated the north group at will. Sami points out:

> I remember one year in particular, when our goal difference was 142–1 and we had barely played ten matches. The final scores were wild, like 18–0 or 24–0 throughout the season. We could have probably played blindfolded and still won, so dominant were we in that north group that year. It could have gotten out of hand and we could have started joking about our opponents, but we always played every match with the fullest commitment. Then, at the finals, we always matched up against the teams from Kotka – first Kotka Youth League and then KTP – who left us no chance and took the trophy home. Despite the Kotka teams' dominance, though, we did manage to win the regional championship in my youth team years a few times, and then made it a rule as we grew older.

Sami won his first regional championship in 1984, when he was playing for the Under-11 juniors, the youth team a year older than his age. Sami's own team, the Under-10 juniors, finished second after a disappointing rematch of the final. In his busiest seasons, it was no exception that Sami played for as many as three different youth teams. 'When I was still in the Under-10 juniors, PaPe's Under-14 juniors had a tournament in Denmark,' Sami remembers. 'My dad was part of the coaching staff for that team as well, so I travelled along with the team as a team mascot, but I actually ended up playing a few games in the tournament as well.'

Although it was clear that Sami was a talented youth player, he was never considered the most outstanding in his team. Janne Pahkala, who later made a name for himself as a wrestler, was the first player to make it to the regional team and his potential was valued the highest. But Sami's achievements in his early years were not insignificant either. Among others, he won the regional skills championships as an Under-11 junior in 1985 and finished fifth in the nationals, as a representative of his region. So, the ball was tightly in control for Sami already at youth level. Sami shrugs off his success at skills competitions as a delightful but not an unforgettable event: 'It was a surprise for myself, too, that I was so successful in the national skills championships. I didn't expect anything from the competition, and I don't even remember who won it, nor any other participants.'

Since Sami's youth years, his size may have fooled many into thinking that he is merely a stopper who wins a lot of headers. However, Jouko Hyypiä is quick to remind people that, as a younger lad, Sami was not particularly tall, even though he was taller than average. More than anything, young Sami was known for his good skills and intelligent football mind. As he grew taller, it was natural that Sami often found himself playing a position that requires strong heading. Even so, the skilful youth player still lives inside the two-metre centre-back.

Sami was fortunate to develop as a footballer without any particular pressure on his shoulders. For most of his youth years, football was merely one of Sami's hobbies, although an important one, of course. Sami also played ice-hockey at Kuusankosken Puhti until he was 14, but decided to call it quits when football began to require more time in the winter, too. Even then Sami didn't make any great future plans based around football, and he was content with playing football at the small-scale level of his home town.

It was no different then than it is now – the players of the small-town teams are often ignored by regional coaches, and invitations for the youth national team try-outs don't exactly come easy for the small-town boys either. National team scouts never attended youth matches in Voikkaa or Kuusankoski, even though the best teams in the region, especially in the older age groups, were consistently from either town. Unlike the talented players from Voikkaa or Kuusankoski, players from bigger cities were in the headlines already at a young age. Joonas Kolkka (currently at Panathinaikos in Greece), Sami's teammate in Finland and Holland, as well as in the Finnish national team, is a good example of such a player. A year younger than Sami, Joonas, a product of Lahden Reipas – the team that also brought up Jari Litmanen – became a familiar name in Finnish football as a youth player. Of course, Joonas's only credit was not his big home town, he also won the national skills championships many years in a row and represented his country at schoolboy level. Whereas Joonas and other players in Lahti practised at the city's great indoor stadium, Sami and his teammates at PaPe spent their winters playing small-side games in small school gymnasiums, far from any publicity. There were no indoor facilities for football in the neighbourhood, and the youth teams practised on the snowy pitches even in freezing temperatures. Sami describes the winters of his youth years:

> When I was a kid, the conditions for football were quite dreary, and still we were practising the same drills as the teams with fancier facilities. The only indoor stadium was in Lahti, and we only paid a visit there when there was a tournament. Otherwise, the small club didn't have the money for practising hours at the stadium. Besides, travelling to Lahti would also have required time and money, so it was the most convenient option for our teams to practise wherever we could. I remember practising on a pitch with ten inches of snow on it, and players wearing boots with spikes as studs. Even a touch on another player's boot with your own tore the boot apart, so it was often quite dangerous as well.
>
> The wooden floor in our gymnasium was also a surface that increased the possibility of an injury even in the safest drills. A hardwood floor strains your ankles and knees heavily and the stall-bars on the sides add yet another dimension of risk to a training session. Back then, it was not unusual for you to get a nosebleed when someone tackled you up against the wall. These days, the youth are fortunate to practise in such high-quality facilities, and I have to say that it pleases the eye of an old youth player like myself to watch the huge development that has taken place as far as the training facilities in Finland go.

The meagre training facilities Sami had as a youth were not necessarily a disadvantage to his development as a player. Toni Huttunen and Mika Hernesniemi, the two other players from Sami's youth team who made it to the top of Finnish football, are a reminder that personal motivation and willingness to work hard are key characteristics in the development of any successful football player. Huttunen explains: 'If you are willing to do the work, the conditions will not become an issue. Sometimes I think that some things come too easy for today's youth players, and their motivation may run out.'

Hernesniemi continues:

> Today, many youth players are extremely skilful. What they don't
> realise is that it is not always enough in a game. When you practise
> in a snowdrift, the one thing that is guaranteed is that you have the
> right attitude. Our youth team always stayed together and we
> enjoyed the training, and I don't think anyone thought that much
> about the conditions or how poor they were.

There is an advantage in playing for a small-town team as a youth, too. In
the summertime, PaPe's youth teams practised and played their matches at
'Voikkaa's Wembley', the main pitch in town and certainly a grass field
worthy of pride for any youth team. On the contrary, the youth teams in
bigger cities seldom get to practise on grass.

THE DIFFICULTY OF LOSING

A coaching relationship between a father and his son has been questioned
time and again, but both Sami and Jouko confirm, as if speaking with one
voice, that the relationship in the Hyypiä family has always worked well.
Jouko recalls:

> I never had to press Sami to practise, and I don't believe that any
> success in sports is achieved through coercion. The will to work for
> one's own success has to come from within. There were times when
> Sami didn't feel like going to training and he might complain about
> a sore foot or something else. I always told him to stay home if he
> felt like it and then left to go to training, and usually Sami followed
> me a few moments later.
>
> Sami has always been very dutiful and he has always been able
> to concentrate on what he does. Still, I wish his temper wasn't as
> short as it sometimes is. He may explode at times, but he also calms
> down quickly.

It may be hard to imagine Sami as a temperamental person, for he has
always kept his cool in matches. Neither Sami nor Jouko, nor his former
teammates Hernesniemi and Huttunen, remember Sami being sent off in
his career. Sami hasn't been booked that often either, but his emotions
have surfaced occasionally on the pitch and, in particular, losing has
always been a source of anger for Sami. 'I have always had a strong drive

for winning. I hate losing, no matter what the sport,' Sami admits without hesitation.

Sami's distaste for losing has become familiar to his teammates, too. If, for example, Sami was on the losing side at the end of a training session, he might kick all the balls out of the training ground. Sami was never shy with his feelings, especially if he felt that someone was taking the training too lightly. Sami's circle of friends know quite a few legends about his outbursts. With a smile on his face, Mika Hernesniemi recalls one in particular, this time on the badminton court:

> This was a time when we were playing doubles in badminton at the Kuusankoski indoor facility with Toni Huttunen and 'Miso' Sipola. Since Sami is so good at all sports and he has such a good reach, Miso and I decided to play every shuttle at Toni and avoid playing them to Sami if we could. Well, we happened to win the match, and Sami lost it so badly he refused to ride home in the same car with us and walked the five kilometres to Voikkaa instead.

Still, Sami's childhood friends don't remember Sami as a hothead. At school, for instance, Sami was usually well behaved, and on the football pitch he always had the patience to stay calm and focus on the job. At training, he has always done what's been required and often a little extra. According to Jouko, it was easy for him as Sami's father to work as his coach at PaPe because playing Sami was never in question. Thus, playing Sami never evoked any bitter feelings among the other players on the team or gave reason for a quarrel between father and son. Sami earned the spot in the starting line-up with his talent and skills, not because he was the coach's favourite player. Also, the squad at PaPe was always so small that nearly everyone had to play anyway.

It would be hard to imagine any major disagreements between Sami and Jouko off the field, too. Both the father and the son are serious and calm, and they never stir things up without reason. As a youth, there were never any signs of arrogance in Sami's behaviour, just as there aren't today. Both Sami and Jouko remember one occasion from the past when their views didn't quite match. It was in the early years of Sami's career, a game in the town league when Jouko substituted Sami after the win was assured. However, this substitution was one that Sami could not tolerate, for his father substituted him for a girl! Sami thinks back at the incident about 20 years ago, saying: 'It was a tough spot. After I was subbed I walked under a tree, sat down and cried – it was so hard on me.'

Sami has since been able to reminisce about the bitter substitution during every visit to Toni Huttunen's home, because Jonna, the girl who was always in the same football camps with the boys in town, happens to be Huttunen's wife. The bitter childhood event didn't leave any grudges between the two and since then Sami has learnt to take substitutions more calmly.

Wrestling was one thing that never aroused any strong feelings in Sami, although it had been one of Jouko Hyypiä's interests as a young boy. One of the players in PaPe's '73 team, Janne Pahkala, was a successful wrestler at national level. Jouko thinks that wrestling is a good way for a footballer to improve coordination and balance, but Sami never became interested in it. This is one of the few things that troubled Jouko a little as Sami's coach. But Sami explains: 'When I was about 12 or 13, Janne was wrestling at Voikkaan Viesti and I paid a few visit to the gym as well, but I was never that inspired by the sport.'

As Sami never took up wrestling seriously, in hindsight it seems that Sami's selection of his favourite sport hit the bull's-eye, although I have to admit that a 196-centimetre-tall wrestler in the under 90 kg class would have been an interesting sight!

Another short experiment that Sami had with a hobby outside football was in cinema. Sami recalls with warmth a video film put together with friends. The boys were busy filming a lot of footage, but the epic, with a showing time of more than an hour, was never completely finished. Sami explains and laughs:

> It was fun to do and watch, and still is, even though our performances on the tape don't quite give any promise for sequels or sitcoms. There is one scene in the film where this person starts to climb down the stairs, and as he reaches the ground he has lost his hair and his clothes are different than they were at the top. It was the same guy we were filming, though, and we didn't mind about little details like that back then. It was more about the big picture.
>
> I had one of those multi-roles, if you will. We didn't have enough people for a cast, so I had to play several parts. We had all kinds of masks and everything, and the characters were versatile as well, from a ninja to a drug dealer and so on. But I've never considered continuing with my career in the film industry since then.

THE STAKES BECOME HIGHER

Until upper secondary school, Sami's football career proceeded steadily without much extra effort. His success and development were regular, and Sami became a familiar face in the regional team, too. The PaPe '73 team stayed together and most of the team still attended the same school. Sami and other PaPe youth team players attended Hirvelä Upper Level School, next to the athletic field, and the team were successful in school tournaments throughout the upper level. Sami reminisces about his successful school years, saying:

> Once we made it to the national schools' championships in football. Even though we finished last in the tournament, it was unusual for a school team from a town of 2,000 to make it among the best three or four school teams in the nation.

When the boys went to upper secondary school, the school team broke up. The only players from the PaPe '73 team who attended Voikkaa upper secondary school with Sami were his future teammates at Kumu and MyPa, Mika Hernesniemi and Toni Huttunen, and Tommi Janhunen, who called it quits as an Under-17 junior in his first year in upper secondary school. With such limited player material, it was difficult to succeed in the school tournaments any more, but it was an honourable task to keep the reputation of Voikkaa as high as possible. Sami recalls his first encounters with his future teammate and coach at MyPa:

> There were only three of us playing regular club football at upper secondary school, so it was quite difficult to win matches with three against eleven match-ups. I remember one match in particular, though: it was against the sports upper secondary school of Salpausselkä from Lahti, in 1991, I think. Their team was full of talented youth players from Reipas and Kuusysi, among them Joonas Kolkka, and they were coached by Harri Kampman.
>
> I think we ended up losing by a narrow margin of 3–2, but it was well fought considering our clear underdog status. We led the match twice before they tied it up and scored the winner, and I remember how furious Kampman was on the sidelines, particularly when we were winning. After all, all their players were regular starters for their youth teams and we were practically playing with three men.

When the boys reached the Under-17 age group, players from the PaPe '73 team started to find other interests more appealing, and the team was losing a lot of players. Tuning the engines of mopeds and other typical pastimes of the youth at that age were familiar to Sami, too, but his passion for football never diminished.

With a population of only 20,000, it was difficult to maintain more than one Under-17 team in Kuusankoski. At this point, PaPe barely had enough players to form a squad, but the player loss at Kumu had been even worse. Although there had always been a fierce rivalry between PaPe and Kumu, the two clubs of the region decided to unify their strengths. Kumu loaned its Under-17 juniors to PaPe, and thus remarkably improved the team's potential for success. That Under-17 team then took PaPe close to the top national level. In 1988, PaPe won the regional championships for Under-17 juniors. This achievement was by no means a common one, and it was particularly sweet for Jouko Hyypiä: exactly 25 years before, he had been a member of the PaPe Under-17 team who were crowned regional champions.

The success story of PaPe and Sami Hyypiä continued as Sami's team were promoted to the Under-17 First Division in the same year, which is yet another tremendous achievement for such a remote small-town team. PaPe's first year in the Under-17 First Division was successful, too, as the team finished fourth in the final standings. At the end of 1989, Sami, Toni Huttunen and Mika Hernesniemi made their debuts in first-team football, when they played a few matches for PaPe's first team in the Finnish Third Division. The best achievement of a PaPe Under-17 team ever is also from the same year. Sami's team reached the semi-final stage in the international Kokkola Cup, and faced KuPS, one of the best youth teams in the nation, in an exciting and even match-up. After a goalless draw in regular time, the match went into extra-time and then to a penalty shootout, which the Kuopio team won, advancing to the tournament final. PaPe won the bronze medal match and earned third place and a Fair Play trophy. In the autumn of the same year, KuPS were crowned the national Under-17 champions, which demonstrated how close to the top PaPe actually were.

> In 1990, it was time to move on to Under-20 juniors, the oldest youth-team level in Finnish football. At the same time, the first transfer in Sami's career became a reality, and also for the first time in his life he was now coached by someone other than his father. 'PaPe was the club when we were Under-17 juniors, but as Under-20 juniors we were playing for Kumu, with the name Kumu-Peikot [coined from *Kumu* and *Pallo-Peikot*].

At Kumu, the rising careers of the '73 team players continued under the guidance of Jari Haapala, the coach, and Jouko Hyypiä, who stayed with the team as Haapala's assistant and the team physio. Kumu's first team had been promoted to the Finnish Premier League for the 1990 season, and the club's Under-20 team were carefully watched with regard to first-team potential. Sami's development was as steady as ever. Up until that point, football had been more of a hobby, but it was now time to start systematic training with a daily programme.

In the summer, Sami and a few other Under-20 juniors were called up to practise with the first team. Still, the boys earned their match minutes with the youth team, who were dominating the Under-20 First Division. The coach at Kumu's first team was Derek Fazackerley, and Sami had a good opportunity to learn more about British football culture through him. 'I wouldn't say there was much difference. He just spoke English and didn't understand if I said something in Finnish,' Sami says with a smile, shrugging off any notion of cultural differences.

> Later, Fazackerley worked as Kevin Keegan's assistant with the English national team and as a coach at Blackburn Rovers. He also played a part when I was given a chance to train with Newcastle United in November and December 1995, as he was then Keegan's assistant there. I didn't think he had changed one bit since our time together at Kumu.

Sami's debut in the Finnish Premier League was actually quite close during Fazackerley's spell, but Sami left for a language course in England in the middle of the busiest time in the season. Sami remembers the reasons behind the trip clearly:

> I had booked the trip to Bournemouth early in the spring when I didn't even know that I would get to practise with the first team. It might be that I still wouldn't have played any matches if I had cancelled the trip to England, although Mika Hernesniemi did play a few matches while I was gone.

Sami's football experiences in Bournemouth were limited to leisurely matches among the language course students, although an attempt had been made to arrange something more serious with a local club.

> Clubs in England were preparing for the season then, and it was supposed to be arranged so that I would get to practise with some

club there, but nothing like that ever materialised. No one ever contacted me concerning training with any local team.

Otherwise, the trip was a wonderful experience and, as far as learning the language, it was definitely worth it. My friend Pasi Myller and I lived with a Scottish family, and we could barely make out one word of what the father of the family was saying. The mother spoke a little more clearly and our conversations with her were slightly easier. Pasi and I talked Finnish with each other, of course, but otherwise it was all English or shut up. We also had classes and we made excursions to London and the Isle of Wight.

When Sami returned to Finland, he kept practising with Kumu's first team and played matches with the Under-20 team. The youth team were successful, but the first team's flight in the Premier League was cut short as they were relegated at the end of the season.

THE APPRENTICE OF 'THE WIZARD' VOUTILAINEN

The following winter Kumu hired the Finnish coaching legend Keijo 'Velho [the Wizard]' Voutilainen, who had made a name for himself by winning several national titles at Kuusysi as first-team coach. Voutilainen began building the team with a clean sheet and included Sami in the squad from day one. Hernesniemi and Huttunen were also part of the first-team squad. Sami describes his early times on the first team:

> Voutilainen didn't know anything about the players in advance, but I suppose such an experienced coach sees the abilities of each player rather soon even when he starts from point zero. Anyway, we were on the team from the very beginning and we kept our places from then on. Sometimes Voutilainen had some special tricks for us youngsters, but otherwise he treated us equally with all the other, older players.

The young players often went to training half an hour early, and Voutilainen ran them through extra drills with some dribbling and other basic techniques. The winter training apparently went well for the youngsters at Kumu, and well ahead of the 1991 season, Voutilainen announced his reliance on the 17-year-old Sami Hyypiä. In an article in *Kouvolan Sanomat*, the local paper, he said that Sami had everything it takes to become an international-level player in the next few years. In the same article, he mentioned that Mika Hernesniemi and Toni Huttunen were also true prospective talents.

Along with an experienced coach, there was another person at Kumu who was a tremendous mentor for Sami. The team's other starting centre-back was Esa Pekonen, a veteran in the Finnish Premier League and an experienced international player. Pekonen was paired up in the back with the Estonian Urmas Hepner, and Sami's position in the original plan was in the anchoring role at centre-half – the position where the future centre-back had played in his youth years, too. Pekonen's consistent and routine-like performances at stopper were a perfect example of leading the central defence, and Sami paid careful attention to this.

It is also much to the credit of Voutilainen that Sami was offered a chance at the youth national team try-outs. It was wintertime when Kumu's first team were playing a tournament in Lahti at the same time as the Finnish Under-18 national team had a training camp there. Voutilainen hinted to Jyrki Heliskoski, the national team coach, that he had a player in his team at whom he should take a closer look. Heliskoski decided to pay heed to his colleague's advice and wasted no time on the matter, inviting Sami to the youth national team camp immediately. Heliskoski's call was so unexpected that Sami was a little confused as he returned from the tournament and explained that he needed to get back to Lahti in the morning, to train with the youth national team, Jouko Hyypiä reminisces about Heliskoski's unexpected call.

From that first camp in Lahti, Sami was one of Heliskoski's key players, and he has never been dropped from the national side since. During that first weekend with the national team, the Finnish Under-18 squad played a practice match where Sami got his chance and after that he played almost every possible national team match at all levels.

Sami played his first boys' international match at the age of 17 against Yugoslavia in a goalless draw in Italy on 23 March 1991. In hindsight, it is easy to proclaim that the star of Sami Hyypiä was truly born on that night, but the young talent handled the situation calmly and modestly. He assured the media that a year ago he hadn't even dreamed about playing for his country. Even though ten years have passed, the secret behind the quick rise to the national side is not completely clear to Sami. Although he had been a member of the regional team in the Pohjola Cup (the regional team cup in Finland), he never even made the initial list of 60 players who were selected for the first, preliminary national team try-out camps. Only Janne Pahkala of PaPe had once made it to the first camp, but he never made it to the eventual team. Ten years on, the star player of

Liverpool FC thinks back on his career as a football player in this way:

> I had never even thought that I would make the national team at
> that point. I was never a prodigious talent, and I hadn't really
> played on the first team either, so it felt a little unusual to make the
> national side all of a sudden. It took a while before I even realised
> what was going on. If someone had come to me then and told me
> what was going to happen in the next ten years, I would have
> laughed straight in his face.

Lennart Wangel, who also worked as a youth trainer for the Finnish FA in
the 1980s, remembers Sami from the Pohjola Cup as a Bambi-type centre-
half who was almost as tall as he is today, but at least 20 kg lighter. He
slipped through the scouts' net that time, and it is astounding that, a few
months later, the unknown youth from Voikkaa emerged as a top-level
talent who immediately became a regular starter and a key player for the
boys' national team. It will always remain a mystery how much interest
Sami would have aroused as a youth player had he played for any of the
teams from Helsinki, where youth players are automatically more visible
to national team scouts.

On the other hand, it may also be an advantage for small-town players
that they don't achieve much competitive success or receive opportunities
to represent their region or country at such a young age. The recipe for
success with the Voikkaa '73 team is similar to that of the Åland island
clubs. Several talented youth players have emerged from the islands, with
Daniel Sjölund and Kristoffer Weckström being the latest. It has been
argued that, because the islanders struggle to succeed as a team, they can
improve the basics of their game with time. The small towns don't offer
too many leisure activities for the youth, which is why they are favourable
ground for the development of young athletes.

No matter what the secret behind the success of the Voikkaa '73 team,
1991 will be marked in the history books of Finnish football as the year
when Sami Hyypiä broke into the national and international football
scene. Before that, the prospective football player from Voikkaa had been
a familiar name only among the most enthusiastic fans of youth football in
the Kuusankoski region.

3

The Tests of First-Team Football

SAMI HYYPIÄ'S FOOTBALL CAREER HAS BEEN MARKED BY HIS ABILITY to seize an opportunity whenever one has been offered. Spring 1991 passed quickly as Sami was training with Kumu's first team and travelling with the Finnish Under-18 national team. The season started well for Sami and it became clear that youth matches were a thing of the past for him.

The youth national team coach, Jyrki Heliskoski, put Sami in central defence, where he was to play in all future national squads. At Kumu, Sami played a variety of positions. Usually, he played at centre-half, but when necessary, coach Voutilainen played him as a sweeper or stopper, and sometimes even as a full-back. The future 'perpetual stopper', explains how responsibilities at centre-half widened his view of the game and improved his footballing skills:

> For Voutilainen I played mostly in a defensive role at centre-half. I
> don't know if that was a good position for me or not, but no matter
> what the position, when you get playing time on the first team as
> a young lad you'll always give your best effort. In the midfield,
> there isn't much time to hold the ball, but you have to control it
> quickly and pass it on with speed. Therefore, playing at centre-half
> certainly improved my game quite a bit.

'I did play in the midfield in the youth teams, too, but as I grew taller I think my turns became so slow that I didn't do that well at centre-half any more,' Sami explains with a big smile.

Voutilainen followed the development of his young talent carefully, and helped Sami improve every aspect of his game. The example set by Esa 'Peksa' Pekonen, the team veteran, was also important for the budding talent in Kumu's first team. Having played professional football abroad and earned a respectable number of caps for Finland, Pekonen's mere presence at training guaranteed a certain level of diligence amongst the players. Peksa gave appropriate feedback to the young lads as well, praising them for solid performances and bringing them down to earth if they were too full of themselves. Sami recalls: 'Peksa had so much experience that he knew when was the right moment to encourage us and when we needed a kick in the backside. I really enjoyed playing with him, and he has helped me forward in my career.'

Coach Voutilainen also had a good understanding of how to treat young talent. Voutilainen would always praise his players when it was appropriate, but he also let the boys hear if things didn't go as planned. He was systematic and just in his feedback. 'As a coach, Voutilainen had experience of all types of players, and I don't think I was among the most difficult to coach, especially since I was such a young lad then,' Sami remembers.

The previous season in the top flight had taken an enormous toll on Kumu's finances, and so the budget for the first team in 1991 was cut to the minimum. Fortunately for the young players, this meant that they would get a fair chance of playing for the first team, as there were no funds to acquire any new players from the transfer market. The team played with no pressure, and the main objective for the season was not to get relegated to the Second Division. The season in the Finnish First Division was important for Sami and it helped him mature as a player. Playing First Division football, or first-team football overall, is quite different from playing in youth matches, and Sami didn't expect much from the forthcoming season. He was happy to be part of the team and learn as much as possible. Nevertheless, he got a fair share of playing time and responsibility. Sami explains:

> I had a great deal of respect for Voutilainen. He was one of the best-known coaches in Finland, and he had won a lot of trophies for the clubs he had coached. For me as a player, he had all sorts of tips and advice that would never have crossed my mind.

Playing first-team football at Kumu did not have that much of an effect on Sami's everyday life. He lived at home with his parents and attended Voikkaa upper secondary school. In the summer of 1991, Sami also got his first summer job.

I worked for about a month that summer and it still remains the only experience I have had of working life. My friend, Janne Pahkala, and I were working at this industrial paint shop, and I have to say that sometimes when we got home I felt a little dozy after working in a room filled with paint fumes all day. It was fun to gain some experience from the so-called normal working life, although I must admit that working as an industrial painter is not my cup of tea. With all due respect for painters, of course.

The early '90s was a time when the young first-team players at Kumu could not earn a living from football, even though the club did pay some compensation for points earned in the league table. For the lads still eligible for Under-20 matches, the source of inspiration was more honourable than money: for young boys still in school, it was an honour to play for the first team. At the same time, they learned a great many things for their future careers and money didn't play any significant role. Playing first-team football in Kuusankoski didn't equate to a significantly improved popularity in the community either. According to Sami, there were neither backstabbers nor many people giving praise after the matches in Kuusankoski. Practically everyone knew each other in the small town, so Sami was a familiar face to many from his youth-team years.

Kumu secured its place in the mid-table early in the season and remained there throughout Sami's first season in the First Division. Local press took notice of Sami's solid season, but he didn't stir any sensational headlines. Sami developed steadily with no hurry or extra fuss around him, and Voutilainen was careful not to burn out his talented youth players. He gave them enough playing time and responsibility so that the strain on them wouldn't come too hard. There were times when Sami started a match, and sometimes he came on as a substitute, but the bottom line is that he got regular playing time throughout the season. Toni Huttunen, Mika Hernesniemi and Janne Pahkala were the other players from the PaPe '73 team who gained experience from first-team football, but Sami was a step ahead of them and he was clearly the top player in his age group. His career in international football, which had started for Sami in the winter, accelerated this development considerably.

A KEY PLAYER IN THE YOUTH NATIONAL TEAM
Practising and playing with the Kumu first team were crucial steps in Sami's career, but he learned a lot of valuable things from Jyrki

Heliskoski, his coach in the Under-18 national team. Heliskoski thought that Sami's talent hadn't been used in the way it should be and after a few full 90 minutes with the Under-18 team, Heliskoski was convinced of his sweeper's top-level potential. Particularly impressive to the national team coach were Sami's eye for the game and his mental strength, and Heliskoski was also delighted that Sami was playing club football under the quality training of Keijo Voutilainen. A demanding club coach is vital for the development of a talented youth player, for even the most talented players have to learn the value of hard work and that nothing comes for free. Like Voutilainen, Heliskoski, too, predicted a glorious career for Sami, if only Sami would keep working as hard as he had up to that point. The past decade hasn't changed anything in Heliskoski's view on Sami:

> At the first camp I saw that I had a real talent in him. Although he was lacking in physical strength and he was a bit lanky, his eye for the game was remarkable. It often looked as if he wouldn't make it to the ball, but somehow he was always there. Later, he began adding some of the needed strength, but I always thought his best talent was winning the ball because of his perfect timing and view of the game. When he added the extra strength, he became a superior player in the youth national team.

One of the most important things I see in Sami is that he is a tremendous person, a wonderful human being. It is easy to imagine that he would be the favourite son-in-law for every mother on this earth, and I don't think there are many people who have any bad things to say about him. As a player, you could tell Sami hated losing more than anything. Still, it doesn't show as unnecessary boasting or anything like that – it is the way he goes in for a ball. He seeks certain types of challenges and is often not satisfied with the easiest solution. He knows what he can do with the ball. For example, a basic inside pass always comes hard and on the ground from Sami, and it takes a lot of confidence and will to win to do that. He leaves nothing undone and never tries to offer an easy way out. It is clear that Sami has set simple goals for himself, such that improve him as a player. Mastering the basic passes perfectly is one of those things.

In the beginning, Sami was hesitant about his future with the youth national team, but his confidence in his own skills grew with time. Of course, the first call-up for the national team was delightful news, but Sami didn't get carried away with his success. After all, his international career might just as well have stopped with the first camp – at least that's how Sami thought back then. Some ten years later, Sami considers the early days in the youth national team as the turning point in his career, because making the national squad gave him an extra push, encouraging him to work even harder and improve himself as a player.

Even though Sami had travelled in southern Europe with his parents, and the language course in Bournemouth had offered him some experience of living abroad, Sami had never seriously thought about an international career. Playing for the youth national team gave him more reasons to start thinking about one. Sami talks of his outlook on life:

> Becoming a professional football player was probably some sort of a dream in the back of my mind, but in 1991, my main career objective in football was to make it to the Finnish Premier League some day. I have never been one to try to take a bigger bite of the cake than what I'm capable of. 'Slow and steady' is a more suitable motto for my career.
>
> When I secured my place in the national side, I gained experience in many international matches and saw countries outside Finland, too. I knew that playing for the national team was the best way to show your talent to foreign scouts, and it was around that time when I first started to think about a potential professional career seriously.

On his first trip abroad with the Under-18 national team, Sami played two matches. It was in March 1991, and Finland played Yugoslavia in a goalless draw and lost to the USA 2–1. The team played yet another match, against Italy, but Sami missed it because of a cold he caught during the trip. The two matches Sami played were enough to convince Jyrki Heliskoski of the young player's ability and Sami was selected for the team travelling to play Holland in a qualifying match for the European Championships in April. Among others, goalkeeper Teuvo Moilanen (Preston North End) and forward Antti Sumiala (Yozgatspor, in Turkey) were members of the same team. Like Sami, the two have also have had fine careers both in club football and with the national side.

From then on, Sami played the full 90 minutes in each of the youth national team's matches in 1991. In Holland, the qualifying match played in Alkmaar ended with an impressive score of 3–0 to Finland. In June, the Finnish team were beaten 3–0 by Austria in another European Championships qualifier at home. In August, the boys' national team played Poland twice at home. The first match ended with a goalless draw, but the final score in the second was again 3–0 to the home side. That was also the match where Sami scored his first goal for his country. Later in the same month, Finland travelled to Norway for another European Championships qualifier and came back with a valuable 1–0 victory. A rematch against Austria in September produced yet another victory, this time 2–0, and Sami once again added his name to the list of goalscorers. In October, the Dutch were beaten by the same number of goals at home in the final European Championships qualifier. Despite the impressive record of the Finnish youth national team, it was Norway who packed their bags and headed for the Under-18 European Championships tournament. Finland and Norway shared the number-one spot in their qualifying group, but Norway got the ticket to the tournament due to their better goal difference. Although Finland once again failed to qualify for a championship tournament, Sami's international career had started well. An interesting little detail worth mentioning about the qualifiers in 1991 is the fact that the Dutch goalkeeper in those matches against Finland was Sander Westerveld, who was to become a good friend of Sami's during his early years with Liverpool FC. At least back then, Finland were ahead of the Dutch, and, as we know, Sami's career at Liverpool FC has been more successful than that of Westerveld, who transferred to Spain during the 2001–02 season.

His international career had now taken off and Sami's development was progressing. Sami refused to talk about any major steps of improvement, though, and he'd much rather give credit for those who helped him move forward in his career. Sami thinks back over the tactics that were practically tailored to his tall figure:

> The system we played in the Under-18 national team was perfect for me. Defensively, our aim was to make the opponent kick the ball long and high, and we had two tall centre-backs who went in for the first balls. For most of the time, we played with one marking stopper and one sweeper who'd cover the back.
>
> Our system for building the game from the back was also very effective. We tried to make one of our midfielders free and then pass the ball to him on the floor instead of kicking the ball high and far. After getting the ball to the midfield, we tried to play in the back of the opponent's defensive line. We practised the system over and over at camps, and I think it has helped me pass the ball from the back in the later years, too. The tempo in the international youth matches was quite quick, and I think

that's another factor contributing to my improvement as a player. After getting such good results against solid European teams, it was a shame that we didn't qualify for any championship tournaments, but I'm sure that the matches I played for the youth national team helped me make the transition from First Division football to the Premier League level.

If Sami thought that the tactics of the youth national team suited him well, Heliskoski clearly agreed with his newly found talent:

As for tactics, Sami always had a key role in the team. For example, in the older youth national team, there were many lads like Mika Nurmela, who had good stamina and ran miles in every match. One of our tactics was to put pressure on the ball and make the opponent kick the ball long and high, so that we would win it back quickly with Sami being the dominant force at the back. He won practically every ball in the air. Already then, I noticed that one of Sami's strengths was not only winning the ball, but also dishing it off to a teammate instead of playing it just somewhere. In a few matches I had someone keep statistics, which showed that four out of every five balls that Sami won in the air ended up at the feet of a teammate. He usually won the fifth ball as well, but still the battle often ended with the opponent fouling more often than Sami playing the ball to the other team. The percentage of the successful passes, 80 per cent, is remarkably high for a defender and says a lot about Sami's level. In every situation on the field, he had the time, skill and vision required. This showed up particularly in the Under-21 team.

Sami played for three different age groups in the five years I coached him at youth national teams. Already then, I thought he was among the top three centre-backs in Europe. I dare not say that he was the best, for I didn't see every centre-back in Europe play, but I never saw anyone better than Sami either.

The changes related to playing that came along with the step from youth football into the first-team matches and the youth national team were huge. Previously, Sami had only represented his home area at the regional team and, with all due respect to youth football, that was not quite top-level football. Although he had earned some local success at PaPe, the level of football in the region was not that high in national terms. Therefore, making the first team and the youth national team were the first major steps forward in Sami's football career. Until then, Sami and the other youth players in Voikkaa had played only for fun and mainly because there were no other options. The groundwork had been done at PaPe, but taking the step to the next level became possible only through tough challenges and bigger matches.

The transition from youth football to the men's level was painless for Sami. In his first season with Kumu, he played in 19 matches in the First Division, starting some and coming on as a sub in others. Marko Helkala was only the player in the team who played the full 20 matches, and the only other person besides Sami who played 19 matches was the team's reliable Estonian stopper, Urmas Hepner. The other key defender, Esa Pekonen, ended up playing one match less than Sami. Altogether, coach Voutilainen's squad was well used: 18 players made an appearance during the season, with 15 carrying the main load. The young talent got their share of responsibility, too, as the PaPe boys played a respectable number of matches as well: Toni Huttunen played 11, while Mika Hernesniemi and Janne Pahkala both played 4. Huttunen managed to score four goals and Pahkala one, but Sami had to wait a little while longer for his first goal for the first team.

Although Sami trained and played with the first team throughout the season, he paid a short visit back to youth football when he played a few matches for the Under-20 team who were playing for promotion. The first team had lost its chances for promotion a while back and they weren't threatened by relegation either, so Voutilainen was happy to let his key players show up for the youth matches. With quality youth players who had first-team experience under their belts, the Kumu Under-20 team got promoted to the highest level of youth football in Finland, only to find out at the beginning of the next season that they were short of players and had to withdraw from the league.

Kumu's first team finished fifth in the 1991 First Division standings – a good performance considering the low expectations. Out of the 20 matches, they managed to win 8, draw 6 and lose 6. The champions and the club that got promoted to the Premier League were MyPa, Kumu's rivals from the neighbouring town, who would make their first appearance in the top flight since 1975 when they played their first season in the Premier League. Sami reminisces over some of the more memorable moments of his first season as a first-team player:

> Although we didn't finish at the top of the table, we had the best
> goalscorer in our team, Igor Danilov, whom we called Igor the
> Great, and we also took four points in two matches from MyPa,
> beating them 3–1 at home and drawing the away match 0–0. I had
> a tremendous chance to score the winner in the away match, and I
> headed the ball down obediently according to all the football
> guides in the world, but to our misfortune the ball bounced off the
> ground and over the bar.

The missed scoring chance and away win may have turned out to be
favourable for Sami after all, as he played his first matches in the Finnish
Premier League for MyPa the following season.

At the end of 1991, Sami got one more considerable piece of recognition
for the work he'd done when he was awarded the Finnish FA Talented
Player of the Year trophy. Winning that particular trophy means more
than many might think, for the winners have almost always made it to the
very top of Finnish football. Some of the better-known players who've
won the trophy before Sami include Olli Huttunen, Pasi Rautiainen, Ismo
Lius, teammate Esa Pekonen 11 years earlier, and Teuvo Moilanen. After
Sami, the names added to the list of winners include Janne Saarinen
(currently with Rosenborg, Norway), Janne Salli, Teemu Tainio (Auxerre,
France) and Petri Pasanen (Ajax, Holland) of his current teammates in the
Finnish national team, and Mika Väyrynen (SC Heerenveen, Holland),
Otto Fredrikson (Borussia Mönchengladbach, Germany) and Antti
Okkonen (still with MyPa) between 1999 and 2001. Usually, the players
who have won the trophy have gained many more caps for the youth
national team than Sami had, whose rise to the elite of Finnish football
took place with astounding speed. Obviously, Sami was very appreciative
of the recognition. In the same year he was also awarded the Finnish
Ministry of Education's Scholarship for a Youth Athlete and the award of
Best Local Youth Team Athlete in Kuusankoski.

THE GRADUATING CLASS OF MYPA

The tall, promising centre-back had been noticed outside the award
councils, too. Harri Kampman, the coach who took MyPa to the Premier
League, was especially interested in the young star of the local rivals. Sami
remembers:

> Kampman began calling me after the season, asking if I would like

to join MyPa. Kuusysi were also interested in me, and I drove once to Lahti for negotiations, but they didn't quite go as I had planned. After all, I'm not that sure of how much they really wanted me there.

The trip to Lahti ended up in a surprising manner regardless:

As I was leaving the Lahti Stadium, where Kuusysi had their office, Kampman happened to be at the parking lot in his car. As soon as he saw me he told me not to sign with Kuusysi and join MyPa instead. It was a funny little coincidence, even though Kampman did live in Lahti then.

As a new team in the Premier League, MyPa were very active in the transfer market in the autumn of 1991, and after a short period of consideration, Sami decided to join the club in neighbouring Anjalankoski. Esa Pekonen and Toni Huttunen were the other two players from Kumu who transferred to the same club. Sami reminisces about the transfer decision that he has never had to regret:

They made some really good acquisitions for that year, and it certainly felt like the right place for me. I didn't even have to move away from home, which was particularly important because I was still at school. Moreover, as Kampman acquired a few other players from Kumu, too, MyPa felt like a safe club to sign with. In all possible ways, transferring to MyPa seemed like the most convenient and practical option for my career at that point.

Sami remembers that the people in Kuusankoski, and particularly in Voikkaa, were very encouraging about his attempt to make it to the top.

I felt that the folk in Kuusaa were happy for me when I signed with a Premier League club. They never thought of me as a traitor or anything, even though I transferred to a local rival. The relationship between Kumu and MyPa was not so intense. PaPe and Kumu had been a little sensitive with each other, but already during my later years in youth football, the clubs were cooperating.

It seemed that not even the status of a Premier League player touched the people in the community that much, and Sami was still able to live without any extra pressure. He also didn't have any will or need for showing off his football stardom in his free time. Sami notes: 'Myllykoski is also such a small place that almost everyone knew each other there. People never pointed their fingers at me or whispered mysteriously as I walked by or anything like that. I was treated no differently than anybody else in town.'

The transfer didn't even make a big financial difference in Sami's life, but he was not interested in the economics of football. Sami explains:

> Of the ones who got to play regularly, I probably had the lowest wages in the club. At that time, I didn't feel any need to start negotiating for more money, and why, after all, should they have paid me any more than what they did? I thought it was fun to play in the Premier League, and there wasn't much arm-wrestling about the wages when I first had talks with MyPa.
>
> We did revise the contract a little, right before the start of the season, as it began to look like I was going to get a fair share of responsibility during the season. We had agreed about that already in the first contract.

Regardless of the matters smoothing the transfer to another club, playing in Myllykoski did cause a significant change in Sami's life. Sami was in his final year of upper secondary school, and the spring 1992 exams were ahead of him. MyPa trained twice a day throughout the winter, so the young players attending school were extremely busy. Sami's mother, Irma Hyypiä, remembers that it was the first time ever that she was worried about her son's busy life. Sami had always been a good student and now, with the most important year of his school life ahead of him, Sami was committed to football training during school hours and national team camps during the week. Sami had decided to take proper care of his school work and the teachers at the Voikkaa Upper Secondary School were very understanding of his football activities. Although the trip from Voikkaa to Myllykoski is only about 20 km, it was a trip that had to be made several times a week, often twice a day. Sami talks about his attitude towards school:

> The first winter was tough. I drove to the morning training session, then back to school and off to another training session in the afternoon. The days at school were long, as I was studying

45

advanced mathematics and German, but I still never left anything undone even though I was often more absent than present during a course. I asked my friends what had been covered in class, and I always did the homework. I knew that if I had slacked off one bit, I probably wouldn't have gotten all the freedom that I was now enjoying. Sometimes I woke up early in the morning to do my homework, and sometimes I stayed up later to finish it, but I always got it done. In a way, school work has been a good compensation for the work on the field, and I think that success in school came rather easy for me. Besides, studying gave me things to think about other than football.

Their son's combination of school and Premier League football required some new arrangements in the Hyypiä family. They bought another car, because Sami could no longer borrow his father's car for the trips between Voikkaa and Myllykoski. This helped to relieve the burden of the dual duties of football and school from Sami's shoulders. Sami's familiar recipe for success – 'a lot of work and a little talk' – was successful. He got a good amount of playing time in the winter friendlies, and he also performed well for the team. In school there were no reasons for complaining either, as Sami finished upper secondary school with a good grade average.

The new league level also brought along changes into the training methods. The training facilities at Kumu had been pretty much alike with PaPe, only the amount of time spent on training and the output required from the players had increased. Voutilainen had such a long history in top-level football that he could plan the training sessions on the basis of his past experiences. Harri Kampman also had a respectable career in coaching behind him, but his approach to coaching football was more modern than Voutilainen's. The other important change was the indoor training ground in Myllykoski, which is rather small, but nevertheless a quality indoor training facility for the severe Finnish winters:

> Kampman brought along a lot of his own stuff, but, overall I think that coaching remained pretty much the same. Perhaps Kampman had more modern thoughts, and his training sessions always had many match-type drills. We used the ball as much as possible, which was refreshing in otherwise hard and strenuous training with a lot of running. I think using the ball even in running drills is wise because, after all the ball is there all the time in the match, too.

Even then, the training conditions weren't that good. When you train twice a day in such a small hall, the walls get closer and closer. I think it was crucial that Kampman's drills were so interesting and diverse.

The indoor training ground in Myllykoski was too small for playing matches, so the first team had to travel elsewhere for training camps. Cyprus has long been the club's traditional campsite, and Sami's years at MyPa were no exception: they had a training camp in Cyprus every year he played there. The winter matches in Finland were played in the indoor stadiums that were available in the early 1990s – most often in the Lahti indoor stadium, which has an artificial turf pitch. Sami recalls the winter facilities:

When we went from our small indoor training ground to the regular-size field, it always took some time to adjust to the different surface. However, playing in the small indoor training ground made the players play quickly and left no time for thinking about the plays, which surely must have helped us handle the ball with speed. You didn't have much time with the ball, and you had to pass it on quickly.

The surface in our training ground was grit, so the ball often bounced in the most unexpected direction. Today, in the high-quality indoor stadiums, the surface is as level as a pool table. I remember how much it bugged you if the ball hit you on the shin or knee, but then again, we all knew it was part of training there. Besides, the best players often come from countries where you don't find many level fields. A training ground with grit surface is good for your body, too, as the surface does not make your joints ache like some other surfaces do. I liked practising there a lot.

In March 1992, MyPa's preparations for the club's second-ever season in the Premier League were at full throttle. At the same time, Sami Hyypiä and Toni Huttunen were preparing for their exams, and fitting the schedules so that everything would work was not always that easy. The situation required a great deal of flexibility from both sides and, simultaneously, Sami and Toni got to learn all the different aspects of the life of a Premier League player.

Towards the beginning of the season, coach Harri Kampman had arranged a friendly against the Swedish side Hammarby in Stockholm.

The match was scheduled for the weekend of an important exam, and the coach wanted his future graduates in the game. The trip to Stockholm was also supposed to be the team's motivational and inspirational trip before the season, so the Voikkaa boys left for the trip, even though Huttunen was recovering from a fractured foot and therefore not even able to play. A little break from the daily routine seemed to be a good idea before another stressful week of exams. The boys took their schoolbooks with them for the trip, but didn't really study them at all.

The team took a boat to Sweden, leaving on Saturday night for the Sunday match. The rest of the team were going to return by boat, too, but Sami and Toni had to fly back in order to make it on time for the Monday's exam. Because of this arrangement, the boys were going to miss the free night out on the return trip. Due to the match the next day, the programme for the trip to Stockholm was rather strict: the players were ordered to go to bed early, but the wives and girlfriends who were travelling along were obviously allowed to stay and enjoy the night activities on the cruiser. After the dinner, Sami and Toni didn't want to go to their cabins straight away, and they decided to stay up for a while because they would miss the fun on the return trip. When the wives and girlfriends decided to go to the nightclub, Toni and Sami were bold enough to follow.

'We thought that Kampman and his wife had already gone to bed and that he would definitely not be at the nightclub,' Sami says, shedding some light on the clever ideas he and Huttunen had that night. 'Nevertheless, we decided to take a longer route to the night club, so that we would definitely not run into Kampman. We had to walk through a long glass corridor and as we reached the halfway point Kampman and his wife stepped in from the other end. There was no place to hide, so we turned around and ran away.'

The young daredevils didn't go straight back to their cabins, though, for they thought they had escaped without getting caught. They decided not to go to the nightclub, however, and stayed on the cruiser's promenade deck for some time.

> It was pretty late when I noticed someone next to me, pulling my sleeve. It was Kampman, of course, telling me it was time for bed. I went to get 'Bottoms' Huttunen from nearby, and off to our cabins we went, both very embarrassed. When the boat arrived in Stockholm the next morning, we were as subdued as we could be, and expected the worse from the coach.

That night, the coach had not got mad at the boys, but, to the shock of Sami and Toni, in the morning he headed straight towards their table. Instead of a much-dreaded reprimand, however, Kampman explained that he understood the boys' situation. It was the time of their exams and they would miss the fun and excitement of the return trip on the boat. Sami recalls Kampman's way of educating young lads:

> We realised that Kampman was a person who understands things like this. Of course, he later let us hear how Toni's leg was fit for running away but not on the field, and during the match Kampman gave Toni stick by asking if the night before would have much effect on my game. I think the final score of the match was 1–1, and on Monday morning we were back in the exams.

Both his exams and the Premier League debut went well for Sami. On 26 April 1992, at the age of 18, he played his first match in the Finnish Premier League against FC Jazz in a 2–0 victory for MyPa. A little over a month later he graduated from upper secondary school with a Magna Cum Laude Approbatur overall grade.

1992: THE YEAR OF DEBUTS

During his first season in the Finnish Premier League, Sami immediately seized the opportunity he had been given. Already in the previous season, his rise to Kumu's first team and the youth national team had surprised pretty much everyone, but his opening campaign in the Finnish top flight was even more astounding. Sami played every minute of every single match MyPa played that season. Harri Kampman describes the rise of his young talent into the Premier League side:

> Sami impressed me very quickly. The starting point was that Esa Pekonen would play as a sweeper and Sami as a stopper, so that Peksa could make use of his experience and instruct Sami all the time. At our training camp in Cyprus in the winter, Peksa told me he didn't have much to do, playing behind Sami, and that he was of no use playing there without getting involved in the game. So, we switched their positions, so that Peksa stepped up to stopper and Sami played sweeper.
>
> It was a perfect position for Sami to develop as a player, for, in addition to Pekonen, our defence was formed by two other

experienced players, Janne Mäkelä and Mika Viljanen as full-backs, so it was easy for a newcomer to adjust to the style and form.

MyPa finished the 1992 season in fourth place, and the club's defence was the tightest in the league, much to the credit of Sami. They conceded only 29 goals in the 33 league matches, seven less than HJK, the champions, who conceded 36 goals. Sami's first season in the Finnish Premier League was almost perfect, and yet he never forgets to share the honours with the coach.

> Some coaches might have thought back then that I was too young to be given such responsibility, after all, I was only a 19-year-old kid then. Still, Kampman was courageous enough to rely on me, and I played the full 90 minutes in all 33 league matches that year. So I guess you could say that it was a successful season for a youngster like myself.
>
> The crowning event for the year was winning the Finnish Cup. We beat Jaro at the Helsinki Olympic Stadium 2–0, with goals from Esa Pekonen and Jari Litmanen.

Sami Hyypiä's name was no longer unfamiliar to Finnish football fans.

MyPa's team in 1992 was full of familiar names from the Finnish Premier League, with Jari Litmanen, who transferred there from HJK, being the brightest star. Litti transferred to Ajax Amsterdam in the middle of the season. Names like Mauri Keskitalo, Janne Lindberg, Janne Mäkelä, Esa Pekonen, Jukka Turunen and Mika Viljanen were familiar to all Finnish football fans, and now Sami Hyypiä, initially from the small PaPe of Voikkaa, was added to the list. Another Voikkaa product who made his debut in 1992 was Toni Huttunen, who played in 14 league matches and scored his first goal in one of them. Sami didn't manage to score that year.

Sami's career in international football was proceeding favourably, too. Even though the player was a year younger, in the late autumn of 1991 Jyrki Heliskoski had included Sami in the youth national team. So, as an 'under-aged' player, Sami entered the Finnish Under-21 national team and joined his current teammates in the Finnish national team, Mika Nurmela (SC Heerenveen in Holland) and Antti Niemi (Heart of Midlothian, Scotland). Other players from that Under-21 team who have since played senior football for Finland are Antti Heinola, Jokke Kangaskorpi, Tommi

Kautonen, Sami Mahlio, Jussi Nuorela, Ville Nylund, Kai Nyyssönen, Panu Toivonen, Sami Väisänen and Harri Ylönen, so Sami joined a talented group of players. During the 1992 season, Sami played five matches for the Under-21 team and four for the Under-19 team, his own age group.

Sami's life was not totally filled with football that year, though. On his 19th birthday in October 1992, Sami entered the Häme Regiment in the Finnish Defence Forces as a conscript, to serve in the Sports School unit in Lahti. After finding out about his acceptance to the Sports School, Sami had decided to put off his plans for further education to a later date. Sami had planned to studying physical education and then look for a job in that field. During his time in the army, however, Sami began to reshape his future plans in a completely different direction, although physical exercise was still a key part of his future profession. Sami decided to aim for a professional football career, and acknowledged that he still had a lot to learn in the domestic league, too, before aspiring to the leagues abroad.

As early as the turn of the month, Sami got some relief from his dull army routine when he was invited to train with Ajax Amsterdam for a few weeks. When he transferred to MyPa, Sami had agreed with the club that they would arrange an opportunity for him to visit some top European club to train with them and to get a sniff of the atmosphere in professional football was like in Europe. As coach Harri Kampman had good relations with Ajax Amsterdam, the club who had just recently purchased Jari Litmanen, Sami got to enjoy the fruit of that special clause in his contract with one of the top clubs in Europe.

> Training abroad was a tremendous experience for me. My advice to any young player is that if you get the chance to go abroad for even a short period, go. I think the best way to enter any training camp of a professional team is to think that you'll make the most out of the opportunity you have been given. At least until 1995, I went to those camps to gain experience and I never thought too much about trying to get a deal with the club. I wasn't too stressed about succeeding, I just went in to do what I could and train with 100 per cent effort. I think those trips were good for me, and I really enjoyed them. They showed me what teams in Europe were doing and, perhaps more importantly, that the players aren't that much better there.

Sami's year in football reached a peak during his visit to Amsterdam when he was called up for the Finnish national team match against Tunisia. Sami had to cut short his camp with Ajax, and he travelled to play his first full international on 7 November 1992. The head coach, Jukka Vakkila, had surprisingly selected the young newcomer from MyPa to play against Tunisia, and brought him onto the pitch in the 82nd minute. The match ended in a 1–1 draw, and the Finland goal was scored by Ari Hjelm, the joint highest-ever scorer for Finland. Sami made his debut in a full international only two years after entering the Kumu First Division squad as a lanky youth player, and only seven months after he had made his first appearance for the Under-21 national team.

The Sports School of the Finnish Defence Forces did not restrict football that much, although the first few weeks in the army were quite difficult. The Finnish football season was still running when Sami and Toni Huttunen started their national service. MyPa had training on the boys' first day in the army and it was supposed to be agreed that they would get leave for training. Sami and Toni had gone early to the garrison to make sure everything was in order before training.

> So we went into the sergeant-major's office and asked if we could leave for training. Instead of the 'yes, everything is clear' we had expected, a raging sea of yelling was the only reply we got, as the sergeant-major let us know that you don't go anywhere on your first day in the army. Toni and I were in quite a panic, and we didn't dare say anything back. We called Kampman and explained the situation and that we couldn't go anywhere.

The worry the boys had was unnecessary, though: club administrators from MyPa called the garrison and took care of the matter, and the boys got their leave for training. According to Sami, getting leave was no problem from then on, but still, the 11 months in the army were tough – both mentally and physically. In addition to doing his national service and playing for the youth national team, the training, matches and camps of MyPa were part of Sami's weekly routine. Managing the different duties required a lot of travelling, and the road between Lahti and Myllykoski became all too familiar for Sami. Even though football took up a lot of Sami's time during his national service, his attitude towards it was similar to his attitude towards school: Sami did everything faultlessly and he was a successful student in the Reserve Officer School, too. When Sami was discharged from the army, he had earned the rank of a second lieutenant and the Finnish infantry medal for excellent service. Sami recalls:

I did travel a lot during the year in the army, but I think the Sports School was the perfect place for serving. Although we spent a lot of time away from the garrison, we always did everything as well as we could when we were there. I was fortunate to room in the same barrack as Toni, so we were able to share the driving. Sometimes we were so tired when we were driving that I can't remember a thing about some of the trips.

Even though Sami reminisces about his time in the army with a smile, it was not always easy for him. Antti Niemi, the current Finnish national team keeper who served with Sami, verifies this with a colourful story. Already then, Sami and Antti were teammates in the youth national team and they were both key players on the team. Niemi explains that Sami did well in the service, although the workings of army life did make Sami's blood boil on one occasion. On this day, Niemi was the unit's duty officer and he had been reprimanded because the stairs to the Soldiers' Home had frozen over. The ice was dangerous and had to be removed immediately.

Sami happened to walk by and, without any further thought, I ordered him to chop the ice off the stairs. Of course, Sami didn't say a word and left to take care of the duty, but as I was on my break in the Soldiers' Home, others came to tell me that Sami was out there, chopping the ice and cursing. He was furious because I had asked him, even though the place was filled with shot putters and discus throwers. He thought that us football players should have pulled together.

The incident didn't affect Sami and Antti's friendship and they still like each other. According to Niemi, the years as a professional football player haven't changed Sami one bit, and he is still the same as he was in his first camps with the youth national team in 1992. 'Thank God, though, the mullet and the perm he had back then are now a thing of the past, but otherwise, he's the same lad I've always known,' Niemi affirms.

UPHILL IN LEAGUE MATCHES

The 1993 campaign started out in a promising way for Sami. Training at MyPa was going well and Sami got a fair share of responsibility in the national team. Altogether, Sami earned seven caps for the Under-21 team in 1993, scoring two goals. His first goal in this team came on 12 May 1993 in a European Championships qualifying match against Austria. Sami started the scoring and Antti Sumiala finalised the score at 2–0. The other goal Sami scored was in the match against Israel that Finland lost 2–1. Yet again, Finland did not qualify for the Championships, although the performances of the team had increased the hopes of the nation. For a third year in a row Sami had been the backbone and in those three years he had played the full 90 minutes in all but one match in his age group. The only match he missed – because of a cold – was the match against Italy during his first trip with the youth national team.

The season didn't meet the club's expectations either. In the previous season, MyPa had surprised many because they had just been promoted to the Premier League, but now other clubs knew them better and took them seriously. The squad at MyPa had remained pretty much unchanged, and the club had acquired Saku Laaksonen, Marko Rajamäki and Anders Roth to strengthen the team. Nevertheless, they had trouble getting started and the effective defensive line of Viljanen–Hyypiä–Pekonen–Mäkelä failed to achieve the level they had played throughout the previous season; the poor overall performance of the team forced Kampman to try alternative line-ups. National service had some influence on Sami's performances in particular, and his place in the starting line-up was no longer evident. On top of all that, Sami broke his foot in June, which sidelined him for a month. After Sami was back in shape, he found himself out of the team, as Mika Viljanen had moved to centre-back, pairing up with Pekonen. The team was playing well again and Kampman kept it unchanged. Although playing only 12 matches in a season was a huge disappointment for Sami, for another Voikkaa product – Toni Huttunen – the second season in the top flight was a breakthrough: he played 27 out of the 29 league matches. Kampman thinks back over the 1993 season and Sami's part in it:

> We were playing for the championship in our final match against FC Jazz in Pori, and Sami only got to warm up as a substitute and didn't get to play. I remember noticing how hard he took it, and you could see it from his face that he wanted to be on the pitch, working things out for the team instead of watching on the sidelines while others were doing it.

When reminiscing about the same situation, Sami says that he understood why Kampman kept him on the bench but, nevertheless, the experience was hard on him:

The team was doing well and I understood that Kampman didn't want to change a winning team. But it did bug me, and I'm sure it also taught me a number of things both as a player and as a human being. It made me kick myself on the backside and work even harder than before, so that I would make the starting line-up again.

By winning the final match against FC Jazz, MyPa would have won the Finnish Premier League, but a crushing 6–3 loss meant that the trophy stayed in Pori. The longed-for championship was replaced with silver medals and the record crowd at Pori, of 11,193 spectators, witnessed how the Pori team celebrated the league championship after two goals by Miika Juntunen and Luiz Antonio, and a goal apiece by Antti Sumiala and Piracaia. MyPa's goals were scored by Jukka Turunen (two) and Saku Laaksonen.

Sami's future in the silver-medal team didn't look that bright. Esa Pekonen had decided to transfer back to his home town of Lahti after the season, but MyPa had prepared to go in for the transfer market in search of an experienced centre-back to replace him. The arrival of a new centre-back might have meant another season on the bench for Sami.

There were talks that Jarmo Saastamoinen was coming to MyPa, and I must admit I wasn't that happy when I heard about it. He was a national team player, and surely he would have been brought in to play, if the club had signed him.

I had already thought about the possibility of looking for another club, but then I had a meeting with Kampman where he explained that he had decided to rely on me and that he was going to give me great responsibility at the back. In hindsight, I think Kampman had been happy with that decision, and, certainly, I felt better after that and my confidence got the boost it needed. As far as my playing went, things went back to normal in the next season, and we finished second in the table again.

Harri Kampman also thinks that the conversation he had with Sami in the autumn of 1993 was a crucial moment in Sami's development. Kampman explains:

Club management gave me permission to find a new, experienced centre-back for the team, but before I made up my mind on whether or not to go to the market, I wanted to have a one-on-one conversation with Sami. As we were talking, I realised that I didn't need any other centre-back, experienced or not. I had one right in my hands! I noticed that there was no way I could let the most talented defender in the nation go and I told Sami that I had full confidence in him, and that the position was his if he was willing to take it. Sami walked out of the room, but returned immediately and shook hands with me. The moment gave me shivers, because I realised that right then and there, Sami stepped into a man's boots and became a leader. He decided that he would take the position and carry the responsibility on his shoulders. It was no surprise, then, that he dominated the whole league that season.

Sami played in the centre with Mika Viljanen and I'm not sure if there ever has been as good a pair of centre-backs in Finland. They worked tremendously together, covering each other and sharing the responsibility everywhere on the field.

Teammate Toni Huttunen thinks that the difficult 1993 season ended up being good for Sami's career:

> The season probably made Sami more mature as a player. Until then, he had always been a starter, and this was the first setback. Knowing Sami, I'm sure he just decided to work harder and show everyone the following year. It was probably the crucial turning point in Sami's development.

At the end of the 1993 season Sami got yet another opportunity to train abroad with a top-level professional club. He spent a month in England, training with Leeds. 'Even though my own situation wasn't an ideal one then, the trip was very rewarding. I gained more experience and learnt about yet another type of coaching style.'

Sami's trip to Leeds started out under not-so-lucky stars. On his first day at Leeds, he watched the first team play a league match, accompanied by the players left out of the side:

> We were watching the match from a box and there was plenty of food to eat – chips and other greasy food. After the journey from Finland, I was starving and ate myself full while watching the match. Right after the match, one of the coaches came in and said that I could go change in the dressing-room. I was supposed to run a 12-minute test and, of course, I didn't really feel like it, after

56

eating my stomach was full, but I obviously didn't dare to say anything about it. So, I got changed, went to the track, and actually ran quite well, which surprised the others completely. It did feel horrible, though.

For some reason, the blood in my legs stopped circulating during the test and I got really cold. When we were back in the dressing-room, the coach and the physio laughed together at this crazy character. The lad was feeling cold after running a 12-minute test!

At Leeds, Sami got to train with a few legendary players, among them Gary McAllister, his future teammate at Liverpool FC. His first encounter with the Scottish veteran left a permanent mark in Sami's mind:

Leeds were preparing for a match, and I was training with the first team before it. I was young and eager, and I made the mistake of tackling Gordon Strachan a little late. Gary came to me immediately and told me: 'Take it easy, son, and don't ever tackle like that before a match.' I still remember the situation clearly.

SAMI BEGINS TO SCORE

In 1994, the Finnish youth national team took part in the qualifications for the European Championships, which were also the qualifiers for the 1996 Atlanta Olympic Games. Finland's chances of making the tournament were considered good, and Sami was the leader of the defence in that team, together with Jussi Nuorela. The goalkeepers on the team were the current professional keepers, Teuvo Moilanen (Preston North End) and Jussi Jääskeläinen (Bolton Wanderers). The skills of Sami's long-time teammate, Toni Huttunen, had also been noted by Jyrki Heliskoski, and the PaPe product was called up for the team as well. Another current Finnish international player in that team was Joonas Kolkka (Panathinaikos, Greece), who had transferred to MyPa in the same year.

MyPa's goal for the season was to turn the silver from the previous years into gold and to progress in the UEFA Cup. In 1993, MyPa had been knocked out of the Cup-Winners' Cup in the preliminary round by the Icelandic side Valur, but this time MyPa were eligible for the qualifying rounds of the UEFA Cup. In addition to Joonas Kolkka, MyPa had strengthened their team for the upcoming season by acquiring Petri Tiainen, the former Ajax Amsterdam player, for the midfield, and Niclas Grönholm to add scoring power up front. The defence of the team was anchored by the national team keeper Petri Jakonen. The number of players with Voikkaa background also increased on the team, as Mika Hernesniemi joined the team from Kumu. When Ilpo Hellsten, a veteran ten years older than Sami, had joined MyPa already the year before, the total number of players from Voikkaa on the first team became four! In 1994, Mika Hernesniemi played only one match for the Premier League side, gaining more experience at Reipas in the First Division.

MyPa started the season strongly and the team were among the highest placed throughout the season. Sami was playing consistently and with class, and in May he managed to score his first goal for the first team. Sami's first goal was a nice Mother's Day present for Irma Hyypiä, as it was scored on 7 May 1994 against HJK. MyPa took the lead with Sami's goal, but Ismo Lius scored a late equaliser, finishing the match with a draw. Once Sami had got started with the scoring, it seemed for a while that he was going to stay with it. Two weeks from scoring his first ever goal in first-team football, Sami scored twice with headers against Kuusysi.

> I scored twice against Kuusysi, which is quite unusual for me. Towards the end of the second half we were already winning 3–0 when we got a penalty. The lads were asking if I should like to go and have the shot, so that I would score a hat-trick. There were 15 minutes on the clock, and I must admit that if there had been a little less time left I might have taken it, but my confidence wasn't strong enough then. Rajamäki scored from the spot, and today, I hate to say it, but I regret not taking the chance. After all, it would have been a nice little detail on my career record, scoring a hat-trick in a league match.
>
> Since then, I've once shot a penalty in regular time. It was in 1995 against FinnPa, and I scored, but we lost the game at home 2–1.

In 1994, Sami scored two more goals. The one against Valkeakosken Haka in June was a brilliant shot from a long distance past the legendary keeper Olli Huttunen, but MyPa lost the game 3–1. A month later, Sami's goal counted a lot more, as he scored the only goal of the match when MyPa beat FC Oulu 1–0. So, the total number of goals Sami scored in 1994 was five – still the highest number of goals Sami has scored in one season. There were only two players at MyPa who scored more goals that season: Marko Rajamäki and Joonas Kolkka. As for playing time, Sami missed one match during the whole season and played the full 90 minutes in all other matches.

Once again the championship trophy slipped out of MyPa's hands at the end of the season, but this time the final league standings were clear only after a nervous wait on the final score in Pietarsaari. Before the final round, MyPa were two points behind TPV Tampere, who played their final match in Pietarsaari against FF Jaro. In the final round, MyPa destroyed KuPS 8–0 at home, and the crowd in Myllykoski were listening to the radio for the score in Pietarsaari. The crowd at Saviniemi went silent as the news of Jari Aaltonen's leading goal broke into the stadium, but as Teemu Ingi's equaliser was announced moments later, everyone went wild again. People in Myllykoski were already preparing for a rematch for the title, but Dionisio, the Brazilian striker for TPV Tampere silenced the whole town by scoring the winner five minutes from time. TPV were the unexpected champions and MyPa were left second yet again. After so many wasted chances, the silver medal tasted bitter.

In the UEFA Cup, MyPa were drawn to play against Inter Bratislava from Slovakia. The 3–0 away win in the first leg was enough to take the team to the next round, despite the shameful 1–0 defeat at home. In the first round, MyPa played the Portuguese side Boavista. In the first leg, MyPa fought bravely and returned home with only a 2–1 defeat. This provided a good starting point for the home leg. At Saviniemi, MyPa scored early in the match and were already hoping to qualify with the away goals, but a goal from a late penalty tied up the match and Boavista advanced to the second round to face Naples. The disappointment of the home side was beyond description.

In the youth national team, Sami had a big role and the team performed well. In April, the Under-21 team gained some exotic experience by playing Zambia, India and Iran in a tournament in India. Again, Sami played the full 90 minutes in each match, but the really important matches started with the Olympic team in the autumn. In their preparation for the qualification matches, Finland got beaten by Sweden, but the opening match of the European Championships qualifying campaign was successful, as Finland beat Scotland 1–0 with a penalty shot from Sami Ristilä. The success of the team continued in October, when Finland beat Greece away 4–3. Sami Hyypiä started the scoring for Finland, while Sami Väisänen scored the next two and Jasse Jalonen the winner. Sami also scored in the international friendly against Germany, which Finland lost 2–1. When the Under-21 team next played a qualifying match, Sami scored yet again, this time against San Marino when Finland beat the Mediterranean country 4–0 away.

The league season, as well as the youth national team matches, had clearly shown that Sami was among the elite centre-backs in Finland. This was also noted by the management of the full national squad and Sami played another match for his country in October 1994. Sami had made his debut in the full international squad two years before when Jukka Vakkila was the coach, but his successor, Tommy Lindholm, had not picked Sami. However, Sami felt that the youth national team matches were enough for him and he had no hesitation in taking the next step. At that time, Sami thought it was important to get as much playing time as possible and sitting on the bench during full internationals would have done no good for his development.

Two consecutive losses in the European Championships qualifying matches in the autumn of 1994 meant that Lindholm had to go. He was replaced by Jukka Ikäläinen, who showed no prejudice when he called up the team for the first match under his command. Ikäläinen invited a number of young players to the team, including Sami, Toni Huttunen, Lasse Karjalainen and Joonas Kolkka from the Under-21 team. Antti Sumiala, who was also eligible for the Under-21 team, had already been called up for the previous matches. The first match under Ikäläinen was against Estonia in Tallinn, and Finland won 7–0 although the team was mainly selected from the players in the Finnish Premier League. Sami played the full 90 minutes.

Sami was called up to the full international squad for the next match, too, even though he had played with the Under-21s against Germany the day before. Sami watched from the bench as Finland beat the Faeroe Islands 5–0 in a European Championships qualifying match. Two weeks later, Finland played a friendly against Spain and Sami played the full match again. The next match was another European Championships qualifier, against San Marino, but Ikäläinen let Sami take a rest and he played only for the Under-21 team that time.

In November, between his national team duties, Sami trained two weeks with Newcastle United, under the guidance of Kevin Keegan and Derek Fazackerley, the familiar coach from Sami's first season with Kumu. In January 1995, Joonas Kolkka accompanied Sami on a similar trip, and it started to become clear that Sami would not delight the Finnish football crowds much longer. A career in the European professional leagues was not far away. 'As years went by, I had reached my goal of playing in the Finnish Premier League with MyPa and I could set my new goals a step higher,' Sami explains.

THE FINAL SEASON IN FINLAND

Sami's contract with MyPa lasted through the 1995 season. Coach Kampman was very much aware that the season could be Sami's last in Finland. Already in the previous season he had told Sami that he could leave whenever he wanted and when the opportunity was right. Already in 1994, Sami had played so well that the clubs in Europe were lining up to talk to him. In that same year he was selected as youth national team Player of the Year.

The Finnish full international squad relied on Sami all the more, although the Under-21 matches were still his priority. The full squad's chances for qualifying were minimal, and the coaches Jukka Ikäläinen and Jyrki Heliskoski considered that it was better for both Sami and the Under-21 team if he played with them. Still, Sami was called for duty with the full squad in February 1995, the first international match of the year. However, Ikäläinen did not let Sami play in his usual position of central defence.

> Ikäläinen played more experienced players at centre-back, and I usually had to play in a defensive role as a centre-half. Neither position is best for me, but I suppose those matches taught me something, too. At the end of the day, when you're young, you want to play for the full squad, and when you get to play, you do your best no matter what the position.

In the first European Championships qualifying match for the Under-21 team in spring 1995 against San Marino, Jyrki Heliskoski made a tactical move which turned out to be perfect. He played Sami in an attacking role at centre-half, where the tall talent controlled everything in the air. Sami scored twice in 20 minutes and teammate Joonas Kolkka added another pair before half-time, making the score 4–0 at the break. At this point, Heliskoski gave Sami a breather, for Ikäläinen had asked to use Sami in the full squad's qualifier the next day. Lennart Wangel, who was then the team leader for the full squad, remembers that the San Marino match with the Under-21 team was the match where he finally registered the talent of Sami Hyypiä. Wangel describes the impact the product of his home region made in the qualifier that ended with a 6–0 victory for Finland.

> Sami really stood out in the middle of the small San Marino players. He reminded me of Elmo, Juhani Peltonen's heroic literary character who was invincible in all sports. It felt as if Sami had kicked the goal

61

kicks, then received them in the midfield and run to the attacking
third to score the goal, too. It was a stunning performance.

The next day, Ikäläinen substituted Sami in the 83rd minute, which
marked his first qualifying match for the full squad. Finland beat San
Marino 2–0, with goals by Jari Litmanen and Antti Sumiala. The next
opponents for the full squad were the Faeroe Islands and Sami played the
entire match. Although Sami earned his fourth cap in a match against
Turkey in October, the matches with the Under-21 team were still the
priority because, for the first time in a while, Finland had a really good
chance of qualifying for the Under-21 European Championships and then
to compete for the place in the Olympic Games. But as so many times
before, Finland failed to qualify. 'Our qualification was up to the last two
matches. First we lost 5–0 to Scotland away and then 3–1 to Russia. That
buried our hopes for qualification,' Sami says, recalling the disappointing
qualifying campaign.

MyPa entered the season with high hopes, although the team had gone
through some changes. At the end of the 1994 season, Janne Lindberg and
Marko Rajamäki transferred to Greenock Morton in the Scottish League,
and Janne Mäkelä, a key player at the back, left MyPa for FinnPa. Still,
the team remained strong, as the new players from FC Haka – Sami Mahlio
and Tommi Kautonen – were quality players. During the 1995 season, six
players from MyPa played for Finland: Sami, Petri Jakonen, Joonas
Kolkka, Jukka Koskinen, Sami Mahlio and Petri Tiainen. In addition, Toni
Huttunen and Jarkko Koskinen were regulars with the Under-21 team and
Jukka Lindström, Antti Pohja, Miikka Multaharju, and Jani Uotinen with
the boys' national team. With this much talent at the club, it was no
wonder that people in Myllykoski expected nothing less than a
championship from its team.

The beginning of the season followed a similar script to the previous
season. MyPa were again among the top clubs from the very beginning,
holding the top position from mid-June until early August. With Sami
Hyypiä as the natural leader in the club's defence, the other regular
starters at the back were Toni Huttunen, Mika Viljanen and Jukka
Koskinen. In the midfield, Mika Hernesniemi made a breakthrough in the
Premier League and played 20 matches. Sami didn't miss a single minute
during his final season in Finland. His scoring spell fell in July this time,
as he scored three goals in three matches. Sami didn't score any more goals
that season, which means the total number of goals he scored in the
Finnish Premier League was eight in four seasons.

In the UEFA Cup, MyPa advanced from the preliminary round against the Scottish side Motherwell, and were drawn to play the top Dutch club PSV Eindhoven in the first round. In the home leg, played in September, Sami Mahlio scored the leader for MyPa, but PSV's Brazilian star Ronaldo equalised. The club's expectations were high after a 1–1 draw at home, but the away leg a week later ended in a disaster. After fighting evenly for the first 45 minutes, MyPa collapsed completely. Ronaldo scored four goals and the match ended with a final score of 7–1. The biggest news on trip, however, was that Joonas Kolkka had signed a professional contract. The Dutch Premier League side Willem II would acquire Kolkka immediately after the end of the Finnish season. Club technical manager Martin van Geel reveals that Willem was developing an idea of another acquisition as well:

> The MyPa–PSV match where we had come to watch Joonas Kolkka was the first time we saw Sami Hyypiä play. This is why we also saw Sami play against HJK in a league match and in the away match between PSV and MyPa. We signed Joonas immediately after the match, but Sami remained strong in our thoughts, too. From the first glimpse, he was an interesting player, and we decided to contact him later.

At the end of the season, another club from beside a paper mill, FC Haka, the pride of Valkeakoski, interfered with MyPa's plans for a championship and took the title. FC Haka secured the title in the penultimate match and MyPa had to settle for yet another silver medal, for the third time in a row. MyPa had also made their way to the Finnish Cup final and the team that lined up against them on 28 October at the Helsinki Olympic Stadium was FC Jazz from Pori. The Cup final was Sami's final match for MyPa, and his career in Finland could not have ended better: MyPa took the Cup title 1–0, with a header by Sami.

A charter train from Myllykoski had brought hundreds of fans to Helsinki and the atmosphere at the stadium was tremendous. The players left to celebrate the victory and took the same train home with the fans; there was no limit to the festivities. Sami could not participate in the celebrations, though, for he had to stay in Helsinki for a season-closing ceremony. There, for the second time in a row, Sami was awarded the youth national team Player of the Year. Sami recalls the party: 'I couldn't make it to the Cup train even though I wanted to. Other players got off the train in Lahti and went out to celebrate the win, and as soon as the award ceremony was over I took a cab and made it to the party after all.'

Sami's final match for MyPa left a sweet memory. It was a memory of a team where Sami had loved to play and, even after several years abroad as a professional, Sami still thinks about his time at MyPa with warmth. The unreserved atmosphere at the small-town club appealed to the young lad from the first day. The players were carefully looked after, and they had their own premises at the MyPa house, where many of them spent a lot of free time as well. The first team's kit manager couple, Arja and Erkki Leppänen, particularly impressed Sami:

> They were always ready to help, no matter what the time or the problem. At first, I really didn't have the courage to ask for anything, but in the end I dared and knew to turn to them if I needed something. There's this one time in particular that I remember, when we had just come back from an away match in the middle of the night and we were a bit hungry. It must have been around three o'clock, but our physio 'Käärö [Bundle]' called his wife Arja immediately and sooner than we realised, she brought us warm pastries for a snack.

4

The Professional Career Starts in Holland

FOUR YEARS IN THE FINNISH PREMIER LEAGUE WITH MYPA HAD BEEN good for Sami. Competitively, two Cup titles and three silver medals in the league were magnificent achievements. Individually, Sami had achieved success on many fronts: *Pallokopla*, the Finnish football journalists' association, had selected Sami in the Premier League All Star line-ups for 1992, 1994 and 1995. He had been a key player for the Under-21 national team and his place in the full international squad had become secure. The years in Myllykoski had left a lot of good memories but it was time to move on. In November, Sami flew to Tilburg, Holland, to train with the local Premier League side, Willem II, for two weeks. Willem already had world-class centre-backs Jaap Stam and Jean-Paul van Gastel, so Sami was not immediately offered a contract. Stam rose to the world's elite of central defenders in the Dutch national team, and after Willem he made a name for himself at PSV, Manchester United and Lazio. Van Gastel became a familiar name in Feyenoord's line-up.

Sami also paid short visits to Oldham and Örgryte in Sweden, but the most exotic visit, however, was to Turkey, where he trained with Samsunspor for five days.

> It was a pretty wild experience. Honestly speaking, it was not in my best interests to sign with a club in Turkey, for if you are at the beginning of your professional career in football, Turkey is probably not the first place that comes to your mind. But I went there regardless, just out of general interest if nothing else.

In Germany, Werder Bremen also tested Sami for about four days, but that visit didn't produce any lucrative offers either.

> All the clubs were interested in me, but the offers were such that accepting them would have made no sense at all. At that point, I think only Örgryte's offer was a realistic one, but it still didn't attract me enough to go pack my bags and sign with them. From the visits I paid to the different clubs, I got an idea that many clubs were looking for a chance to sign players for as little money as possible.

During his stay in Germany, however, things suddenly began to happen for Sami. Harri Kampman called him and said that Willem II needed a centre-back. Sami sheds some light on the background to his first professional contract:

> I had visited Willem in the autumn, on a sort of a test camp, and back then they had Stam and van Gastel playing in central defence. Stam's departure was already an issue of speculation then and I was told I was a potential replacement for him. As soon as Stam's transfer materialised during the winter break in the Dutch league, they called from Willem and said they wanted me to replace him. So, even though I had planned for the move for a while, when it was time to go, it all happened rather quickly,

MyPa didn't set any restrictions on Sami's transfer. On the contrary, Harri Kampman played an active role in helping his players sign with foreign clubs. 'The offer Willem made for Sami was good, but not top level,' says Kampman. 'Nevertheless, the timing was just right, for Willem II was a very good club for Sami's development. I knew that Sami would quickly mature as a player while playing for the Dutch side.'

In the late autumn of 1995, Sami had moved to Myllykoski with his girlfriend Niina, but the couple lived together only for a few months. Sami moved to Tilburg, a small town in Holland, on his own, in February 1996. Niina was going to follow along in the summer, when all practical matters had been arranged. Jouko and Irma Hyypiä were happy and proud of their son's success, but the move abroad made them a little uneasy. Although Sami had travelled round the world, living abroad was a completely different matter. After all, Sami was only 22 years old.

'Sami has always kept in contact with the family, and our relationship has remained strong throughout his career,' Jouko Hyypiä explains. 'We talk on the phone at least two to three times a week, and Sami always calls after a match to let us know how it went and how he played.'

Sami's transfer did not yet mean any major news headlines, for Willem II had not been that successful in the past few decades. Traditionally, the top positions in Holland were divided between the three big clubs, Ajax Amsterdam, PSV Eindhoven and Feyenoord. The last time the Dutch League title was won by a team outside the three was in 1981, and the time before that was in 1962. So, the three clubs had held a superior, dominant position in Dutch football for the past 40 years, and Ajax Amsterdam, with Jari Litmanen as one of their bigger stars, had been in control for the past few years.

Willem did have strong traditions, though. The club was founded in 1896 and had won the league title three times: in 1916, 1952 and 1955. They were victorious in the Dutch Cup title twice, in 1944 and 1963, which meant that they had not made it to the European club competition for over three decades. Therefore, Willem were best known as a club that produced star players for the bigger clubs. For a young player from Finland, Tilburg was an excellent place for growth and development, because the pressure put on the team's shoulders was not overwhelming. The club organisation was very professional, which was reinforced by its technical manager, the former Ajax Amsterdam and Dutch national team star player, Martin van Geel. Under his command, Willem II were actively looking for promising talent and refining them into full-scale professionals for the use of the big European clubs. The club's Willem II Stadium has a capacity of 14,000, and the crowd in Tilburg always expects an attacking style of football from its team. Winning was not as important as the style of play.

Sami's way to Willem was paved by Joonas Kolkka, who had transferred to the club in autumn 1995. Kolkka had suffered from injuries, and he had not yet made his debut in the Dutch top flight. However, the town of Tilburg had become familiar to Joonas, and he was a great help to Sami when he was taking care of the practical matters related to the move. Sami talks about his early days in Tilburg:

> When I arrived at Willem, I lived in a hotel for the first four months. There were no apartments available at that time and, of course, the club couldn't know what type of apartment I was looking for.
>
> Joonas already had a flat, which he shared with another player, and I spent a lot of time there. The fact that Joonas had been there for six months before me helped a great deal, for he knew his way around town and how everything worked. I only stayed at my

hotel at night, and I think if I had just stayed in the hotel room watching TV all the time, the walls might have started closing in on me. Besides, I think that my arrival helped Joonas, too.

Joonas Kolkka welcomed Sami to Tilburg with pleasure. The two had a long history together, so they got along really well – and they still do. Joonas laughs as he recalls:

> I had been Sami's roommate on several away trips at MyPa and the youth national teams. Everything went well between us, except for the few occasions when Sami demonstrated why one of his nicknames during our MyPa years was 'Hot Hyypiä'. Sometimes he lost it really bad . . . I think 'Hot Hyypiä' was originally thought up by Toni Huttunen during their time in national service, and it remained at MyPa. Even now I sometimes have to remind him about the old nickname, when he needs to be brought down to earth.

Moving to Holland was not a big culture shock for Sami because the Dutch lifestyle isn't that much different from Finland. The language was one thing that felt complicated, though, so Sami decided to work on it purposefully.

> The club had arranged a Dutch teacher for us, but we only had a class once a week, 45 minutes at a time. It wasn't very useful, so I started practising my Dutch with the team, too: I tried to listen carefully to what the lads were saying, and I also decided to have the courage to speak up. Of course, I made a lot of mistakes in the beginning, but no one cared about it. On the contrary, I think they were happy because I made the effort to try to speak their language.
>   It took about a year and a half before I knew enough Dutch to handle everything in Dutch without having to resort to English. The best way to learn was to keep talking, whenever possible.

The difference between Holland and Finland was far greater on the pitch than off it. Sami didn't have much time to worry about adjusting, though, for his career at Willem got off to a flying start. Sami put on the club's white, blue and red striped jersey sooner than he had anticipated. 'We had a match the day after my arrival at Tilburg,' Sami remembers. 'I was on the squad and substituted on with about ten minutes remaining in the match. So in that sense, it all started out well for me, coming on as a sub immediately. Joonas and I made our debuts in the same match, on 9 February 1996.'

On Sami and Joonas's debut, Willem were beaten 5–0 by Vitesse, but all the goals had been scored before the two Finns came on. Willem's results were poor overall anyway, and soon Sami's promising early position had become uncertain. Only a few weeks after Sami's arrival, the club sacked the manager, Theo de Jong, and named his assistant, Jim Calderwood, as his replacement. 'I did think that this was not the best possible start for me, as the manager who had wanted me at the club was sacked. Fortunately, I got along just fine with Calderwood,' says Sami.

Getting used to the Dutch style of play took a little time, but new manager Calderwood was patient with his new centre-back.

> I don't think our team was that good back then. The manager trusted me and gave me responsibility, even though I was playing inconsistently. It was difficult to adjust to the new style of play and my performances changed from weak to solid. One of the more difficult new things was playing man-on-man in the back, with no cover. The full-backs stayed with their marks and didn't pinch in towards the centre to cover for the centre-backs. You were on your own against the forward.
>
> From a football point of view, Holland was a good step forward, although the level was not that much higher than in Finland. I think that if MyPa had played against Willem at that time, it would have been quite an even match. Still, the transfer was very important for me in terms of the future.

As a manager, Calderwood was more a friend than a serious authoritative figure. His easy way of coaching was perfect for Sami, who was adjusting to the new style of play.

> The first season and a half at Willem were crucial in terms of adjustment, for the playing system and rhythm were so different from Finland. Later, when Co Adriaanse was the manager, the coaching methods were not so lenient. If you played inconsistently or had a poor match, you were out of the line-up immediately.

In Sami's first campaign with Willem II, the club finished 12th in the league, with Ajax winning the title. Sami made an appearance in 14 matches, stepping into big boots as both Jaap Stam and Jean-Paul van Gastel, the club's reliable pair at the back, transferred in the middle of the season. In addition to Sami, Willem acquired Bert Konterman to fill the gap left by Stam's and van Gastel's departure. Konterman has since also made his way to the Dutch national side. Even though the results were poor in their first season, Martin van Geel, Willem's technical manager had strong faith in his new Finnish players. Van Geel looks back:

> I think the team changed a bit too much, for before Stam and van Gastel's departure we were near the top in the table, and yet we finished the season in 12th place. Too many changes confused our game, although we acquired quality players to replace the ones who left.
>
> Joonas and Sami made an immediate impact, but still, the rise to the top takes a little time. At first, Joonas was injured and Sami took a while before he learnt the Dutch style of play. We were patient, though, for we knew Sami's potential. Patience paid off, as Sami improved his game continuously and developed into a brilliant professional with us. Already in his second season, he proved that we had made a really successful acquisition. He always has the right attitude towards football, and he was willing to do the work in every match and in every training session.

TO A TOUGH SCHOOL

Sami settled down comfortably in Holland. In the summer of 1996, he moved, with his girlfriend Niina, to his own apartment. Tilburg is an attractive little town in the south of Holland and its citizens have a rather dishonourable nickname, *kruikenzeiger*, which translates as 'piss-porter'. The nickname refers to the ammonia factory that once lay in the area and whose repellent-smelling odour the citizens carried. The people of Tilburg are not ashamed of the name, however, and are actually proud of it. A brewery in the area even has a beer called *Kruikenzeiger*!

In terms of football, the years at Willem were educational for Sami. Since the club and its fans preferred to play an attacking style of football, the defenders were often on their own when protecting their goal. Added to the fact that the whole defensive line played man-on-man, the mistakes at the back showed on the scoreboard immediately. The defenders had no chance for a breather at any point in the matches. 'The Dutch one-on-one system is more difficult than the one we had used in Finland,' Sami explains. 'During my three and a half years at Willem, I learnt the style, though, on a personal level, it was easier to go back to the old, familiar system that we use in England, too.'

The days as a professional football player were not any longer in Holland than they were in Finland, but the season was much longer. With the longer season, you have to concentrate on important matches one month after another. 'I think that the amount of training is smaller in Holland than in Finland, but the tempo is quicker,' Sami estimates.

Away trips in Holland were easier to get to than in Finland. Finland is ten times larger than Holland, where the distance from the northern end to the southern border is only a little over 200 km, and even shorter from the eastern border to the western border of the country.

> We always took a bus to the away matches in Holland. I think that the longest trip was about three hours, and already after an hour and a half the players thought it was a really long trip. When I told them that the shortest away trip in Finland is about the same length, they were shaking their heads in disbelief. In Finland, we never took a bus to Rovaniemi, for example, but we drove the bus to Helsinki and flew from there.

In his second season with Willem, Sami played a lot of minutes and got a fair share of responsibility. Still, the team continued to do poorly and Calderwood's style, based on being friends with the players, did not bring the most out of the squad. 'Some players took advantage of their friendship with the manager and trained only when they felt like it,' recalls Sami. 'It didn't do any good for the team, and it was really no surprise that we didn't produce any results either.'

In the 1996–97 season, it was Feyenoord's turn to win the Dutch league title. Willem II finished 15th in the table, only a point above the relegation play-off zone. Sami played 30 matches and scored his first goal in the Dutch Premier League on 5 April 1997. Willem lost the match 3–1 to SC Heerenveen and Sami's goal was a late consolation goal. That goal was the only one Sami scored that season, but Joonas Kolkka scored a respectable 7 goals in the 32 league matches he played. In his first season with Willem, he had played only seven matches, but the second year was a success for Joonas, who scored one-fifth of the team's goals for that season. In a team which finished near the bottom, it was enough to share the top scorer title in the club.

Martin van Geel did not rest on his laurels and watch his club wander in oblivion: he hired Co Adriaanse, a manager who has become a legend in Holland, to run the first team. Adriaanse, a manager who is known for his autocratic coaching methods, had learned his coaching style during his many years on the staff of Ajax Amsterdam, and he treats his players with an iron-clad touch. In broad terms, the gentle methods of Jim Calderwood were changed into grind and hardship by Adriaanse. There are some wild legends about Adriaanse, who later became manager at Ajax, and most of them are true. The players feared and respected the cold-hearted man who might punish the team with 20-km runs after a weak performance. Democracy was not in his vocabulary. Sami recalls:

> When Adriaanse arrived and started listing his rules, I thought I was back in the army.
>
> Everything changed completely and the players who had taken advantage of the situation during Calderwood's reign were kicked out of the team. The same sluggish training did not work with the new manager. We didn't acquire many new players and I don't think the club even had that much money to go into the transfer market. Adriaanse did want a few players, and he got what he wanted, but otherwise the team remained the same.

Sami and Joonas were accompanied by another Finn when Jukka Koskinen joined Willem in the summer. Koskinen was familiar to the boys, for he also came from MyPa and had played for the Finnish national team. He never managed to convince Adriaanse of his skills, however, and he ended up not playing much: during his stay at Willem, he played 20 matches in his first season, but only five in the season after. Sami says of his former teammate:

> The situation was difficult for Jukka back then. He had been signed before Adriaanse arrived, and the new manager didn't have any idea of him as a player. The season started out well for him, and he played a lot, but then he unfortunately got injured. After he was back in shape, it was difficult for him to make the squad again.

Sami wants to emphasise that even though Adriaanse's way of treating his players was strict, he was a very competent and just manager. All players were treated fairly.

In a way, I like strict discipline. I think it is good for the team when the rules and penalties are the same for everyone and individuals don't get to horse around.

I think Adriaanse was a very good manager, and he could improve us individually and as a team. As a person, he could have been different, of course, but that's his style. It is difficult to change who you are and I don't think Adriaanse changed me during the two years he coached me at Willem.

Both Sami and Joonas Kolkka attest that players can talk about football matters with Adriaanse, even though there was never any doubt about who has the ruling power. 'I always thought I could talk with him face to face if I needed to and tell him my views on the game,' Sami notes. 'What he actually took into consideration is a different matter, though. He had his own ideas, and he wouldn't change them no matter who said what.'

For Joonas Kolkka, the season with Adriaanse was productive and training under his command wasn't too hard either. However, Joonas is quick to point out that he only spent a year training with Adriaanse before transferring to PSV Eindhoven. This is how Joonas evaluates Adriaanse's methods:

> I played the most successful season of my career so far with Adriaanse, and I have only positive things to say about him. Physically, the training was hard, but that style has always suited me fine. As for the communication, it worked for me from the first day, although I am aware that there are differing views about him, too.

In Sami's opinion, Adriaanse was the right type of manager at the right time for a small club like Willem II. Under his command, the players were in strong physical shape and the club achieved its best results for decades. He simply knew how to get the most out of the players. Sami explains:

> For the club, hiring Adriaanse as the manager was like winning the lottery, but it was probably not the same for the players. For me personally, it wasn't exactly the happiest time in my life. Adriaanse made us work enormously hard throughout the year, and you could see it in the matches. We were in shape to go at full speed the whole 90 minutes, and we often wore out our opponents.
>
> We ran a lot in training. I even lost a few kilos in weight though

I wasn't overweight. Weight-lifting, for example, was totally forbidden, for the manager thought it didn't do any good for a football player. You could go to the gym if you were hurt, but not otherwise.

Sami remembers a time in pre-season when there were two training sessions and a match on the same day. After a tough session in the morning, Adriaanse freed the players who were going to play in the evening from the other training session. Back at the hotel, two players decided to pay a visit to the gym and loosen their muscles after a demanding session on the pitch.

> The manager noticed this and ordered the two to the afternoon training as well, since they had so much energy left. The other one of the players was also in the starting line-up for the match, but he was so worn out already before kick-off that he simply couldn't play. Adriaanse wasn't interested in things like that, though. It was pre-season.
>
> When we played friendlies, he used to tell us how many goals we should score against each opponent. The scores depended on the opponent's level: we had to beat First Division teams by one goal, Second Division teams by two, and so on. If we were playing part-timers or amateurs, the score might have been seven, for example. If the match then ended with a 7–0 result or more, he was grateful for a job well done, but if we failed to score the required number of goals, he punished us in the next training session. It was pretty tough back then.

No matter what people say about Adriaanse's coaching methods, he brought results to the club. In his first season with the team, Willem finished fifth in the league and were granted admission to the first round of the UEFA Cup. It was the first time the club had got into the European contest in 35 years and Tilburg went wild. People on the streets cheered for their heroes and, according to Sami, the atmosphere in the town was unbelievable. During the 1997–98 season, Sami played 30 matches, Joonas 29 and Jukka Koskinen 20. While Sami didn't score for the club that season, Joonas managed to score nine goals and Jukka also got his name on the scoring sheet once.

If Adriaanse's first season at Willem delighted Tilburg, the best was yet to come. Though the team had trained hard in the summer, the following season started out with mediocre performances. As the season progressed, however, Willem kept improving, and at the end of the season they were second. Finishing second in the Dutch league also meant that the small-town club had won a place in the Champions League. In the middle of the season, Sami Hyypiä had been promoted to team captain, and he wore the captain's armband honourably until the end of his final season at Willem. Looking back at his final season at Willem II, Sami, then the favourite player of the Tilburg fans, recounts: 'The fans' expectations for the team were a bit higher that season, but no one probably thought we would be that successful. We lost only one game after New Year and that was after we had secured our second place, and we only drew a couple of times, so it was a tremendous season in all respects.'

In the 1998–99 season, Sami played 26 matches for Willem and scored two goals. The first came at the end of August, when Sami scored the winner against Fortuna Sittard. The second goal was scored when Willem crushed Feyenoord 4–1 at home in March. Sami scored his goal in the 21st minute, and interestingly, Feyenoord's consolation goal was scored by van Gastel – the player whom Sami had replaced at Willem.

In the autumn of 1998 Sami suffered his first serious injury since the summer of 1993. He hurt his knee but it didn't require a big operation and Sami walked home on the day of the surgery. Still, he had to sit out a couple of matches because of the injury.

Willem's European campaign didn't bring any success for the club. The team beat Dynamo Tbilisi from Georgia in the first round and advanced to the second, where their European campaign was cut short by the Spanish side, Real Betis. In the home leg against Real Betis, Adriaanse named Sami team captain. He wanted the captain to be able to communicate with the referee properly – and the referee was Mikko Vuorela from Finland. Janne Kosunen, a Finnish football journalist who followed the home leg at the Willem II Stadium, remembers that at that time Sami was the dominant figure on the pitch and clearly the crowd favourite. Kosunen's emotions surfaced after the match, as he describes the atmosphere at the Willem II Stadium: 'It was a tremendous match. Willem won 3–0 and the crowd were singing Sami Hyypiä's name at the top of their voices. It felt great that a Finnish player had done all this.'

The celebrations of the Tilburg fans after Willem were granted admission to the UEFA Cup were soon forgotten in the spring in the face of an even greater achievement. The whole town was celebrating the place in the Champions League, but the celebrations were overshadowed by the news that broke at the end of the season. Sami Hyypiä had signed a contract with the famous Liverpool FC in the English Premier League. In his final match in front of the home crowd, Sami was substituted at the end of the match so that the fans had a chance to say goodbye to their hero. His teammates carried Sami off the field as the crowd cheered wildly. The work had been done. When describing the significant role Sami had on that Willem team, Martin van Geel doesn't hold back on superlatives. 'In addition to his brilliant talent as a player, Sami Hyypiä is a wonderful human being,' van Geel enthuses. 'There wasn't a single person in our club who didn't like him. He is polite, friendly, and he has a good sense of humour. And another important asset is that he learnt the Dutch language really fast.'

THE NATIONAL TEAM KEEPS IMPROVING
The years at Willem II had elevated Sami to a group of respected professionals. His appearances for the Finnish national team added an extra level of depth to Sami's career development, for the tall stopper had become the leader of the Finland defence. In the autumn of 1995, the Dane Richard Møller-Nielsen had been appointed the head coach of the Finnish national team. The Dane had coached his home country to the European title in 1992, and his achievements speak for themselves.

'The years under Møller-Nielsen were fruitful,' Sami says of the former national team coach. 'He was an experienced coach who gave us a lot of good advice on tactics. He often spoke about confidence and built our faith in ourselves and our abilities.'

Møller-Nielsen accepted his position in the summer of 1996 and Finland began to prepare for the World Cup qualifiers that would start in the autumn. As an increasing number of the national team players played in the European leagues and the coach had a proven record of achievement, the qualifying group didn't seem too difficult this time (Finland were grouped with Azerbaijan, Norway, Switzerland and Hungary). The expectations set for the national team were high.

The qualifying campaign got off to a poor start. In their first two matches, Finland lost to Hungary away and to Switzerland at home. The schedule became tighter the next spring, when Finland beat Azerbaijan both home and away and drew 1–1 with Norway away in between. The good away result against Norway, who had made it to the previous World Cup, was overshadowed by the poor performance against them at home, which resulted in an ugly defeat. Nevertheless, the away win against Switzerland took Finland back to the battle for second place and admission to the play-off against Yugoslavia. Sami missed the Norway and Switzerland matches due to an injury, but he was back in the squad for the decisive match against Hungary at the Helsinki Olympic Stadium on 11 October 1997. A win in that match would have meant that Finland would play Yugoslavia in a two-legged play-off for a place in the World Cup. When Antti Sumiala scored a beautiful goal and Finland took the lead, it started to look promising for the Finnish hopes of finishing second in the group. The victory was almost in the hands of the Finland team, when the whole world seemed to collapse: in the final minutes of the match, the Finnish players scored an own goal in a goal-front scurry after a corner kick. The Hungarians stood and watched in awe as the ball bounced off five different Finns before crossing the line. The capacity crowd at the Olympic Stadium went silent in disbelief and the players seemed to share the feeling.

The poignant defeat by Hungary raised the debate over the age-old topic: do Finnish football players have the mental strength to make it to the top of international football? Sami admits that the loss was an exceptionally hard blow for the players, too, but he would still prefer not to make any large-scale conclusions on the basis of one single result. Sami considers the Finland national team:

> You have to keep in mind that even if we had won the match, we would have only made it to the play-off against Yugoslavia. Yugoslavia gave a severe beating to Hungary and qualified for the World Cup with the aggregate score of 12–1 so, unlike us, the Hungarians didn't have much reason for any shilly-shally.
>
> Of course, the result bugged me, but I've seen even more embarrassing goals and other last-minute setbacks during my career, too. Despite the poor result against Hungary, we have pulled good crowds for our home matches, and today, the Finnish fans also cheer for us instead of the traditional silent viewing.

Even though Finland failed to qualify for the Championships yet again, the performances of the national team began to consolidate Finland's position on the European football map. In the summer of 1998, Finland played friendly matches against Germany and World Cup hosts France, and the decision of two football superpowers to meet Finland in the last stages of preparation for the World Cup was a good demonstration of the improved status of Finnish football. The match against Germany ended in a goalless draw, but the forthcoming world champions, France, turned out to be the stronger side of the two, winning by a narrow 1–0 margin. In association with the French national team's visit to Finland, for the first time in his life – and at least until now, the only time in his life – Sami played for a national team other than Finland. After their friendly against the Finland full international squad, France played against HJK Helsinki, so that the players who didn't play against Finland would get some action as well. For one reason or another, France were short of players, and Aimé Jacquet, their national team coach, asked if Finland could lend a few players. Sami accepted the offer and played at centre-back, wearing Marcel Desailly's jersey. Sami still has the jersey of the world champion centre-back as a memento from the unusual match. Sami describes this rare experience:

> Originally, I was supposed to be a substitute, but just before the match the coach gave me a jersey with Desailly's name on it, and wrote my name on the starting line-up. The French players were laughing at how Marcel had changed all of a sudden. The international friendly we played the night before had worn me out, so I was exhausted at around 70 minutes into the match and asked to be taken off. Despite being tired, I really enjoyed playing with the world champions. I was paired up with Frank Leboeuf at centre-back against Mika Kottila, a teammate of mine from the Finnish national team. Other players whom I remember from our side were Vincent Candela, Bernard Dioméde, Alain Boghossian and Thierry Henry. Zinedine Zidane rested that day.

After the match, Janne Kosunen wrote in his column for *Veikkaaja*, a Finnish sports paper: 'Of course, Hyypiä is not a Desailly just yet, but he has no reason to be ashamed of his performance either.' Kosunen's view hit the mark quite accurately, for the French stopper was generally considered the best centre-back at the World Cup that summer. Since then, the roles have probably been reversed.

Autumn 1998 started yet another qualifying campaign for the national team, as Finland were drawn in a tough group with Germany, Turkey, Northern Ireland and Moldova for the qualification for the European Championships in 2000. The campaign started with a home win against Moldova, but Finland were humbled by Northern Ireland in Belfast, losing the away match 1–0. The Finnish media scolded the team and gave them no chance in the next match against Turkey in Istanbul only four days after the match in Belfast. The players didn't mind the media prejudice and won the match 3–1. In pouring rain, Finland gave a sensational performance at one of the most dreaded stadiums of international football and rose to top spot in the group. Finland's goals were scored by Mixu Paatelainen (formerly of Bolton Wanderers, currently with Strasbourg in France), Jonathan Johansson (Charlton Athletic) and Jari Litmanen. Defensively, Antti Niemi made numerous remarkable saves and Sami Hyypiä dominated the air in the middle of the Turkish attacking frenzy. Beating Turkey on their home turf is an achievement that even some of the most successful football nations have failed to accomplish, and the win was particularly important for the Finland team, who were doomed to lose according to the Finnish media. Sami recalls the atmosphere at the Ali Sami Yen Stadium:

> The mere journey to Turkey made me a bit unsure, for the Turkish crowd is famous for its fanaticism and wild nature. We knew that we were headed for a real witch's cauldron, and the stadium was already packed with 20–30,000 wild fans when we went in for our warm-up. Coins, cigarette lighters and all sorts of things were thrown at us, so we had to choose our place for the warm-up carefully. We ended up warming up almost in the centre circle, and I've never experienced anything like that anywhere else. The hostile crowd were shouting, screaming, booing and throwing things on the pitch throughout the match.
>
> I honestly didn't believe we'd win until we scored from a counter-attack in the end to make it 3–1.

After the match, Sami appeared in front of the Finnish media representatives. As his first statement, he reminded the reporters about their articles before the match. The journalists who had underestimated Finland's chances were now quiet and listened to Sami's lecture carefully. Sami explains:

> I told them that they should think about the things they print on paper. It was nice to have the chance to shoot back at the reporters, for it has usually been the other way round. It is more common that the reporters get to criticise us after losses and, frankly, I don't really like it. I think I can take criticism when I deserve it, but if I get the blame undeservedly, I may lose my temper and shoot back. As for the match against Northern Ireland, we could just as well have won it. The goal they scored was an easy one, and that time we just couldn't equalise.

One target for Sami's reproach was Janne Kosunen of *Veikkaaja*, who had predicted at least a two-goal defeat in his article before the match. Sami's words and the whole situation left a clear mark in the reporter's memory:

> We were in some dark hallways, in catacombs underneath the stadium and there were soldiers with machine-guns not far from us. There was a loud clamour in the Finland dressing-room, and Hyypiä was standing right in front of us. For a moment, he was looking around and didn't look anyone in the eye. I felt that, by his presence and confidence, he was a head taller than everyone else.
>
> It really made me stop and think. I could tell it was an important thing for Sami to say. At that point, he wanted to remind us about the persistence and tenacity of the Finland team. Sami has always believed in his team and their chances, and in that sense, he is a hard-headed lad. It seems that pessimistic reviews are particularly troublesome for him.

The win over Turkey took Finland to the top of the qualifying group for a moment, but as the campaign progressed, things changed. In March, Germany beat Finland in Nurnberg, and in early June, Turkey paid a visit to Helsinki and got their revenge with a 4–2 victory. Immediately after that, Finland were forced to a goalless draw by Moldova and yet another qualifying campaign ended unsuccessfully. The heroes of Istanbul had once again become underachievers. After the match, Sami wanted to face the media again. The first thing he said was that he couldn't remember playing so poorly for the national team in his life.

Sami's substandard performances against Turkey and Moldova have a legitimate and human explanation, though. Just before the matches, Sami's transfer to Liverpool FC had been finalised and he had just played his final emotional matches for Willem. It would be hard for anyone to put on his best performance in a similar situation. A transfer of this scale can be compared to a win in a lottery: it is excellent news, but it turns your world upside down and messes up your normal daily life. Sami played the next international matches as a Liverpool player, and he hasn't played a poor game for the national team since.

Richard Møller-Nielsen, the head coach of the Finland team from 1996–99, joins the list of people who praise Sami's consistency and attitude. In the autumn of 2001, the experienced Danish coach reminisced about his reliable defender in the Finland team:

His attitude towards playing is tremendous and his hatred for losing immense. Sami Hyypiä is clearly one of the most professional-minded players I have ever coached.

His performances with the national team were consistent, but one match in particular remains in my memory. The away match against Turkey showed the desire Sami had for winning more clearly than in any other match. The whole team wanted to show the nay-sayers, and everyone played well, but Sami's performance was the best in my time with Finland. Of course, I'm also happy that he scored the first goal in his international career in my last match as the Finland coach against Northern Ireland in Helsinki.

HEADED FOR LIVERPOOL

Transferring from Holland to Liverpool was the end result of a long process. Representatives of the famous English club had seen Finland play Germany before the 1998 World Cup and Sami Hyypiä's name had been marked in the match report. In the autumn of the same year, a Liverpool scout saw one Willem match, but Sami didn't hear from Liverpool for quite a while. Sami looks back:

> The Dutch league match the scout saw was not a particularly strong performance from me. We lost 4–1, and I don't know if that diminished their interest in me, for they didn't pay a visit for six months. There are always rumours, and I never stress out about them. If someone is watching our match, it is still a long way away from an actual contract.

Throughout the first half of the season, both Sami and the team improved their performances, and Sami also stepped it up in the national team. In Liverpool, the plans for acquiring Sami started to progress in the spring. In April 1999, Ron Yeats, Liverpool's main scout and a legendary player himself, saw the international friendly between Finland and Slovenia in Ljubljana, Slovenia. Liverpool scouts also visited the Dutch league matches regularly, and Liverpool's level of interest started to become clear to Sami. Sami recalls the spring of 1999:

> In the spring, I think about ten different people from Liverpool attended our matches, so I guess the system is such that everyone in the coaching staff has to see the player in action before any deal

is finalised. I also met a few people from the club a few times. As for Gérard Houllier, I met him once at our stadium after one of our matches, and he told me what he had in mind. He explained that he was going to build a new, successful Liverpool side and he needed someone at my position. I got the idea that he was planning on using me as the other one of the two central defenders, and after the meeting I really started to believe that they meant business.

Just before the end of the season, Sami was invited to Liverpool and the transfer was finalised. Sami considers how quickly the process developed:

I had reserved tickets for a *Lord of the Dance* show, but it had to wait because of the unexpected trip to Liverpool. I had my physical during the trip and signed the contract right after that.

I think it was a Thursday when I returned from Liverpool, and our last away match of the season, where we secured our second place and admission to Champions League, was on the following Sunday. It was an emotional moment, and I was sad leaving everything behind and moving on to another club. When I was thinking about the other players and the fans, I felt as if I were letting them down. We had just accomplished something big, and now I was going to leave. With all these feelings in my head, it felt nice when everyone was happy for me and wished me luck.

Sami's transfer was announced the following week, before the last match of the season. Willem II got a transfer fee of about £2.7 million. Although the amount is not that great for Liverpool FC, it was significant for Willem. Their investment in Sami had paid off. 'Willem didn't object to the transfer at all, and I'm sure the clubs had already agreed on everything before I even knew about it,' says Sami. 'Willem has a tradition of selling players, and they always look to bring in new talent and develop them for the use of the bigger clubs.'

For Martin van Geel, the technical manager at Willem, Sami's transfer to Liverpool meant recognition of a job well done, on behalf of both Sami and the club. Van Geel ponders:

When Sami transferred to Liverpool, I was proud of him. He developed into a top-level professional at Willem and we have always had a reputation of finding the right talent and developing them to the next level. Sami is a model example of a player who always worked hard in order to succeed in his career. In the end, everyone was happy – Sami, Willem II and, apparently, Liverpool FC too.

I was certain that Sami would succeed at Liverpool, for I had seen the type of person he is, both as a player and as a person. I still have his jersey hanging on the wall, reminding me about our way of working with the players.

The seasons at Willem had refined Sami into a full-blooded professional and he felt ready for the English Premier League, which had developed into perhaps the most competitive league in Europe at the end of the 1990s. According to Sami, the timing of the transfer could not have been better, all things considered. Liverpool FC were seriously aiming to get back to the top of European football, and Holland didn't have much to offer any more. Even though the years at Willem had gone well for Sami, Co Adriaanse's exhausting training methods had already done their job. 'Now, when I think about it afterwards, I think that I would not have lasted a third year with that stress. So I guess, in a way, I had to get out of Willem.'

The years in Holland had taught Sami that the life of a professional football player is not always a bed of roses. For any professional player, football is hard work.

> Particularly towards the end of the second season with Adriaanse, I was feeling so worn out both mentally and physically that I lost the enjoyment I got from training and playing almost completely. That was when I noticed how hard a job I had. Good results were the only pleasure you got from the work, and sometimes when I woke up in the morning I didn't feel like going to training again. Football had ceased to be fun.

At Liverpool, Sami felt immediately that he had rediscovered the fun and joy in his game.

> Here, I found the enjoyment again. It feels great to wake up in the morning and leave for training. Football is fun again and the passion is there again, too. The move to England wasn't that difficult either. I think life has been pretty much the same here, too.
>
> As a person, the boss [Gérard Houllier] here is different and

deals with his players in a totally different manner from Adriaanse. If a player complained about being tired to Adriaanse, he told him to train more. Houllier understands his players better. If you tell him that you're tired or that you're muscles are sore, he may advise you to take a day off and to have a little rest. And still, it is not that he merely tries to please his players – he gets fired up when necessary.

5

Big Sami in the Premiership

SAMI HYYPIÄ'S NEW LIFE IN A NEW CLUB AND IN A NEW COUNTRY
started in the summer of 1999. He had left Holland and Willem II after a
brilliant final season as team captain and an indisputable key player.
Willem had finished second in the league and earned a place in the
Champions League. After the season, Sami had a few weeks' holiday,
which was mostly spent preparing for the move to England and taking
care of all the essential matters. Sami's first task was to find a pleasant
home for himself and his girlfriend Niina. For the first two months, Sami
lived in a hotel, but then he found a nice apartment and Niina followed
Sami from Holland to England and Liverpool.

As usual, Sami wanted to live near work, in this case the Melwood
training centre and Anfield Road. The new home was found in a small
block of flats, next to Sefton Park. Sami didn't want to buy a house,
because, as he said himself, he is not much of a gardening person.

> I want to live so close to work that I don't have to drive much.
> Thirty minutes is about the maximum amount of time that I would
> drive for training. After all, during the season, we spend quite a lot
> of time on the road, so I think it is unnecessary to waste time and
> energy driving long distances on your daily trips, too. You can
> always find an apartment nearby.

Training and spending time on the road are standards in a professional
football player's life, and you just have to get used to them. With the
European cup competitions and the Finland international matches,
Sami spends almost as much time on the road as he does at home.
According to Sami, however, it is all part of the profession he has

chosen for himself, so there really isn't much to complain about.

The move to England didn't bring up any great changes to Sami's daily routine, but he soon found out that football is taken even more seriously at Liverpool. The standards at one of the most successful club in England are very high, and, as the club wants to return to its glory days, each employee at Liverpool FC can feel the pressure on his shoulders. The legendary fans of Liverpool FC, particularly the crowd at the Kop end, add their share of the pressure. Sami explains:

> Of course football is bigger here than in Holland. When I moved from Finland to Holland, football seemed to mean so much more to the Dutch than to us Finns. And yet when I came to England, I noticed that football's importance to the people in Holland was nothing compared to England.
>
> Here, people live for the game, and they are so passionate that they'll spend their last penny on a season ticket. Although it feels great to have an influence on so many people's lives, it also creates additional pressure. People expect a return for the investment they make, and it sometimes feels horrible when we fail to give the crowd what they want. But then again, that's how football is.

Sami reported to his new employer and manager Gérard Houllier on 1 July. He was by no means the only new player in the squad and in particular the defence had been totally renewed by the French boss. Houllier had left his position as the technical director of the French FA to join Liverpool FC as an assistant to Roy Evans on 17 July 1998, and the new rise of Liverpool FC began on the same date. The partnership of Evans and Houllier didn't produce good results, however, and Evans was released from his duties after serving the club for many years. Houllier now carried the responsibility completely on his own shoulders and he began building up his new dynasty from day one.

In the summer of 1999 Sami was one of the new faces at the Liverpool FC training camp who were going to form the foundation of the new, successful Liverpool side. Other future key players who joined Liverpool then were Stéphane Henchoz, a Swiss international from Blackburn, Dietmar Hamann, a German international from Newcastle, Vladimir Smicer, a Czech Republic international from the French side Lens, and Sander Westerveld, a Dutch international from Vitesse. In January, the club had acquired Cameroon international Rigobert Song, who was expected to secure his place in central defence. Since the Number 4 jersey, which Sami had worn for years, had been reserved for Song, Sami had to settle for the Number 12 jersey. As for publicity, Sami was the least known of the new players, largely because of the low status of the Finnish national team in the eyes of the English media. Henchoz and Hamann, for example, were already familiar players to the English football world because they had played in the Premiership for some time already. Even in Finland, not everyone believed in Sami's success at his new club. Jyrki Heliskoski, the coach of Sami's youth national team, reminisces.

> It seemed that only a few believed in Sami's permanent position in the Liverpool defence. Of course, this is hindsight and it feels foolish to say this, but I believed in Sami from the first and with no hesitation. I knew that there weren't many stoppers in Europe who could match Sami's talent.

Sami himself was also careful about his expectations and future responsibilities in the top-level squad. Even though he played a good number of minutes in the summer friendlies, the Voikkaa product kept his feet firmly on the ground. In an interview right before the season, Sami noted that it was no use thinking about a position in the starting 11. Nevertheless, he believed that he would get his chance sooner or later, if only he kept working hard. 'I have a chance to make the 11 if I believe in myself and my abilities,' Sami said back then.

When the 1999–2000 campaign opened, Sami had shown his ability to Houllier. In the opening match of the season, Sami was part of the reformed Liverpool defence alongside Westerveld, Vegard Heggem, Jamie Carragher and Dominic Matteo, who was later sold to Leeds. Sami paired up in central defence with Jamie Carragher and the defence worked well. Liverpool started the season with a 2–1 away win against Sheffield Wednesday with goals from Robbie Fowler and Titi Camara. Sami's ratings for the match were excellent, and he secured his place in the team during the August matches against Watford and Middlesbrough, despite the fact that Liverpool FC lost both matches. The match against Watford was Sami's first appearance in front of his new home fans at Anfield.

> I will always remember the feeling I had when we entered the field from the tunnel before kick-off. Fans were shouting at the top of their voices and the atmosphere was tremendous. The memory I have from the match itself is not as sweet, of course, as we lost 1–0 in my home debut.

SAMI HYYPIÄ

The Premiership had a break for the international match day, but Finland had to do without Sami against Belgium. Richard Møller-Nielsen, the Finland coach, had agreed with Houllier that the centre-back, who had played the full 90 minutes in each of Liverpool's matches so far, would stay in Liverpool and take a rest before his club team returned to action. Møller-Nielsen remembers the occasion well and says: 'It was the right decision to leave Sami out of the squad then, for he had a tremendous performance against Leeds after the break.' In August 1999, Møller-Nielsen said: 'I spoke with Houllier and he said he was very pleased with the way Sami has played. Sami will remain in the squad in the future, too.'

The Danish coach was right in his decision, for Sami remained in the squad. However, Liverpool's form was not yet solid: after beating Leeds they also beat Arsenal, but lost to their fiercest rival, Manchester United, at home. The match will be remembered by many as an entertaining one, and in Finland people will always remember it as the match where Sami Hyypiä scored his first goal in the English Premiership. Sami scored a consolation goal after a corner, making the score 2–1. Sami remembers that goal:

> I usually go up for all set pieces. In that particular case, the ball came just perfectly to me and it was actually quite easy to score. It was magnificent to score the opener in front of the home crowd, but the feeling was gone after the match. A loss is a loss no matter what, and scoring a goal when you lose 2–3 doesn't make you any happier.
>
> It was my first match against Manchester United, and I could still see how important the match was to everyone. The meetings between us and Manchester United are always charged with extra emotion, both among the players and the fans, and I could really sense all that.

AT THE CENTRE OF ATTENTION

In a few months' time, Sami's success in the Premiership had also been noticed in Finland, and any doubts about his chances to make it in England had disappeared. Later in the autumn, Finland played Germany in a European Championships qualifying match and Sami was the most wanted interviewee before the match. Not long ago, the quiet centre-back from Willem II had been able to focus on the international matches in privacy, far from media attention, and now everything had changed completely. Now the Liverpool star player was expected to be available for every reporter. 'It was quite big a change, for practically no one was interested in what I was doing when I played in Holland,' Sami explains with a smile. 'All of a sudden, everyone seemed to think that I had stepped up my game so vastly in only a few months' time that everyone had to ask something from me.'

The match itself did not bring a smile to Sami's face. Oliver Bierhoff scored two goals in the first 15 minutes, which was enough for Germany to win the match, and one of the goals was deflected off Sami's foot. Despite the defeat, the match also marked another historical point in Sami's career as he was the captain of the full Finland team for the first time in his career because Jari Litmanen was suffering from an injury.

> We got off to a miserable start in that match, but we had a good second half. The first few months at Liverpool had taught me that no player, no matter what his name, was unstoppable. Bierhoff did manage to score twice, but after that he and the other German players were under our control. It was yet another one of those matches that taught us a lot as a team, too.

After international duty, Sami returned to the routines of Premiership football with Liverpool. The renewed squad was slowly growing tighter and becoming more uniform but the results were not that good early on in the season. Until October 1999, it seemed that the team was struggling to find the right harmony. However, in October, the Liverpool defence started to play particularly well together and the rest of the team improved their level of play as well. For Sami, the month of October was significant in two ways. At Liverpool, the important change was that Stéphane Henchoz, who had been sidelined with an injury for the first few months of the season, was fit again and was paired up alongside Sami in the centre: Houllier had found the dominant duo for central defence. In addition to that, the team was playing well and the direction on the table was up. The other significant change in Sami's career happened with the full international squad, when Sami scored his first goal for Finland. On 9 October Finland beat Northern Ireland 4–1 at home in the final match of the qualifying campaign for Euro 2000. Sami's goal was the winner, while Finland's first goal was scored by Jonatan Johansson and the other two by Joonas Kolkka.

Liverpool suffered only one loss in October, but it was all the more bitter. The loss came against Southampton in a Worthington Cup match, and it was a tough setback for the club who were thirsty for success after so many years without a title. In contrast to many other major clubs, success in the Worthington Cup would have been important for Liverpool. 'I must admit it was a bitter loss,' Sami recalls. 'I had heard a lot about the cup tradition in England, and everyone, myself included of course, had always dreamed of playing at Wembley. The one good thing that came with the loss was that we could then focus completely on the Premiership.'

Going out of the cup meant that the players could have a short break, and Sami knew a very pleasant place to visit. On his day off he travelled to Tilburg to watch his former club Willem II play Sparta Prague in the Champions League, the most highly respected of all cup competitions in Europe, back where Sami had led his former team in the previous season. Even as a spectator, Sami wanted to experience how the fans in Tilburg supported their own in the Champions League. At the same time, the trip provided a tremendous opportunity to see his former teammates and friends make Willem II history on the pitch.

Sami's visit did not remain a secret and before the kick-off the announcer at the Willem II Stadium told the capacity crowd that their former favourite player was sitting among them. As soon as they heard this, the crowd stood up and started singing Sami's name. At such a moment even the taciturn lad from Voikkaa was moved.

> It was a very emotional moment, especially because I had been there to build the dream. Of course, it felt fantastic that my former home crowd received me in such a wonderful way. The visit also gave me a sense of how significant a matter the Champions League is. At that moment, I knew that I wanted to play there with Liverpool, that I wanted to be there and compete against the best players and teams in Europe.

Lennart Wangel, the long-time team secretary for the full Finland squad, was UEFA's event manager in all Willem II's matches in the Champions League. The favouritism earned by the kid from his home town impressed him:

> He was extremely popular there. No matter what the occasion, Sami had always done everything carefully and with style, including charity events and other PR matters. His reputation was excellent, and I have no doubt that it is the same at Liverpool now.

Liverpool kept playing well and rising up the table in November, too, keeping a run of clean sheets throughout the month, much to the credit of Westerveld, Hyypiä and Henchoz. November 1999 will also always remain an important date in Finnish football history. On 27 November, in an away match against West Ham, both Liverpool's captains, Jamie Redknapp and Robbie Fowler, were sidelined with injury problems, and a great piece of Finnish football history was made. To the surprise of many, Sami Hyypiä included, Houllier named Sami the captain of the legendary Liverpool FC and made him the first ever Finnish team captain in England. Sami explained the day after the match:

> The severity of Jamie's injury was verified only a few moments before kick-off. Houllier announced that I would wear the armband, and as everything happened at the last minute I didn't have time to stress about it. Obviously, the selection was a complete surprise for me, but a positive one, of course. Being a team captain was not new to me – I had been the captain at Willem II for the latter part of my final season there. As the captain, you just have to try to set as good an example for the other players as possible.

Sami did not think that his term as team captain would be that long. In the same interview he predicted that Robbie Fowler would return to the squad in a few weeks and would take back the armband. 'Robbie will wear the armband next weekend,' Sami said back then.

As we now know, both Redknapp and Fowler's injuries turned out to be so severe that Sami wore the armband until spring. According to Sammy Lee, Liverpool FC's assistant coach, Sami was a natural choice for team captain and his foreign nationality was not a problem. Sami's whole appearance embodies the essence of Liverpool FC. Lee remarks:

> We don't have foreign players, we have Liverpool players. As soon as you walk in from the door, your nationality goes out the window. We don't sign a player because he is foreign or British, we sign him because of his potential to play for Liverpool FC. And when you look at Sami on the pitch, it is evident that he is a Liverpool player.
>
> Sometimes foreign players have had problems adjusting to England and to a new environment, but Sami convinced everyone from day one with his personality and appearance. He is a leader, both on and off the football pitch.

HARD BUT FAIR

November 1999 was also the month when Sami made the headlines for the first time in a negative context. In a league match against Derby, Sami tackled County's Italian player Stefano Eranio – it was a hard-but-fair challenge. Unfortunately, the tackle sidelined Eranio for the remainder of the season as he broke his fibula in the event. Jim Smith, who was then Derby manager, was very outspoken about the incident and demanded a suspension for Sami. According to Sami, the injury was a complete accident.

'Things like that can happen in hard tackles. I've never meant to hurt any opponent intentionally,' Sami said after the match. 'I went in for that tackle as hard as I always do, and collided with Eranio. It was unfortunate that I happened to hit his fibula. Things like this are part of the game. Football is a physical game.'

The whole event troubled Sami's mind so much that he later sent Eranio a letter. 'I wrote to him and told him that I was sorry about the injury. I felt bad about it afterwards because I was thinking about myself in his shoes. You don't want something like that to happen to you,' Sami ponders.

The incident also raised extensive discussion because already during his first few months in the English Premiership, Sami had earned a reputation as a hard-but-fair tackler. Had Eranio been sidelined by a tackle from some other player, there would have been less of a fuss in the press. Sami's reputation as a hard-but-fair defender has followed him, and it is best demonstrated by the minimal number of bookings he has received in the Premiership: in his first two seasons in England, Sami was booked only twice.

Sami's football mentality and motto – hard but fair – came from his father, Jouko. Although many defenders in the modern game go round or bend the rules, or play purposefully dirty defence, Sami always wants to win the tackles in accordance with the rules. You will never see him play dirty or hurt an opponent intentionally. He hasn't changed his style in the English Premiership either, although opponents more often than not like to elbow him or stamp on his toes. It seems obvious that Sami's style of play has been one of the more important factors in his rapid rise to respect and appreciation in England and particularly among the Liverpool fans. More than anything, the English football fans hate unsportsmanlike behaviour, intentional fouls, diving and time-wasting, and these are also the characteristics that Sami hates the most in his opponents. To please British fans, a player has to give and receive hard tackles with no complaints – and this suits Sami fine. In fact, this is one of the things that Sami – a truly typical and honest Finn – and the British way of thinking have in common. The rules of the hard-but-fair game are deep, inherent characteristics both in life and in football.

With the help of live TV matches, the Finnish football fans have also been treated to a selection of examples of Sami's 'British' attitude towards playing. It seems that TV directors have learnt to pick out close-ups of Sami's expressions and gestures which speak for his attitude. TV crowds all over Europe have become familiar with the wide, politely disapproving smile on Sami's face if the referee happens to see the 'hard' in his hard-but-fair tackles. Moreover, fans know the intense stare in Sami's eyes when the opponents have fouled his teammates, or the scornful look on his face when someone has dived in the hope of a free kick. Little details like these are important when the fans pick their favourites, and, more crucially, they are important when a foreign player has to earn the respect of the British fans.

Sami has also made it easy for the referees to approve of his style. During his career, he has never really been booked for mouthing off, although you see him talk back every now and then. In international matches, it is also helpful to be able to express oneself in a language that referees more often than not don't understand. Besides, Sami's comments are usually accompanied with a wide smile. Sami explains:

> When you say something with a smile on your face, you often go without a booking. And to be fair, the referees' decisions more often make me laugh than make me angry. If, for example, a penalty kick against me makes me angry, I may still laugh at the referee for calling a penalty for such a tackle, or something like that. Arguing never changed any referee's decision, so I don't see any point in doing that.

Overall, November 1999 was an excellent month for Liverpool FC, mainly because the side's defensive game kept improving. More specifically, the understanding between the three newcomers – Westerveld, Henchoz and Hyypiä – became ever more solid. In the past few seasons, the Liverpool defence had been close to a bad joke, but the performances of the side's renewed defence silenced the loudest of critics. From then on, the Liverpool defence began to be noted as one of the best – if not the best – defences in the league.

In early December, the Liverpool defence in general, and Sami Hyypiä

SAMI HYYPIÄ

in particular, received nationwide recognition as Sami was historically selected as the Premiership's Player of the Month. Awarding the recognition to a defender or a newcomer is rare, and as central defenders are among the most respected players in England, usually only British players have been included among the elite of the position. In the 1998–99 season, Jaap Stam had had a breakthrough campaign with Manchester United and paved the way for other foreign stoppers, like Sami, to be recognised. As Sami was awarded with the Player of the Month award, comparisons with Stam as well as with the legendary Liverpool defenders from the club's glory days increased. In addition to the Premiership Player of the Month, the Liverpool fans had already voted Sami the team's best player. In the Internet poll, Sami received 63 per cent of all votes, while Titi Camara, the runner-up, gathered 23 per cent and Jamie Redknapp, team captain and second runner-up, received only 3 per cent of the votes. Although Sami's popularity was in a class of its own, the man himself was quite modest about it and shrugged off the comparisons with Stam and Alan Hansen, the legendary Liverpool defender. In November 1999, Sami said:

> Of course, the fans' appreciation has been a delightful and positive surprise for me. However, I would like to keep in mind that I have a long way to go to achieve what some of my predecessors have achieved, and any comparisons with the brilliant Alan Hansen, for example, are completely unnecessary.
>
> I regard Stam as a world-class player so, naturally, I am pleased if people regard me as highly as they regard him. However, I would much rather be 'the first Sami Hyypiä' than 'the next Jaap Stam'.

Janne Kosunen, a Finnish football reporter who has followed Liverpool FC for a long time and with dedication, does not think that comparisons with Alan Hansen are unfounnded, and yet he understands why Sami feels uncomfortable about it:

> Sami is not only dominant in the air, but his passing is also accurate and reliable. I think his qualities as a playmaker are still undervalued in Finland. In the past, Alan Hansen was often responsible for starting the Liverpool attacks, and there are similar elements in Sami's game today.

Another person who emphasises Sami's ability to pass the ball accurately and sharply is Mika Nurmela, Sami's teammate from the national side and also a player who has had a successful career in the Dutch league. According to Nurmela, Sami evolved into a play-making centre-back in his years with Willem II:

> In Holland, Sami played a difficult position because the centre-backs in Holland play man-on-man in a large area. The other thing that is required from the central defenders there is the ability to start the attacks from the back. In Holland, Sami's tactical knowledge improved and that development is now bearing fruit. In England, he stands out as a stopper who can play it on the ground, with accuracy and ease. After all, there are numerous centre-backs in England who are good in the air, but the whole world is short of defenders who can also build up the game.

The Liverpool side kept its form throughout December, celebrating the New Year with a month-long unbeaten run. In the home match against Sheffield Wednesday, Sami scored his second goal of the season, tying the match at 1–1, before Liverpool went on to win the match 4–1. Sami's successful season was recognised in Finland, too, and the Finnish FA awarded him with the Erik von Frenckell trophy for the Finnish Player of the Year. The award ended Jari Litmanen's seven-year dominance, recognising Sami with the distinguished honour for the first time. In his acceptance speech, Sami said: 'All I have to do is to have a look at the past winners of the award, and I feel very honoured to be included in such esteemed company. Now I have to show that I'm worthy of the recognition, both at Liverpool FC and with the Finnish national team.'

At the same event, Daniel Sjölund, who then represented West Ham and since has joined Sami at Liverpool FC, was awarded the Finnish FA Youth Player of the Year award.

Two weeks later, the Finnish sports journalists also recognised Sami as the Player of the Year in his sport, which Litmanen had won seven years in a row before Sami. At the end of 1999, Sami earned yet another recognition at the annual vote for Finnish Athlete of the Year. The voting is traditionally dominated by individual sport athletes in Finland, and Sami was very honoured to finish 14th, as the highest-ranking football player.

At the end of the year, Sami was introduced to the intense match schedule of the English Premiership for the first time. In Holland, the league always had a break in the middle of winter, but in England, the schedule is at its busiest at the turn of the year. The 1999 Boxing Day match against Newcastle is one of the matches Sami remembers best in his first year with Liverpool – it was the first time he played against Duncan Ferguson, who was to become perhaps Sami's toughest opponent in the following years.

> Our Christmas holiday was very short, for we had training on Christmas Day. It was no surprise to me that the English Premiership has fixtures throughout the holiday season and the winter months, and I reminded myself that I chose my career myself, aware of its ups and downs.
>
> The reason why I still remember the match against Newcastle so clearly is that it was the first time I met Duncan Ferguson, who is still probably the toughest opponent I have faced here. The battle has only intensified now that he plays for Everton, our local rivals. Anyway, the Boxing Day fixture against Newcastle was the first time I played against him and Alan Shearer. I was paired up with Jamie Carragher in the centre, and I remember the match was quite a wrestling match for both of us. Elbows were flying in all headers and I got a few hard hits on my head. Thanks to a swing by Ferguson, I spent the New Year with a black eye. Nothing has really changed between us since then, and the battle is fierce every time we play against each other. He comes in for challenges hard and dirty, but he is also a good player.

The match ended 2–2 and both Shearer and Ferguson got their names on the scoresheet. Michael Owen, who was picking up his form with speed, scored both the Liverpool goals.

Liverpool FC manager Gérard Houllier received the Manager of the Month honours in December, and he didn't hesitate in giving the credit to his squad. Houllier told the British media:

> Liverpool are now beginning to play in the style that has made the club the most successful club in England. Our results in the past few weeks have been based on top performances by skilful individual players like Michael Owen and Titi Camara and on the fact that we have the best defence in the Premiership.

Even though the first few months of the 1999–2000 season had been successful for Liverpool FC, the season was only at the halfway mark, and the club were facing a busy and competitive spring as they aimed at the top positions on the table and admission to the European Cup competition. Individually, the spring season was Sami's opportunity to secure his place among the elite group of players in the Premiership.

JARI LITMANEN: SAMI'S TALENT IS BEST UTILISED IN ENGLAND

Jari Litmanen, the most successful Finnish football player ever, has known Sami Hyypiä since the early 1990s. They played together for MyPa in the Finnish Premiership in 1992, they both played in the Dutch Premier League between 1996 and 1999, and they have played dozens of international matches for Finland together. The two have been roommates on the full Finland squad's away trips, and Jari Litmanen joined Sami at Liverpool FC in January 2001.

According to Litmanen, Sami's career began under favourable stars. At MyPa, he had a good, supportive manager (Kampman) and experienced teammates in the defence who gave advice and support to the young talent. In the interviews conducted for this biography, Litmanen says that despite the factors at MyPa which have contributed to his success, he couldn't have predicted in the early '90s that Sami would embark on such a tremendous career:

> At that time it was difficult to say who would succeed abroad because leaving Finland to go play professionally in Europe was much more difficult back then. The Bosman ruling changed everything and the transfer market opened up on a whole new level.
>
> Of course, Sami had some very good qualities for a centre-back. His height provided for a good reach, and already then I noticed in particular how calm he was with the ball, which I think is an exceptional characteristic in a defender. Calm is a word that describes Sami both as a person and as a player. He keeps his head cool even in the tightest spots. It was also characteristic of Sami that he wanted to play the ball instead of just clearing it out from the back. That suited Kampman's style perfectly, and I'm sure Voutilainen had also emphasised similar things in the previous year. Sami already stood out from the crowd in his passing in Finland.

Litmanen left MyPa for Ajax Amsterdam in the middle of the Finnish season and Sami followed him to Holland a few years later. Litmanen played a part in Sami's transfer, too, for the more experienced Finnish international was asked to give his opinion on the younger prospect before the move.

> I knew Sami well enough from MyPa and the Finnish national team for it to be easy for me to recommend him, both as a player and as a person. He was ready to move on from Finland, and Willem II is a good club to start a professional career, just as MyPa had been the right club for Sami in Finland. So, in that sense, I could recommend Sami for Willem and the club for Sami, too. The pressure on the club was not overwhelming and it seemed that Sami would also get to play. Both of these factors were important for someone who is just starting his professional career, because the first step from Finland to the European leagues is a big one.
>
> In terms of Sami's career, Holland was an excellent place for the first years because Finns have often had problems with the style of play in the European leagues. In Holland, Sami had to focus daily on passing, playing man-on-man and other various tactical aspects of the game that are often on a weaker basis in Finland. The strengths of the Dutch style lie particularly in the technical and tactical side of the game, which is why it is no wonder that Sami developed his game tremendously in these areas. Already at MyPa, I could tell that his desire to learn and develop was immense.

Litmanen observed Sami's next transfer from a close vicinity, too:

> I knew some folk at Liverpool. At some point, they were looking for a centre-back, and they had several alternatives. I knew quite a few of the players they were considering, and when they asked for my opinion I recommended Sami. I think that Sami's talent is put to the best use in England, because he is good in the air both offensively and defensively. At times, it is quite impressive when you see him go in for a header and his head is three metres from the ground.
>
> Sami has a good reach on the ground as well, and his calm style is certainly an asset in comparison with the British centre-backs. He reads the game so well that he stops many attacks by his mere positioning, and his passing and moving, which he refined in Holland, are among the best in England. I think he is one of the most sharp passing and intelligent centre-backs in England.

SAMI HYYPIÄ

Litmanen thinks that Sami's move to Liverpool was a perfect decision at a perfect moment:

> Liverpool FC is a big club that has been tremendously successful in the past, but it had gone without a trophy for some years already. Houllier had bought and sold players and the team was in a developing stage. The pressure on the club was increasing and yet the team didn't feel much pressure for success. So, in all ways, it was a good time for Sami to join the side.
>
> To begin with, the expectations that people in Liverpool set for Sami weren't that high. He was a Finnish player from Willem II, which actually doesn't mean much to the English fans. So in that sense, Sami got to sneak in and show what he had with no pressure. And when people started to expect high-level performances from him, he was up to the task and met the challenge.

According to Litmanen, Sami has earned his position at Liverpool. As one of the three captains in the squad, he is an exemplary professional and a reliable player.

> Sami suits the Liverpool playing system perfectly. In the back, he is a very important player around whom you can build a strong and solid defence. He doesn't talk much in the dressing-room and he never really goes out of his way to do something silly either. Throughout his three seasons with the club, he has been a key player in the squad and he has played most of the matches in all three years, and yet you don't see him making a big number of himself. He is a respected and popular lad who always does his work conscientiously.
>
> It is always a great honour and an esteemed recognition for a foreign player to be one of the team captains on any team. And I would say that out of the three captains on the squad in Sami's first years, Sami was the only one who could be sure about his place in the 11. I would presume that he is among the first players when they select the squad.

Like Sami, Litmanen has supported Liverpool FC since his childhood:

> The English League has always been the most popular European

league in Finland and other Nordic countries. And when it comes to English football, Liverpool FC is clearly one of the greatest clubs: Liverpool were just recently selected the club of the century. I became a Liverpool FC fan through TV, as Liverpool were well represented in the league fixtures every Saturday as well as in the FA Cup final and the European Cup competitions throughout my childhood. The Liverpool style simply just appealed to me, and has appealed to me since.

The 1970s and 1980s teams were my favourites. I remember those times clearly and, in a way, I still idolise those teams. Of course, when you're in the club yourself, you don't feel quite the same way as you did before. And even though we won a number of trophies in the 2000–01 season, we still have long way to go to achieve what the 1970s and 1980s teams did.

THE BITTER SPRING 2000

The triumphal march Liverpool had in the autumn half of the 1999–2000 season was expected to continue in the spring. The team were on schedule to finish in the top three and earn a place in the Champions League for the next season. Early on in the new millennium, Liverpool were in good form and proceeded towards the top of the Premiership. They conceded the least goals throughout the season and the three key players at the back had been reinforced with the club's own reliable product, Jamie Carragher, at full-back. Carragher started the season in the centre with Sami, but he later moved to full-back and secured his position there. In the previous season, Carragher had been an obvious choice for stopper, and Houllier's decision to play him at full-back was a surprise move. Chris Bascombe, a football reporter on the *Liverpool Echo*, was among those who thought the decision was unexpected:

When Sami arrived at the team, I thought that he would be a back-up for Jamie Carragher and Stéphane Henchoz. Jamie had played the whole previous season as a centre-back and he had been selected the team's Player of the Year and I don't think anyone would have thought that Sami's arrival would make Jamie a full-back. Yet now the decision seems to have been the only right decision. No one simply knew how good Sami actually is.

Another important factor in the tight defence of the Liverpool side was Dietmar Hamann's strong input at centre-midfield. The German midfielder brings an extra dimension to the actual centre-backs' game as he plays his defensive role unselfishly and passes the ball to his teammates with almost perfect accuracy. Furthermore, Steven Gerrard, another one of the club's own products with tremendous talent, started to perform on the level that makes him one of the most talented midfielders in the world.

In January 2000, however, Liverpool experienced a major setback when they were knocked out of the FA Cup. Success in the competition had been among the main goals of the side for that season and losing 1–0 to Blackburn at home was extremely disappointing. The fact that 2000 was the last year that the Cup final would be played at the old Wembley Stadium in London made the loss all the more bitter.

In mid-January, Sami got his second yellow card of the season in the match against Watford. As a player who seldom gets booked, Sami didn't think the tackle was worth a yellow card, although it was a foul. Unlike some other players, Sami takes every booking seriously. He wants to play hard but fair and he doesn't allow himself to commit fouls worthy of a booking. Sami recalls:

> The first time I was booked was against Aston Villa in the autumn and the card against Watford was my second for the season. I had caught a bad cold earlier in the week, so I probably wasn't in my sharpest form, but I would still argue that I got the card too easily. I was going for the ball, but the opponent put his body in the way just before I hit it. He fell and I got booked.
>
> The reason why I remember the tackle so clearly is that I wasn't booked again that season and I played the whole next season without one single card in a league match.

Liverpool beat Watford in that January match and stepped up to fourth position in the table. It was the best position the club had reached in years, providing an excellent starting point for the important spring fixtures. Already at this point, Manchester United and Arsenal had demonstrated their power and were fighting their own battle for the title, but the competition for the third place was wide open. Finishing third in the Premiership was important primarily because it allowed for an admission into the qualifying rounds of the Champions League next season. The Champions League was the club's major goal for the near future. Liverpool had also recognised the valuable contribution Sami Hyypiä could make to their future plans and offered him a renewed contract. The new contract guaranteed that Sami would remain with the side until 2004.

Although matches in Europe were Liverpool's goal for the future, many of their players played international matches on a regular basis. The majority of Liverpool players, including Sami Hyypiä for Finland, represent their home countries with their full international squads. Around the time of the win against Watford in January 2000, Finland's qualifying group for the 2002 World Cup was drawn in Japan. Finland were drawn in a tough group with Germany, England, Greece and Albania, and speculation about the fixtures began immediately, not least in the Melwood Training Centre. Lady Luck had her way and made Sami's Liverpool teammates his main opponents for future matches with the Finnish national side.

> The winding-up started immediately after the draw. At that time, Didi Hamann was a regular in the German side and Michael Owen, Robbie Fowler and Jamie Redknapp in the English side. I remember thinking how great it would be to play a World Cup qualifier against England at Anfield. I thought it would be a unique experience for me and for my teammates in the England squad as well, of course.

As we know, Sami's wish came true and he faced his teammates as a beloved opponent in a World Cup qualifier in front of a capacity crowd at Anfield.

February 2000 was yet another successful month for Liverpool and they kept marching towards the top of the Premiership. At the turn of the month, the side had spent a few days at Malta, resting and charging their batteries for the upcoming fixtures. The rest was well timed and helped the team to play its best and most relaxed football of the season. A sweet win over Leeds was accompanied with an away win against Arsenal at Highbury. Sami had yet another superb performance and he was the Man of the Match for the fourth time in the season. This also marked a point in Sami's career when he appeared to have become a regular name at the top of various polls and ratings. Individual success did not change anything in Sami's daily routines, though. In his interviews, Big Sami explained how he was truly enjoying life in his new home town. The team had played well for the most part of the season and there were no complaints off the pitch either. He was still a rather unfamiliar face for the people on the streets, even though they did recognise him better than in the autumn, and he did have to stop to sign his autograph more often than previously.

As Liverpool were in good form, Sami was particularly annoyed by the fact that the side had a three-week break just when things were going well for them. By mid-February, Liverpool had risen to third place in the league and everything was in their own hands as they played for the final standings in the league and a place in European Cup competition – even a place in the Champions League qualifying rounds. The team's performances were even more remarkable considering that the England national-team players – Michael Owen, Robbie Fowler and Jamie Redknapp – were all still injured. For obvious reasons, the injuries worried club management, but for Sami, they meant that he would remain the captain of the team.

March 2000 solidified Liverpool's position at the top end of the league, but injuries to important front players made the club management go to the transfer market. As a result, Emile Heskey, a top talent from Leicester, joined Liverpool FC for a large transfer fee of £11 million. This meant that yet another member of the full England team became Sami's teammate at Anfield and the World Cup qualifying group rivalry in the team got stronger. Another significant acquisition, Markus Babbel, had agreed terms with the club, but he would not arrive at Anfield until the summer. Babbel had been a regular in the German side, but as he declined international duty, Sami didn't get to play against him in the World Cup qualifiers.

The acquisition of Heskey turned out to be yet another masterstroke from Houllier. Titi Camara, who had been in tremendous form early in the season, had started to falter and both Owen and Fowler were still sidelined with injuries. The stakes were high both on and off the pitch, and as the season was nearing the end, it became evident that Liverpool would make it to the European Cup competition unless there was a total breakdown. On various occasions, Sami Hyypiä and other players reminded the media that getting back into Europe was among the club's most important goals. As the Champions League has become the most important competition in Europe, no team is recognised as a top-level side unless they make the competition.

Throughout March, Liverpool kept playing well and they went the whole month without being defeated. Naturally, the team's success was much to the credit of their solid defence, which was generally considered the toughest in the league. Liverpool's first match in March 2000 was against Manchester United and it is a fixture that Sami remembers as one of the most bitter experiences he has had on the pitch. Until the Manchester United match, Sami had played the full 90 minutes of every league match that season. Five minutes from half-time, Manchester United's Norwegian striker, Ole Gunnar Solskjär, came late for a tackle and the stud of the striker's boot cut through Sami's boot, making an open wound on Sami's foot. Gérard Houllier didn't make a substitution and the Liverpool physios tried to get Sami back to the match as soon as possible. When Sami was on the sidelines, Solskjär equalised for Manchester United.

> I still don't understand what Solskjär was trying in that tackle. He was awfully late, for I had already passed the ball on before he hit me. I thought it was a really dirty tackle.
>
> Of course, what made me even more furious was the fact that he scored the equaliser only a few minutes after the tackle. Even today, I still wonder how on earth he got away with it without getting booked. He could have hurt me even worse.

Once again, Sami demonstrated his tremendous pain threshold as he came back on in the second half. The team doctor had sewn four stitches into his foot at half-time, but Sami wanted to keep on playing. After a few minutes into the second half, however, Sami had to face the facts and come off the pitch. His boot was filled with blood and the pain in his foot had become intolerable. It was clear that he was not on top form and he asked to be subbed.

> That was the end of a fine streak. I think it would have been some kind of a record if I had played the full minutes in my first season in the Premiership. The whole thing troubled me so much, also because the boss had waited for ten minutes before making the substitution, and then Solskjär scored while I was being treated. I felt as if I had let the team and the other players down when I couldn't keep playing after that, although I guess you couldn't really blame me for not being able to keep playing.

Gérard Houllier was strongly criticised for not making the substitution immediately. Neither Houllier nor Sami tried to evade the responsibility in front of the media after the match. 'I take full responsibility over the decision. Sami is such an important player for us that I wanted him to play in the second half,' Houllier said afterwards.

SAMI HYYPIÄ

The first injury Sami had in England was painful but it didn't take long to heal. After only a week, Sami was back in his normal position in the Liverpool defence. At the end of the month, Finland played Wales in an international friendly, as the opening match of the new Millennium Stadium in Cardiff. It was the first match Sami played for the new Finland coach, Antti Muurinen, and later the Welsh were criticised for choosing the wrong opponents. Finland were in good form and beat Wales 2–1, and the first goal in the new stadium was scored by Jari Litmanen. It was the first victory for Litmanen and Hyypiä in Cardiff, but the next would follow within a year, this time wearing the Liverpool jersey.

IN THE TOP SIX

April 2000 took Sami Hyypiä's name to yet another level. Both the club and Sami were still playing well and it was generally thought that Liverpool would finish third at the end of the season, even though Leeds were playing well. Of the two top teams in the league, Manchester United had left everyone behind and raced to the title, but the top-form Liverpool side had overtaken Arsenal. Sami was rewarded with recognition off the pitch. He was named among the six players who formed the nominees for Premiership Player of the Year at the end of the season. The candidates were nominated by the PFA, so that the players voted for their own choice, with the exception that you couldn't vote for your teammates. Sami was the only defender in the group, and the other five were Roy Keane and Andy Cole from Manchester United, Kevin Phillips from Sunderland, Harry Kewell from Leeds, and Alan Shearer from Newcastle. The PaPe product had joined a tough group of players.

'Being nominated is a tremendous honour for me, particularly because the selection is made by the colleagues whom I have the most respect for: the Premiership players,' said Sami. 'Personally, I really don't care if I win or not, because being included in the top six is already such an enormous honour.'

A few weeks earlier, Sami had been named the Viewers' Player of the Year in a Sky Sports' Internet poll, where he received an overwhelming 60 per cent of the total votes.

> That selection also made me extremely happy because it was the fans' choice. I'm still not completely sure about all the different polls and selections, for I am merely one player in a tremendous team. In my opinion, the whole team were playing such strong

defence that anyone could have been awarded with the honours. We had conceded the least goals in the league, and the last time a Liverpool side had done that was in 1988.

But really, I didn't think about the poll results back then. The only thing in my mind was that we were second in the table and we wanted to get to Europe.

At the end of April, everything was ready for Liverpool's glorious return to the limelight. The team was second in the table, they were in good form, and the last fixtures of the season seemed favourable. The defence was effective and up front the squad was crowded with stars: Owen, Fowler, Heskey and Camara – a quartet that was feared all over the nation. But the high hopes were about to crash sooner than anyone would have thought.

For Liverpool FC, though, things started to turn sour on 21 April, when they played Everton away. The local rivals managed to keep a clean sheet against the feared Liverpool frontline, and the Merseyside derby ended in a goalless draw. The agony continued in the next match against Chelsea, where the London side beat Liverpool 2–0 at Stamford Bridge. At the same time, Arsenal took second place and regained a firm hold of the admission ticket to the Champions League the following week. Considering the Reds' renowned frontline, the almost incomprehensible goalless streak of two matches continued in May, as Leicester visited Anfield and returned home with a 2–0 victory. Four days later, yet another goalless performance by the Reds left them with a 0–0 draw against Southampton at Anfield. Even after a few years, Sami marvels:

> The goalless streak was inconceivable. Throughout the season, we had managed to score even when we were suffering from many injuries at the top. For some reason, the pressure on us grew too great, and we choked in the crucial moments of an otherwise tremendous season.

Still, even with a four-match goalless streak, Liverpool had everything in their own hands. By beating Bradford away in their last match of the season, they would have secured third place and admission to the qualifying rounds of Champions League. However, the worst nightmare came true: Liverpool went goalless for the fifth consecutive time and lost to Bradford 1–0. The Reds finished fourth in the Premiership and had to be satisfied with a place in the UEFA Cup. There is no doubt that the legendary history of Anfield Road does not know as bitter a goalless streak as the last five matches of the otherwise fine 1999–2000 season.

> In those five matches we conceded quite a few goals in the beginning and thus gave our opponents a chance to build a defensive wall which we were unable to break. I don't know if it was too long since the last success and our routine just wasn't enough or what it was, but it still remains a mystery to me.
>
> Overall, the season was successful, though, for we conceded the least goals in the league. If we had been asked about it before the season, we would have considered fourth place and a place in the UEFA Cup as tremendous achievements, but now that we had been offered so much more we finished the season with a bitter taste in our mouths. Despite performing well throughout the season, we were not mature enough to make it last until the end. I believe that finishing a season like that taught the team a lot and, more importantly, prepared us for the next season.

Although the spring half of the season was a huge disappointment for the whole team, on a personal level, Sami's first season at Liverpool FC was a tremendous success. He made a breakthrough in England and, really, in the whole footballing world. Although he didn't receive the Player of the Year award (Roy Keane from Manchester United won), the nomination and the selections for various All Star teams warmed Sami's heart a great deal. And yet, the season left scores to settle for Sami and the team. Even though Sami was the only Liverpool player who played in each Premiership match during the season and the original goals the team had set for themselves were well met, the season had ended with a disappointment and a thirst for more success. 'In many ways, we had a splendid season, and yet we finished two points from a brilliant season,' Sami explains. 'We returned to the top of the English Premier League and also made it back to Europe with the place in the UEFA Cup, so we had all the reason to be satisfied, and still . . .'

After the season, Sami faced a crossfire of questions in front of the Finnish media. Even after a long and hard season, he was the same old Sami and had the patience to answer everyone's questions from a big crowd of Finnish sports reporters on the media day arranged in Anjalankoski. Sami told the media in May 2000:

> I have never played as many matches during one season and

towards the end of the season I could really tell that my body was not used to it. This was the first season when I had no winter break, and it took a while to adjust to it.

Success hasn't changed me one bit. I'm still the same lad who played for PaPe, Kumu and MyPa and the same things that mattered to me then are still important to me now. I'm really not that interested in the sensation and publicity around me. At the moment, I'm just a very happy human being who makes his living out of his dearest interest. I don't think I could ask for more.

Already then, he believed that Liverpool were truly returning to the top to stay. His hunger for more success was immense. 'The way we ended our season really irritates me, but I'm sure we will learn from it. Next year, Liverpool will be stronger than before and we will fight for the title in every competition we are in. I'm very confident about it,' Sami predicted at the same event. The future was to show that Sami's faith in his club was not misplaced.

For the first time in his life, Sami spent his short summer holiday in Finland in his own apartment. He had bought a flat in Kuusankoski in the winter and he now spent the one-month summer holiday there with his girlfriend Niina before returning to Liverpool.

Before the next season, Sami had a few international matches to play as well. In early June, the full Finland squad played Latvia in Riga and were humiliated in a 1–0 defeat. In August, the Finnish national team returned to good form as they beat Norway 3–1 in the official opening match of the new Finnair Stadium in Helsinki. Before the match, Sami had been on a Liverpool training camp filled with training and friendly matches, and Gérard Houllier had asked if the Liverpool players could be released from duty in the international friendly matches, or at least not play the full 90 minutes. Despite the wishes of the Liverpool boss, the Finland coach Antti Muurinen did not want to rest his key player in a match that was part of the Nordic Championship tournament. The match went well for Sami and the Finland team, but things turned bad when Sami hurt his groin in the closing minutes. Sami remembers the match against Norway:

It had been agreed with Muurinen that I would not play the whole match. However, during the match it started to seem that I wasn't going to be substituted and yet I couldn't just walk off the pitch either. A little before the final whistle I felt a strain on my groin and experienced minor pain. I'm not saying that the strain was a direct result of playing the full 90 minutes, but I was very tired then and the next matches followed soon thereafter.

The worst thing about it all was that things didn't go as planned. When I returned to Liverpool and the boss found out what had happened, I had to go straight to his office and explain everything. Obviously, the gaffer didn't like it, but I think you just have to learn from things like this and try not to make the same mistake again.

Gérard Houllier's dissatisfaction with the Finland national team's decision to play Sami the full 90 minutes in an 'unimportant' match is very understandable, because all the other Liverpool players who were called up for international duty played no more than a single half in their matches. Although the value of the Nordic Championship tournament is greater from a Finnish viewpoint than from the French viewpoint, Houllier's opinion on the incident was totally justified. In addition to a long season in the Premiership, Liverpool faced a tight schedule in three cup competitions, and Sami was among the group of players whom Houllier was counting on the most. Therefore, any injury to Sami right before the season would have been a severe setback for the Reds. On the other hand, the Finnish national team were preparing for a busy autumn as well. The full Finland squad were facing Albania, Greece and England in the World Cup qualifiers, and in the spring, the qualifying campaign would continue with the long-awaited visit to Anfield to face England. The much-debated Nordic Championships tournament was finished in January 2001 without professional players. Finland took the title by beating Sweden 1–0 in an indoor stadium in Jönköping, Sweden.

All in all, the events of the Norway match show how useful it would be to come up with common rules for the ways to best serve the interests of the player, club and national team. Regular playing time and tough matches with their professional club teams are valuable for international players – even from the national team point of view. At least in the English Premiership the players may face as many competitive, world-class opponents as they do in all the international matches in a year. By no means is it in the best interest of the club team or the national team to burn out the key players before the most important fixtures.

6

High Hopes – Autumn 2000

SAMI HYYPIÄ'S FIRST SEASON AT LIVERPOOL HAD COME TO A conclusion after a disappointing winless streak and the second and third places had slipped away from the side in the last rounds. After a one-month holiday in Finland, Sami was ready to face the challenges of the new season. Immediately before returning to England, he gave an interview where he looked back at the better moments in the previous season. Sami said:

> For me personally, one of the highlights of the previous season was wearing the captain's armband. I was the third-ever foreign captain for the club. The two other foreign players who had had the honour to be Liverpool captains were the Swede Glenn Hysen and the Dane Jan Mölby. When you think about the players who have captained the legendary Liverpool FC in the past, it feels all the more amazing. After all, Liverpool FC is one of the most famous clubs in the world.
>
> I have to admit that even a few years back, or when I was a little kid and watched Liverpool play on TV, the thought of wearing the captain's armband at Liverpool one day would have never crossed my mind. Of course, when you're young you always dream about big things like that, but if signing with Liverpool was already a dream come true for me, I'm sure you can imagine how unbelievable it felt to become the team captain. The only other thing I can ask for is that we now begin to win some trophies.

Being a team captain is always an important matter, particularly in a major club like Liverpool FC. In addition to Hysen and Mölby, some of Sami's predecessors include such legendary players as Ron Yeats, Tommy Smith, Emlyn Hughes, Phil Thompson, Graeme Souness, Phil Neal, Alan Hansen and Paul Ince. All very familiar names to British football fans.

During his holiday in Finland, Sami had paid careful attention to his teammates' and future opponents' performances in the European Championships hosted by Holland and Belgium, where the reigning world champions France took the title home. Liverpool were strongly represented in the tournament. Michael Owen, Robbie Fowler, Emile Heskey, and the sensation of the previous season, Steven Gerrard, played for England, while Dietmar Hamann and Markus Babbel, Sami's future teammate, played for Germany. Babbel had agreed terms with Liverpool on the first day he was allowed to – in January 2000 – and would join the side in the training camp. The other three Liverpool players in the tournament were Vladimir Smicer and Patrick Berger for the Czech Republic and Sander Westerveld for Holland. Besides having a number of teammates there, another, more important reason for carefully watching the tournament was the fact that Sami and the Finland team would meet England and Germany in the World Cup 2002 qualifying campaign.

> I was surprised by the poor performances of the England and Germany teams in the tournament. However, I was quite sure that both squads would go through a certain changing process after Euro 2000, and I knew that our qualifying matches against these two football superpowers would be completely different matches. And even though neither England nor Germany played well in the tournament, a few names in particular stuck in my mind.
>
> I've always considered Markus Babbel a top level defender, so it was tremendous news that he was going to join us at Liverpool.

MARKUS BABBEL: SAMI HAS A BIG HEART

The German defender, Markus Babbel, had a long career at Bayern Munich and the German national team before he transferred to Liverpool in the summer of 2000. He soon took his place as the right full-back in the squad, so he knows Sami very well as a player. The two are often seen together off the pitch, too, and Babbel accompanied Sami on his visit to Finland in November 2001 when Sami was awarded the Finnish FA Player of the Year award. During the trip, he also took some time to share his thoughts on Sami and Liverpool FC.

Sami and Markus Babbel became friends soon after Babbel joined

Liverpool. 'I was a new player on the squad and I didn't know anyone. Sami was one of the first who talked to me, and it was nice that we became roommates on our away trips, too. I hardly knew any English when I arrived and Sami knew a little German, so he made my move and adjustment to Liverpool much easier,' Babbel now explains in fluent English.

Nevertheless, football is not the only thing the two defenders have in common:

> Sami likes rock music and cars just like I do and we have a lot in common in our personalities, too. We like similar things and Sami has become a very good friend of mine.
>
> I think he is very funny both in training and in free time. If, for example, the coaches criticise us in training, Sami may swear in Finnish and smile all the time. He has a good way of keeping our spirits high, and everyone at Liverpool likes him as a person and respects him as a player.

The easy-going lad becomes an iron-hard professional on the pitch, though:

> He takes football very seriously. You can tell that he hates losing and wants to win, and I think that is one of the reasons why we won so many titles in 2001. Every team could use a few more players like him.
>
> After a defeat, he might be extremely angry. One time in spring 2001, for example, he cried in the dressing-room after we lost to Leicester. He was so disappointed with the loss and his own performance. At first, I was a bit in awe at Sami's emotional reaction, but that moment only added to my respect for him. Only a few players have the guts to cry in the dressing-room, and to me, it speaks for Sami's emotional charge, attitude and commitment to the game.

Babbel also points out that Sami doesn't exactly fit into the stereotype of an introvert Finn:

> In Germany, the Nordic people are often considered cold, and for some people, Sami, too, may appear cold at first. But now that I have learnt to know Sami better, I know he has a big heart and that

he is always willing to give his maximum effort for the team. He never goes after personal glory. The fans at Anfield have also noticed this, and I think that he has become one of our most popular players.

Another thing about Sami is that he always dares to say things the way they are. He doesn't hesitate to share his opinions with the manager either, and that is another quality in him that I respect highly. I have seen many players who talk behind the boss's back and remain quiet when he's present.

Sami also talks to the younger players on the squad, which is very important for them: 'Hey, one of the star players of the first team spoke to me!'

According to Babbel, Sami's selection as one of the team captains is a tremendous demonstration of respect, trust and appreciation:

> I am sure that Sami is proud of being one of the team captains, especially because he is a foreigner. In Germany, being a team captain is not considered as important as in England, where it is a very significant matter. In England, only top-level players who have the most respect are selected team captains, and Sami is a player who can perform on the same level consistently.
>
> I also have a dream that I will wear the captain's armband at Liverpool one day, even for just one match.

Babbel is used to the fact that the competition for the starting 11 is extremely tight in the top clubs. The competition has never influenced the friendship between him and Sami, at least not negatively.

> Even though I had played in the centre for the most part of my career, I play on the right at Liverpool. So, in a way, Sami is playing in my position. However, the coaches think that this is best for the team, and I agree with their ideology completely. Interestingly enough, the best friends I've had on any team have been defenders, even though they have also been my competitors as far as the position in the squad goes. We understand each other's situation and way of thinking. I always do what I think is best for the team, and Sami thinks the same way. Maybe this is more characteristic of defenders – the strikers might be a little different and more selfish because of the qualities required for their position.

The early season 2001–02 was very unfortunate for Babbel. An extremely rare virus infection prevented him from training and playing, and he had to watch from the sidelines as new players crowded the Liverpool defence. 'Personally, I am not much troubled by having to sit out. What matters the most is that the team is doing well, and if I can help the team after I'm healthy again, things are back to perfect. At the end of the day, though, everything is fine as long as Liverpool are winning.'

Liverpool FC as a club and Liverpool as a city have been a pleasant experience for Babbel.

> When I first arrived at Liverpool, I was surprised by the way the club is run. In Germany, I had heard stories about English football and how unprofessional some things were here, but that couldn't be further from the truth at Liverpool. The club is very well organised, the people in the city are very proud of the team and the players are respected. The fans' relationship with the players is fair, and overall, the life of a football player is much easier here than it is in Germany.
>
> I played 16 years for Bayern Munich, and I will always consider them my team. Although Bayern will always have a place in my heart, after only one year at Liverpool FC I feel a particularly strong connection with the club. Already now, Liverpool FC feels like 'my team', and I really love this club. I like the atmosphere around the club, the people, the stadium, the fans – everything. The chant 'You'll Never Walk Alone' tells a lot about the club and its fans. If we win, everyone is happy, but if we lose, people understand that it is sometimes like that in football. As long as we do our best, we have the fans' support.
>
> Still, this is not to say that winning trophies is not important to Liverpool. The club has a long, winning tradition, and the 1970s and the 1980s were glorious decades. The titles and achievements we won in 2001 were tremendous, but we have to win the league title, too.

Babbel was Houllier's main acquisition for the Liverpool defence for the 2000–01 campaign. The newcomers from the previous year, Hyypiä and Henchoz, and the club's own product Carragher had secured their positions in the starting 11, but Houllier wanted to reinforce the side's defence and went into the transfer market for more players. Right before the beginning of the season, he acquired the German, Christian Ziege, from Middlesbrough and the young French talent, Grégory Vignal. For the midfield, Houllier surprised many by acquiring Gary McAllister from Coventry, and the transfer of the other new midfielder, Nick Barmby, aroused strong emotional reactions in the city of Liverpool. Barmby came to the Reds from their fiercest rivals, Everton. Transfer activity between the two traditional clubs has been quiet throughout history, particularly when it comes to top-level players like Barmby.

Winger Bernard Diomède and goalkeeper Pegguy Arphexad, Houllier's compatriots, were the other two new players in the squad for the upcoming season. As always, when a team gets new players from the transfer market, there are others who leave the club to make room for the newcomers. Between the 1999–2000 and 2000–01 seasons, Phil Babb, Stig Inge Björnebye, Dominic Matteo and David Thompson packed their bags and moved away from Liverpool. Babb and Björnebye's transfers were free, but selling Matteo and Thompson brought back some of the money Houllier had spent when strengthening the squad. Nevertheless, the way Houllier was rebuilding the team did not leave any questions unanswered about the financial investments made to promote Liverpool's return to the top of English and European football.

Interestingly for Liverpool, their 2000–01 season started with the same fixture that had ended the previous season: a match against Bradford. Unlike in the spring, Liverpool managed to score in the season opener and brought their five-match goalless streak to an end with a 1–0 victory through a goal by Emile Heskey. As Robbie Fowler and Jamie Redknapp began the season on the injury list, Sami Hyypiä wore the captain's armband again. Winning the opening match is always important for any club, but it was even more important for Liverpool this time because they played the team that had been such a wet blanket for them in the final match of the previous season. Except for the win against Bradford, the 2000–01 campaign started off inconsistently as Houllier was still searching for his best 11. At the back, Westerveld, Hyypiä and Henchoz were at their usual positions, but the rest of the successful squad was still evolving.

Liverpool's season progressed in search of their best form and there was one match in particular where the team were extremely disorganised. Just before the break for international match day, Liverpool played Southampton at home. The Reds took an early lead in the match, and were winning 3–0 only 17 minutes from time. Sami had scored one of the three goals, but the final minutes of the match were a disaster for the strongest defence in the Premiership. Southampton scored three goals in less than

20 minutes and equalised the match at 3–3. The final score made Houllier furious. 'I am mad because we let three points slip away easily. Considering the size of our defenders, I cannot understand how Southampton could score three goals on us from the air,' Houllier said afterwards. 'In particular, the way they scored their last goal worried me the most because our concentration just failed.'

Sami also remembers the match clearly. For the first time in a long time, the media scolded the Liverpool defence pretty severely. 'Personally, I took the draw hard on myself because I felt that I was blamed for all three goals we conceded. No one said that exactly, but that was the impression I got from the different reports,' Sami says. 'I always accept the praise as part of our defence, and I do the same with criticism. I am never there alone, whether we play well or poorly.'

An interesting detail is that the match against Southampton was the first time when Hyypiä, Henchoz, Carragher and Babbel were all in the team, although not as the back four.

In September, Finland started their World Cup qualifying campaign with a 2–1 home victory over Albania. Jari Litmanen and Aki Riihilahti (Crystal Palace) scored the Finland goals and Sami played in his usual, elegant style in the Finland defence. With Liverpool, the season continued with the first round of the UEFA Cup in addition to the regular Premiership schedule. Historically, September 2000 will remain in the records as the month when Sami Hyypiä missed his first full match while at Liverpool. In the 6 September league match against Aston Villa, Sami twisted his knee in a collision with Luc Nilis, causing a tear in a ligament. The injury sidelined Sami for two weeks, and the next league match against Manchester City was the first match Sami had to sit out at Liverpool FC. Before that, Sami had been in the team on 42 consecutive occasions.

'I got injured during the first half already, but I still played the whole match,' Sami explained at the time. 'The next morning, I noticed that my knee was swollen and it also hurt, so I went in for X-rays. A more careful examination showed that it was only a minor injury.

'Of course, an injury on the knee always makes you worried, but I was fortunate to escape with a scare and a minor injury.'

Because of the injury, Sami missed three Premiership matches and Liverpool's first European match in many years. The club returned to European cup competition on a victorious note as they beat Rapid Bucharest in Romania 1–0, with a goal by Nick Barmby. In addition to the successful return to Europe, Liverpool had found good form in the league, too. Still, October started out in the worst possible way for them: Chelsea beat Liverpool 3–0 in Sami's first match in the squad after his injury. Sami's highlight of the month was still ahead, though, as Finland took on England at the Helsinki Olympic Stadium on 11 October. Four days earlier, Finland had lost to Greece 1–0 in Athens, which made it very difficult for the Finland team to prepare for the England match. Despite the fact that the England coach, Kevin Keegan, had just resigned after the defeat against Germany, the media gave Finland no chance against England.

The fixtures between the teammates from England, Finland and Germany had been a cause for a little tug-of-war at Melwood. Sami told about a deal he had made with Christian Ziege: Germany would first beat England at Wembley, and then Finland would do the same in Helsinki four days later. Before the England match, Sami said that Ziege had kept his part of the deal and now it was his turn to keep his.

As expected, the Helsinki Olympic Stadium was filled with a capacity crowd, the fans enjoying a tremendous atmosphere at the stadium as the two national teams played out a 0–0 draw. The expected match between Michael Owen and Sami Hyypiä was put off for the future because Owen did not play in Helsinki. Nevertheless, Sami had a club teammate on the opposing side, as he measured up against Emile Heskey. Sami's performance in the match was strong, perhaps even brilliant. It seemed that Heskey wanted to remain on the left side of the pitch, trying to avoid any contact with his colossal club teammate in the Finland defence. It seemed as if he would rather give up the ball than challenge Sami in a one-on-one. Nor did Manchester United striker Andy Cole have anything to threaten Sami with. After the match, Cole was the first one who shook hands with Sami.

'He didn't really say anything, but I don't think he talks that much overall anyway. A fair handshake after the match is part of the game, no matter what happens on the pitch,' Sami commented in the match report in *Veikkaaja*.

In the eyes of the Finnish football fans, Sami had risen to a superstar status, alongside Jari Litmanen. He had proven his level in front of the home crowd against the players who are the most respected among the Finnish football fans: the professional English football players. It is they whom thousands of Finnish football fans, Sami and Jouko Hyypiä among them, have followed weekly on TV since the early 1970s.

A DANGEROUS DINNER

A few days after the Finland–England match, Sami made the headlines for the first time for a reason other than football. After a victorious league match against Derby, Sami and a few of his teammates were enjoying a night out at a restaurant in the centre of Liverpool, when the peaceful dinner was interrupted in a dramatic way. Two armed men rushed into the restaurant and opened fire with their handguns. Two people picked up minor injuries in the shooting incident, but the Liverpool players escaped the situation with a scare.

> I actually didn't see anything unusual, but I heard shots from the lobby. All I could do was to go down and look for cover. In the end, we were actually quite far from the actual shooting scene, but, nevertheless, we were in the same restaurant.
>
> At first, a few people in our company just sat and watched what was going on, and when we heard clatter and some banging in the lobby, at first I didn't quite think that someone was shooting there. I didn't even see the gunmen, but I heard that they had come all the way into the restaurant. Fortunately, no one was fatally injured, but still, two people were shot in the leg. I don't think I ever found out why the two men opened fire there.

With Sami at that dinner were Sander Westerveld, Markus Babbel, Christian Ziege, Dietmar Hamann and Erik Meijer. The story does not reveal whether Sami was the first to go down and look for cover or if he was the only one in the party who had done service in the army. The line-up in the dinner party was quite typical, for the foreign players at Liverpool FC often spend their free time in each other's company. According to Sami, it is quite a natural thing:

> I don't think it shows in any particular way that we have a number of foreigners on the squad. Of course, the English perhaps look for each other's company more easily because they have known each other for a longer time. As for us foreigners, it really doesn't matter where you come from, because we're all new to the country.
>
> Perhaps we – those who've come from abroad – spend a little more time together because we know the situation the others are in. The English players don't necessarily notice that it is not always easy for a foreigner to come to a new club. For us, it is important that we have good friends in the team and that you can spend your

free time with someone in the team. The English players often have their old circle of friends in the city, while our old friends are somewhere far away. And because we spend so much time with the team you don't really have time to look for friends outside the team anyway. We have come here on our own, but no one that I know is really truly happy alone all the time. You always need friends and the better friends you have on the team, the better the atmosphere around you. Of course, the English players talk to all the others and enjoy everyone's company no matter what the nationality, but you just don't see them in your free time as much as you see other foreign players.

Due to their common background of Dutch football and life in Holland, Sander Westerveld has been one of the closest friends Sami has had at Liverpool. The Dutch goalkeeper has also been very helpful in terms of Sami's language skills: 'I have started to forget some of the Dutch I learned while I lived in Holland, but I'm trying to maintain my skills as much as possible. On the other hand, though, my English got weaker when I was in Holland.'

The busy training and match schedules ensure that the Liverpool players don't have any problems in finding ways to spend their free time. 'Nowadays, I spend most of my free time just relaxing and resting. I usually just take it easy, sit on the couch and watch TV or something,' Sami confesses, but quickly adds a few activities, too:

We play a lot of table football at Melwood every day, and I've tried to practise some golf. I'm not really that good at it just yet, but practice makes perfect . . . let's just say that I can hit the ball a few yards forward and sometimes straight where I want to. I started out playing occasionally in Holland, but here I've played much more. In a way, England is that much of a golf country that you almost have to play some golf. There are eight golf courses in Liverpool and dozens more right outside the city limits. The drive to a course is never long, and you can also vary the course you play quite conveniently.

A normal working day for Sami begins with a wake-up call at 8.15 a.m. After a light breakfast, Sami drives to Melwood for training. During the season, the training lasts from an hour to an hour and 15 minutes. After showering, Sami often goes for a massage. The players can also have lunch at Melwood, and Sami usually has his lunch there. His favourite food is lasagne, but he also likes Finnish specialities on occasion. 'Now that I have lived abroad for so many years, rye bread and Finnish sausage taste delicious sometimes,' Sami admits.

The day's work is usually done around one o'clock. As Liverpool's recent success has brought along many more matches throughout the year, the amount of training has decreased.

> During my first year at Liverpool, we didn't have as many matches as we do now, so we sometimes had two training sessions in a day. But with two matches a week, the players could never do that. We have so many matches in the season that we don't have time to train much. Most training sessions are either loosening up the day after the match or preparatory training for the next match.

MORE FINNS TO LIVERPOOL

After the break for international match day, the return to routines and Premiership fixtures happened quickly. After the loss to Chelsea, Liverpool won all their matches in October, and the rebuilt defence was starting to look more and more uniform. In November, Liverpool's busy schedule got even busier, as the Premiership and UEFA Cup fixtures were accompanied by the Worthington Cup. Liverpool approached the Worthington Cup with the attitude that winning the cup was the shortest route to Europe for the next season. Although many major clubs in England belittle the Worthington Cup, this has not been the case with Liverpool. Even as early as the first rounds of the cup, Gérard Houllier always plays his best team, which speaks for the commitment the club have for the competition. In a crushing 8–0 victory against Stoke, Sami scored an unusual goal with his foot. 'The ball fell straight in my lap, so it was an easy job to put it in the net with my foot. It was the first goal I scored for Liverpool with my foot, all the others had come off a header.'

Throughout November, Liverpool played consistently, advancing to the next rounds in both the Worthington Cup and the UEFA Cup. In the UEFA Cup, the first leg of the next-round fixture against the Greek side Olympiakos of Athens also produced a good result. Liverpool came away from a tough away match in Athens with a 2–2 draw. Despite advancing in both cup competitions, the most memorable match of the month was between Liverpool and Leeds, the club who had beaten Liverpool in the battle for third place in the final straight of the race for the league. In the

4 November match, Liverpool took the lead only two minutes into the match when Sami scored his second goal of the season. In the end, the match didn't turn out to be a moment of glory for Sami: Leeds striker Mark Viduka stole the show by scoring four goals and taking Leeds to a 4–3 victory.

In November, Liverpool played a total of eight official matches and had Sami played in the international friendly between Finland and Ireland, it would have accounted for his ninth match in one month. However, the Finland coach Antti Muurinen and Liverpool management agreed that Sami would take a well-deserved rest instead.

November was a busy month for Liverpool in the transfer market, too. Rigobert Song, the captain of the full Cameroon squad who had arrived at Liverpool a little before Sami, was fed up with being a substitute and asked to be transferred. As West Ham showed interest in the Cameroon international, Liverpool made a deal with the London club where part of Song's transfer fee was to be paid by the transfer of Daniel Sjölund to Liverpool FC. Sjölund, a native of the Åland islands off the south-western Finnish coast, is a young and talented forward who has been astoundingly productive in the Finland youth national teams. His transfer fee was estimated to be £1 million, and his arrival aroused a lot of interest in the Liverpool dressing-room. Instead of his football skills, however, the interest Sjölund aroused was more due to the peculiar fact that he speaks hardly any Finnish. The Liverpool players were openly puzzled about the fact that the two Finns were communicating in English instead of what they considered their native tongue. Sami chuckles and explains:

> Daniel is from the Åland islands and has never lived on the mainland. The people in Åland speak Swedish as their first language, and although I had studied Swedish for many years and taken the matriculation exam in it, too, I had lost touch with my Swedish skills en route from Holland to England. Undoubtedly, the folk here were quite dumbfounded about our language choice.
>
> I've tried to teach him some Finnish by making him read Finnish magazines, but I think 'Daja' is only flipping through the pictures.

As a football player, Sjölund is tremendously talented. In the future, anything is possible for him, and Sami has a lot of confidence in the young striker. 'He is a player with a lot of potential,' Sami says. 'I hadn't seen him play before he came here, but I had heard a lot of good things about him much earlier. In the future, I believe that Sjölund will bring much delight to this club.'

According to Sami, Sjölund has enjoyed living in Liverpool, and the more experienced Finn hasn't had to look after the youth at all. Since he joined the club, Sjölund has trained with the first team, but he spends his free time mostly with the other youth players. 'Daniel lives in a place with many other youth players, too, so he has a lot of friends there. Every now and then I ask him how he's doing, but I never thought I should look after him any more than that.'

In December, both Sami and the team were playing well. Liverpool advanced to the next round in the UEFA Cup by beating Olympiakos 2–0 at home, with goals from Nick Barmby and Emile Heskey. In the Worthington Cup, Liverpool advanced to the semi-finals by beating Fulham. In the Premiership, the team remained in good standing even though they suffered their first home defeat of the season to Ipswich. In the transfer market, Houllier added another piece to his puzzle by acquiring the Croatian Igor Biscan. The player who had to make room for Biscan's arrival was Steve Staunton, the veteran Irish international. As for individual results, the greatest games of the month were the away win against Manchester United and the home win against Arsenal. The win over Manchester United was even sweeter than usual, as Danny Murphy's winner from a free kick ended Manchester United's 36-match unbeaten run at Old Trafford.

'This was an unbelievable victory for our fans. It was time to end that streak and it was right that we were the side to do it. Our tactics worked out exactly the way we wanted and our defence stood strong throughout the match,' Sami explained afterwards. 'Beating Manchester United at Old Trafford proved to us that if we can keep a clean sheet, we can beat any team in the world. I am sure that we will score goals in the future, too.'

The match at Old Trafford was also the first time Sami had met with Ole Gunnar Solskjär after the Norwegian's dirty tackle in the previous season. Apparently, the events of the previous encounter between the two remained clear in Sami's mind, for there were a few occasions when Sami really tackled the striker hard, and yet clean, as is customary for him. The referee didn't even have to think about pulling the yellow card out of his pocket. 'Solskjär and I were going at it throughout the match. I think I kept him under my control pretty effectively, and we didn't avoid any contacts either,' Sami noted of the rematch between the two.

The next Premiership round gave the famous Liverpool fans even more reason for singing. The fans had barely recovered from the Manchester United win, when the Kop got to witness Liverpool in their best form. The Reds played better than in years and beat Arsenal, another fierce rival,

4–0 at Anfield. The scoring sheet was particularly delightful for the England national-team management, as the Liverpool goals were scored by Steven Gerrard, Michael Owen, Nick Barmby and Robbie Fowler – every single one of them a member of the full England squad. Sami was once again the team captain and this time tamed Arsenal's top gun Dennis Bergkamp.

'The matches against Arsenal are always tough, both teams are always charged with some extra adrenaline in our meetings. Early on in that match, Bergkamp elbowed me pretty hard, so I decided to go in for the tackles a little harder myself – just for self-protection, really,' Sami explained after the sweet victory.

A few changes took place in Sami's life in December 2000. At the beginning of the month, he moved to a new apartment with his girlfriend Niina, but the van did not have to drive far. Sami had grown so fond of the area he was living in that he found a new home in the building next door. The area's reputation as a quality neighbourhood was soon reinforced when a familiar face moved into the same building as Sami. The Liverpool manager Gérard Houllier had bought himself a flat there and on the same floor as Sami. With a smile on his face, Sami quickly points out that he didn't follow the boss, it was the other way round. Living next to his foreman is by no means a problem for Sami either. 'I don't exactly throw many parties, so I have no problems living here. Besides, the boss and I don't see each other that much off the pitch anyway. Sometimes we meet in the garage or the lift, but that's about it,' Sami continues.

Near the end of the year, rumours about a new acquisition were spreading and began to strengthen. Houllier was said to be interested in signing Jari Litmanen, the most successful Finnish football player ever and Sami's long-time teammate from the Finnish national team and MyPa in 1992. Eventually, Litmanen's transfer from Barcelona was sealed at the turn of the year. He was given jersey Number 37 and, like Sami, he also explained that he had been a Liverpool fan since he was a little kid. After his transfer had been sealed, Litmanen said:

> I have always wanted to play for Liverpool and now I had a good chance to make it happen. I wasn't getting much playing time at Barcelona, so a transfer was very welcome. Liverpool are a young and hungry side, and I am sure that we will be successful in the future.

SAMI HYYPIÄ

Sami was extremely happy to be reunited with Litmanen at club level after eight years. 'Jari will bring much joy to this club. He is a true world-class player, he has a good understanding of the game and the ability to score important goals. I think he will play an important part in our success this spring,' Sami said of Litmanen's transfer to a club that was still involved in many different competitions.

The end of the year always marks the time of awards, too. To the surprise of many, instead of Sami Hyypiä, the Finland coach Antti Muurinen selected Jari Litmanen as the Finnish FA Player of the Year. While Sami had played a solid season with Liverpool, Litmanen had struggled for regular playing time at Barcelona. This is how Muurinen justified his decision to the Finnish media, who selected Sami as their Footballer of the Year:

> Both Jari and Sami are tremendous players, and I made my decision completely on the basis of our international matches. In our international matches, Jari Litmanen has clearly been our best player. Of course, Sami Hyypiä could have received this award just as well, but now he has been awarded with the same recognition on behalf of the sports journalists. I am happy for both players, especially because this year we have two remarkable players who are both worthy of both awards.

The sports journalists' recognitions did not end there, though: as the best athlete in a team sport, Sami finished eighth in the annual voting for Finnish Athlete of the Year. Before Sami, only two football players had finished in the top ten in the voting. In the 1950s, Aulis Rytkönen, the first professional Finnish football player abroad, was voted ninth, and in 1995 Jari Litmanen was voted Finnish Athlete of the Year.

'It is a tremendous achievement to finish this high among such a talented group of athletes. This is a great honour for a team player, and I'd like to remind everyone that my teammates, the manager and coaches all deserve their share of this honour,' Sami said after the voting.

Sami received recognition in Liverpool, too. Liverpool FC's largest and most significant fan club, the Merseyside, had selected Sami as the team's Player of the Year in the previous season and they now rewarded him with a Christmas dinner. 'We have the most terrific fans who are always supporting us to their fullest, both home and away. The visiting teams seldom do well at Anfield, and it is much to the credit of our tremendous fans,' Sami said as he thanked the fans for the reward.

In the spring, the fans were treated to a cornucopia of titles that would be hard to repeat.

SEVEN UNFORGETTABLE OPPONENTS
Gabriel Batistuta, AS Roma and Argentina
Batistuta is known as one of the best goalscorers ever, both in the Argentine national team and in the Italian Serie A. With the help of his goals, AS Roma won the Italian league title in 2001, after several years without a trophy. In 1999, FIFA selected Batistuta as the second runner-up for the World Player of the Year, and in 1991 he was selected Player of the Year in South America. He failed to score against Sami both in the UEFA Cup and in the Champions League in 2001.

'He is very quick in his turns and a very good goalscorer. On the other hand, however, he makes it easy to play against him because he almost always goes for the shot himself when he is close to the goal.'

Duncan Ferguson, Everton
Ferguson is one of those players who rank at the top of Sami's list of the dirtiest opponents. The tall Scottish forward has caused a lot of headaches for the Liverpool defence wearing the jersey of the local rivals, Everton.

'I really hate playing against Ferguson because he fouls you a little in every challenge and he always has his elbows flying high in headers. Then again, almost every team has a target man similar to Ferguson.'

Thierry Henry, Arsenal and France
The French Arsenal forward is a world champion and a European champion. He is quick and makes unexpected moves. Sami has played against him on numerous occasions with Liverpool – in the Premiership and in the FA Cup final in spring 2001. What most people don't know is that the two have also played together, in 1998!

'Henry is surprisingly big and strong and extremely skilful. Yet, first and foremost, he is very quick. A really tough opponent, probably the toughest in the Premiership.'

Jari Litmanen, Liverpool (then Ajax Amsterdam) and Finland
Sami played against the most successful Finnish football player in Holland. In the first match between Ajax and Willem II where Sami played against Litmanen, Litmanen scored.

'I played against Jari a few times in Holland, and we never beat them. I'd much rather play with him than against him.'

Ruud van Nistelrooy, Manchester United and Holland

Sami became familiar with the tall Manchester United forward while playing in Holland. The two met again in 2001 when Sami tamed one of the most expensive players in the world and kept him from scoring in the Liverpool–Manchester United match at Anfield.

'In Holland, he proved that he is a good goalscorer and now he is playing for a really good team. A quick forward who will score if you give him the chance. He is not too daring in one-on-ones, though.'

Rivaldo, Barcelona and Brazil

The Brazilian virtuoso plays for Barcelona. He is a tremendous goalscorer and he was selected the World Player of the Year in 1999 and second runner-up in the same voting the year after. He was also selected the European Player of the Year in 1999. The Brazilian national team player played against Sami in the UEFA Cup and in the Champions League in 2001 and failed to score against him.

'An extremely skilful player who is also surprisingly strong, although he may not appear to be so. He could shield the ball against three of our players. If you play against him and can keep his left foot under control, you have already done a great job.'

Mark Viduka, Leeds and Australia

The Australian is breaking through to the elite group of forwards in the world. The tall Leeds forward scored four goals in one match against Liverpool in 2000–01.

'That match was a dream performance for Viduka. He is very dangerous inside the box, he is quick in his turns and shoots the ball well and quickly.'

7

Return to Trophies – Spring 2001

THE YEAR 2001 STARTED OUT WELL FOR LIVERPOOL. DURING THE FIRST month, the Reds played eight matches without being defeated. In the Premiership, Liverpool continued their rise to the top and the side's performances in the different cup competitions were successful, too. In the FA Cup, Liverpool advanced to the fifth round by beating Leeds away with goals by Heskey and Barmby. The Worthington Cup was already in the semi-final stage, where Liverpool beat Crystal Palace in a two-leg fixture. The semi-finals had an extra charge among the Finnish football fans, as both teams had Finnish players in the squad. In addition to Sami, the Reds had just signed a new Finn, Jari Litmanen, who made his debut in the first leg of the semi-final. The Finnish player at Crystal Palace was Mikael Forssell, perhaps the most talented Finnish striker of the moment, who was on loan from Chelsea. Well before the first leg at Selhurst Park in London, Sami and Forssell had engaged in verbal warfare in the media. It was only after the semi-final had been played that the two revealed that they had agreed on most of the things they would say to each other . . . Nevertheless, Forssell was the one who started the wind-up before the first leg and threw a challenge towards Merseyside:

> I have never played against Sami or Jari, so in that sense it will be a very interesting match. Liverpool are strong opponents, but I can guarantee you that it won't be easy for them in London. I will make it particularly hard for Sami, and I have said it a number of times before: I will take him to school, just like I always do in the Finnish national team training.

Sami did not consider his reply for long:

> Playing against Mikael [Forssell] does not make it any different. We
> will forget about our friendship for 90 minutes and be friends again
> after the match. I've heard that he is going to take me to school. All
> I can say to it is, 'Feel free to try, son. We'll see how it is after the
> match.'

Surprisingly, Crystal Palace won the first leg 2–1. Sami played the whole match and Jari came on as a substitute and delivered a quality pass for Vladimir Smicer for the important away goal. For Crystal Palace, Forssell had an assist in the winner, and the young striker did get some credit for his performance from his more experienced national teammate.

'I think the kid did well for himself, except that he had to pull my shirt to have a chance in the one-on-ones. I'm glad he didn't manage to score against us, and I think this result leaves us with a good starting point for our home leg,' Sami said after the match.

In his own post-match comments, Forssell explained that he and Sami didn't really say anything to each other during the match and that the fellow Finn had had a few mean glares at him.

> I think Sami and I had a few really good challenges for the ball. A
> few times we were really going at it on headers and I think we even
> exchanged a few powerful words there. A couple of times, Sami
> also gave me a few of his critical glares that we've all seen on TV.
> Our friendship is forgotten for the duration of the match, but it
> does feel nice to be friends with him again after the final whistle.

Crystal Palace used up all their capacity in the first leg and were completely disarmed at Anfield: Liverpool demolished them 5–0 in the second leg. Although Danny Murphy scored a pair of goals in the win, the best player on the pitch was Jari Litmanen, without question. The Reds' new signing demonstrated his skills and abilities to his new home crowd for the first time. The second encounter between Hyypiä and Forssell was pretty lame due to the dramatic difference in the two teams' levels.

'Our battles were nowhere near the intensity we had in London. Miklu was the best player in the Palace side, but he didn't create much today either. I hope we'll meet again in the future, when he returns to Chelsea,' Sami concluded and wished success to the future star striker.

Another great moment in the history of Finnish football took place in a Premiership match between Aston Villa and Liverpool, as it was the first time a Premiership team had two Finns in the team. As for Liverpool, the most important achievement in the first month of 2001 was returning to a Cup final. By beating Crystal Palace in the semi-final, Liverpool made their way to the Worthington Cup final against Birmingham in Cardiff on 25 February – their first final since 1995. For Sami, January 2001 marked yet another time when he signed a new contract with Liverpool. The contract, whose term had been prolonged already in the previous year, was now made to last until June 2005. Liverpool wanted to hold on to their top defender.

February 2001 was an interesting and strenuous time for Sami. During the short month, he played in five different competitions with Liverpool and the Finnish national team. With Liverpool, he played in the Premiership, the FA Cup, the Worthington Cup and the UEFA Cup, and with the Finland team he played a World Cup qualifier against England. Although it was an exceptionally hard month for Sami, and many other Liverpool players, it has remained in their memory as the time when Liverpool returned to the top – both in England and in Europe.

In the UEFA Cup, the Reds faced AS Roma. Generally, Houllier's army were thought to have no chance against the side who were to be crowned Italian champions later in the year. Football experts were saying that Gabriel Batistuta and company would be too much for the Liverpool side, who were still in a rebuilding phase. The match proved otherwise, however, and the magic formula was no secret. In the first leg at the Rome Olympic Stadium, Liverpool's defence was perfect and they scored two goals from counter-attacks. Michael Owen demonstrated his finishing skills and scored both goals while Sami first tamed the much feared Vincenzo Montella and later kept Batistuta under control, too, when the Argentine striker came on as a substitute. A week later at Anfield, the Reds played with the same tactics, a little less successfully but well enough to advance to the next round. Michael Owen missed a penalty kick and Liverpool were kept scoreless at home. Despite their dominant pressure, AS Roma managed to score only once and Liverpool advanced to the fifth round of the UEFA Cup. Sami recalls that February match:

> The second match at Anfield was really tough, one of the toughest in the season. Roma were really powerful and dominated most of the match, which is very uncommon for us at Anfield. They were really tough opponents – Batistuta, Totti and company are world-class players, and they have a solid defence. Our team effort was absolutely brilliant that evening.
>
> Another reason why the achievement was so important was that

it was only four days before the Worthington Cup final. Beating AS Roma gave us a lot of confidence and taught us another lesson about winning. We were all over-excited about winning a trophy, both for ourselves and for the club. Six years without a trophy for a club like Liverpool FC seems like an eternity.

On Saturday, 24 February, Liverpool took a course towards Cardiff and the stately Millennium Stadium. As a result of the busy match schedule, the team were suffering from numerous injuries and several players who travelled there were still recovering. Jari Litmanen was the latest addition to the injury list due to a calf problem. Although Birmingham, the opponents, were a First Division side, the Liverpool players approached the Cup final with respect towards them. According to Sami, it is impossible that a poor team would make it all the way to the Worthington Cup final. Of course, Liverpool were the clear favourites in the match.

The next day, for the first time in many years, Liverpool, led out by captain Robbie Fowler, took to the pitch for a Cup final. Fowler also had the honour of scoring the first goal of the match 30 minutes into the game. It seemed that the Cup run of the Birmingham side was going to end with a brave one-goal defeat as the rock-hard Liverpool defence – in its usual form of Westerveld, Hyypiä, Henchoz, Carragher and Babbel, with Hamann in front of them – was winning their challenges with ease. In the final minute of the match, however, the whole world seemed to cave in for the Liverpool fans when Henchoz tackled Martin O'Connor inside the penalty box and David Elleray, the referee, pointed to the penalty spot. Darren Purse equalised the score and the match went into extra time.

Extra time remained scoreless and the Cup title was to be decided on penalties. Reflecting the even events of the day, the penalty shootout went to sudden death, and it was only after Sander Westerveld saved Andy Johnson's penalty that the Reds were relieved from their suspense and got to celebrate their first title since 1995. The final score of the shootout was 5–4 and the players' faces lit up with joy – as they had just won their first title together. Sami told the media after the awards ceremony:

> Liverpool has a long winning tradition, and I am sure that this will not be the last trophy this team will win. This is a fine achievement both for the players and the club. I do not understand why the Worthington Cup is so undervalued here, because, for me, a cup is always a cup. You win a cup by winning the final, and cup finals

are the best matches to measure any team's level of play and their mental strength.

I don't think our tremendous fans care much about the name of the cup we won today. What counts the most is that we won a title for them.

AN AWAY MATCH AT HOME

The Liverpool players didn't have much time to celebrate their Worthington Cup title because of the international match the following week. On the Monday after the final, Sami reported to the Finnish national team camp site in Luxemburg. The dark sunglasses on his head seemed a bit out of place at the end of February in a cold climate in Central Europe, but for one reason or another, Sami's eyes were apparently a little more sensitive to sunlight than usual.

Finland won the match against Luxemburg 1–0 through a goal by Mikael Forssell, his first for the full Finland squad. The international match was part of the preparations for Finland's next great challenge, the World Cup qualifier against England at Anfield on 24 March. Before the exciting World Cup qualifier, Sami and other Liverpool players who were members of their national teams concentrated on Liverpool's matches in the Premiership, the FA Cup and the UEFA Cup. Liverpool were defeated in the league match following their Worthington Cup title, but in the UEFA Cup, the Reds advanced to the quarter-finals by beating Porto with a 2–0 aggregate score. The first leg in Portugal ended in a goalless draw and the home leg was won by tremendous defence and goals by Michael Owen and Danny Murphy. In the FA Cup, Liverpool beat local rivals Tranmere and advanced to the semi-finals with a 4–2 victory. The Liverpool goals were all scored by England internationals – Michael Owen, Danny Murphy, Steven Gerrard, and Robbie Fowler each got one apiece – which was a severe warning of Finland's future opponents' current form.

The Finland team came together for the unique World Cup qualifier on Wednesday, 21 March. Jari Litmanen was fit again and Finland appeared to have their best team out. Despite the fact that the members of the Finland team thought they had a rather strong team to challenge England, no one in the footballing world really believed in Finland's chances, except for overly optimistic Finland fans and the members of the full Finland squad, of course. Again, the media in England and in Finland were very interested in Sami Hyypiä's pre-match comments. Sami told reporters before the match:

SAMI HYYPIÄ

I think that Saturday's match will be the most important match I
have played at Anfield so far. For me, this is a unique opportunity,
for I don't think there are many players in the world who get to
play for their country at the home stadium of their own club, in the
opponents' colours. This is a tremendous and unforgettable
experience for me.

Sven-Göran Eriksson, the new England coach, had selected four of Sami
and Jari's teammates from Liverpool for the full England squad. This time
Michael Owen was expected to be in the squad and Sami was eagerly
waiting for this particular encounter. The other three Liverpool players on
the England squad were Steven Gerrard, Robbie Fowler and Emile Heskey.
On the match day, Owen and Gerrard were the two Liverpool players who
walked out of the tunnel at Anfield to meet their Finnish teammates, Sami
Hyypiä and Jari Litmanen, who were in the Finland 11, in front of a
capacity crowd. Of course, the crowd at Anfield was cheering loudly for
its own, but the two Reds in Finland jerseys also received a loud
reception. Without question, this was yet another historical moment in
Finnish football. The wild atmosphere at Anfield went sour in the 26th
minute of the match as Aki Riihilahti headed Finland 1–0 up from a
corner. The Finland defence, led by Sami Hyypiä, held tight until the last
minutes of the first half when Michael Owen relieved the home crowd
from their pain and equalised the score at 1–1. Finland came out for the
second half with a fighting spirit and wanted to come away with a draw,
but fate had it otherwise, though, and Manchester United star player and
England captain David Beckham scored the winner for England in the
50th minute – the Anfield crowd sang Beckham's name for the first time
in his career.

Despite the bitter defeat, the match remains an important part of
Finnish football history. Over 2,000 fans had come from Finland to
support their team. The previous record for Finnish fans in an away match
was 500. Finnish football fans will also always remember that their
national team did not give in to their much more famous opponents at any
point in the match and, in fact, with a little more luck Finland could have
left Anfield with a draw: in the closing moments of the match, David
Seaman made a fabulous save from a Litmanen header. After the match,
Sami Hyypiä and Michael Owen exchanged their jerseys. The two
teammates had finally played against each other and both wanted the
jersey of a much-respected player as a memory.

As for Liverpool FC, the match brought both good and bad news. Owen and Gerrard, who marked Litmanen tight in the second half, played brilliant matches, but Litmanen had played his last match of the season. About 30 minutes from time, the Finland captain fell down in a harmless-looking situation and broke his wrist in eight different places. Even with this severe injury, Litmanen showed tremendous fighting spirit and played the match until the end.

In the second half, there was an interesting incident near the Finland penalty box. Emile Heskey, who had just come on as a substitute, rushed towards the penalty area, ran into Sami Hyypiä and dived in style. Valentin Ivanov, the referee, took the bait and the hook, and gave Sami his only yellow card of the season. Sami was furious after the incident, and his temper had not cooled down after the match either. Sami let Emile hear it loud and clear: 'I've never approved of diving on the pitch, it is totally against my football philosophy. Just as I don't approve of fouling someone on purpose, I despise diving. What Emile did there was really substandard,' Sami stated.

After the unforgettable World Cup qualifier, Liverpool's Finnish players made the shortest of trips home from an away match while the England players left for an away fixture against Albania. After returning from Albania, Emile Heskey had a little surprise waiting for him at Melwood. In front of his locker in the dressing-room there were flippers, a snorkel and diver's goggles in a neat pile. The word around was that Sami was responsible for the little gift. 'I won't comment on the truthfulness of the story, but I can certainly say that I would have liked to give him a surprise present like that,' a smiling Sami explains. 'I still think his dive was wrong, but we have shaken hands about it a long time ago. I think Emile knows what he did and whether or not I hit him at all.'

Since then, quite a few other players have also had to look Big Sami in the eye after wishfully diving for free kicks or penalties. The image of the scornfully smiling, or alternatively, furiously glaring Liverpool stopper is familiar to many fans in England and in Europe.

MICHAEL OWEN: SAMI IS A TREMENDOUS LEADER

Undoubtedly, the Liverpool player who has caused the biggest sensation in recent years is Michael Owen. Owen is a lightning-fast 'little dynamo', whose nose for goals is his golden quality. Owen made his name on the world football stage in 1998, when he was joint top scorer in the English Premiership in his first season in the first team and scored two brilliant goals in the 1998 World Cup.

SAMI HYYPIÄ

According to the English media, the new contract Owen signed with Liverpool in the autumn of 2001 made him one of the best-paid football players in the world. It was the fourth professional contract for this 22-year-old striker and it will keep him at Liverpool until summer 2005.

When asked about Sami Hyypiä's importance to Liverpool FC, Michael Owen answered:

> Sami's selection as team captain shows what the manager, the staff and the players at Liverpool think about him. Everyone looks up to him and he is a tremendous leader. You earn respect by being a good player, and Sami had it from the first.
>
> I think he is one of the top defenders in the Premiership, and the best in the Premiership are among the best in the world.

According to Owen, Sami is first and foremost a leader, with the ability to lead the team with his communication skills. 'Communication on the pitch is vital in football and everyone at Liverpool works to improve this area of the game. As for communication on the pitch, Sami is clearly one of the best in the squad.'

Owen emphasises his view that Sami has earned his respect by his own performances. After all, the players at Liverpool didn't know much about him in advance. 'I don't think many players here had ever heard about Sami when he was still playing for Willem. But already, after five or six matches with us, I think everyone understood how good he is.'

Owen marvels at the small transfer fee – £3 million – that the club paid for Sami. For a player of Sami's quality, £3 million is a bargain.

> If the transfer fee is, say, for example, £10 million, people think that we've gotten ourselves a brilliant player. It was hard to believe that we would get a world-class player with such a small fee, but already in his first year here, Sami was rated among the top in the world. Almost anyone can play well for two or three matches, but Sami was consistent throughout and played well in each match. His second season here proved to everyone that he was exactly as good as his first season had promised.
>
> I don't know if he was this good when he played in Holland, and I would almost like to say that he probably wasn't, because then he would have cost us a lot more than three million pounds.

As for England and Finland being in the same World Cup qualifying group, Owen thinks it was an enjoyable experience at Liverpool. He says:

> I think everyone here was happy with the draw. We English thought we could beat Finland and Sami thought they would give us strong opposition. Although Didi Hamann is a member of the German national team, he is rather quiet and he doesn't talk too much about who is going to beat whom. Sami spoke enough for both of them, and he always said how Finland had nothing to lose against us and how no one expected anything from them. Sami is very patriotic and playing for Finland means a great deal for him. We often talk about the situation between England and Finland.

> We were at the bottom of the group after two rounds of matches and I think Sami believed that Finland would make it at least to second place. Fortunately, we beat Finland at home even though we didn't play particularly well.

Owen scored the equaliser against Finland at Anfield. 'Sami wasn't marking too tight on me, because I managed to score against him – and with my left foot. It is pretty rare for me,' Owen says with a smile.

Nevertheless, the goal did not decrease Michael's respect for Sami. 'Sami is a magnificent professional and it is easy to play with him. Playing against him is tough, but playing with him is a pleasure.'

With the busy match schedule Liverpool FC had, the international matches were soon forgotten. The Reds were after three cup titles and were in third place in the Premiership, which would guarantee them admission to Champions League qualifying rounds – an achievement they let slip out of their hands in the last round of the previous season. In the league, Manchester United had taken an extensive lead despite losing 2–0 to Liverpool at Anfield at the end of March. Already in February, the bookmakers in England had started paying out to those who had bet on Manchester United to win the league title. Mainly because of the inconsistent performance of Liverpool early on in the season, Arsenal were too far ahead as well, which left the Reds battling Leeds for the third place again. In April, every point in the league table was valuable because Leeds' form had picked up after a miserable start.

The win Liverpool achieved over local rivals Everton was extremely important for the side mentally. The closing moments of the match were unforgettable and the win gave Liverpool a tremendous boost of confidence for their remaining battles. Eight minutes from time, Everton equalised the score at 2–2, and it already seemed like an inevitable draw when Gary McAllister scored a brilliant goal from a free kick. Everyone thought that Sami was going for a header from the free kick, but McAllister scored directly and Paul Gerrard, the Everton keeper, was left powerless. The win was also important because it made sure that Liverpool had everything in their own hands. By winning the last four matches of the season they would be in the top three for sure. 'This is the first time in ten years that Liverpool has beaten Everton in both matches of the season. This result will be of great importance to us in the final fixtures of the season,' Sami said back then.

In a match against Coventry at the end of April, Liverpool were struggling yet again, but Sami scored a welcome goal, his third of the season, six minutes from time. Gary McAllister scored Liverpool's second goal, which left the player with mixed emotions. Sami recalls:

> It was an important goal for us, but an extremely uncomfortable situation for Gary. The goals sealed the relegation of his former club and Gary refused to celebrate the goal. I understand his feelings completely and he really wasn't happy after the match, even though the win gave us much-needed points in the table.

In the FA Cup, Liverpool took yet another step towards the final in Cardiff by beating Wycombe, the surprise side from Division Two who made Liverpool earn their passage into the next round. It took a full day's work from the Reds before the lower-league side were beaten 2–1, with goals from Heskey and Fowler.

In the UEFA Cup, Liverpool were drawn to play Barcelona in the semi-final. Barcelona had been in the first round of the Champions League and were now playing for consolation success in the UEFA Cup. The strong Liverpool defence, led by Sami Hyypiä, were faced with world-class attacking football in the form of Rivaldo, Patrick Kluivert and other top-level players. Liverpool's tactics in the away fixture at the Nou Camp were heavily criticised. Liverpool played for a good result and nothing else, and they insisted on keeping a clean sheet no matter what. Almost every player in a red shirt had a defensive role and the Barcelona fans treated Liverpool to a whistling concert they had probably never heard before. The Catalonian newspapers denounced the match as 'The Death of Football' and called it one of the most boring football matches of all time. Despite all this, however, Liverpool got what they wanted: Barcelona didn't score, and the match ended in a goalless draw.

We simply wanted to get to the next round. I'm sure that it was more important for us than it was for Barcelona. I must admit that we didn't deserve any points for style or fancy attacking football, but the result gave us a tremendous starting point in our home leg. I was confident that we could beat Barcelona at home, just like any other team in the world.

Liverpool won the second leg at Anfield 1–0. The match was decided from the penalty spot, when Barcelona's Patrick Kluivert committed an unbelievable foul in his own penalty box. Trying to prevent Sami from heading the ball from a corner, Kluivert handled the ball even though Sami wasn't going for it. The Dutch striker jumped in the air alone and his hand touching the ball could be seen as far away as Anfield. Gary McAllister scored the penalty with confidence and gave Liverpool the lead they would never give up.

Sami was unquestionably the best player on the pitch. He interrupted wave after wave of Barcelona attacks and Rivaldo and Kluivert in particular had to give up in front of the unbeatable Finn. Sami recalls the match:

> I had played against Kluivert already in Holland, so I was familiar with his style. Rivaldo was a difficult opponent, but I was actually surprised at how easily he was out of his game.
>
> When McAllister scored from the spot, winning the game for us, it meant that we would have a chance at an historical cup-triple. In addition to that, we were playing with our backs against the wall in the Premiership, so the month of May offered us a lot to win, or a lot to lose – it was all up to us.

MAY SEALS THE SEASON OF SUCCESS

The world of football will always remember May 2001 as the month when Liverpool FC marched back to the top of English and European football. It will also be remembered as the month when Michael Owen demonstrated that he is clearly one of the best strikers in the world. Moreover, May 2001 will be remembered as the month of the brilliant Liverpool defence which failed only once – in the UEFA Cup final – and even then the rest of the team put on a superb performance to secure a victory in that competition. From a Finnish point of view, May 2001 will be remembered as one of the most significant moments in Finnish football history, as it was the month when Sami Hyypiä lifted a cup as the captain of Liverpool FC on two occasions.

At the beginning of May, Liverpool had only six more matches to play in the season, and yet each of those six matches were extremely important. Liverpool were still after two cup titles – the FA Cup and the UEFA Cup – and a place in the Champions League 2001–02 qualifying rounds at the very least. So, in a way, each Premiership match was also a sort of a cup match.

The work started with an away fixture against Bradford on 1 May. In that match, if not before, Liverpool wiped away the bitter memories from the previous season and the Reds travelled home with a 2–0 victory, with goals by Michael Owen and Gary McAllister. The next league match was four days later at Anfield against Newcastle. Owen scored a hat-trick and Liverpool won 3–0. Three days later, a win against Chelsea at home would have sealed third place in the league, but Liverpool were left to a disappointing 2–2 draw. Again, Michael Owen scored both Liverpool goals. So, Liverpool survived the first three matches well, and yet the stakes were enormously high in the three remaining matches. Before the decisive week of the season, Sami explained the importance of the approaching fixtures:

> The following week will decide whether our season has been perfect or a disappointment. If I were told that we'll win one match next week and I would get to choose which one, I would choose the league match against Charlton. Cup titles are a tremendous addition to league success, but a place in the Champions League next season would mean more to the club.

For the second time in a few months, on Friday, 11 May, Liverpool travlled to Cardiff and the Millennium Stadium. The next day, they would meet Arsenal in an FA Cup final which showed that Cardiff was a perfect location for such a major event. The pitch was brilliant and the atmosphere in the crowd was absolutely fabulous. More than anything, the final will be remembered as 'the Michael Owen final', as the Liverpool golden boy turned the match in the last ten minutes. Arsenal had taken the lead through a goal by Freddie Ljungberg, but Owen's goals from a goal-front hassle in the 82nd minute and after a beautiful breakaway in the 88th minute guaranteed the victory for Liverpool. After the match, Sami Hyypiä unselfishly refused to accept the trophy, although he had led the team from the tunnel. He wanted to give the honours to Jamie

Redknapp, the actual team captain who had to watch the final from the sidelines.

Sami emphasised afterwards: 'We tried to get Jamie to raise the trophy after the Worthington Cup final, but he refused. This time he agreed to do it and I am extremely happy about it. It doesn't matter to me who raises the cup, just as long as it's someone from our team.'

The match was yet another historical moment in Finnish football and Sami played a key part. He was the first Finnish football player to lead his team out of the tunnel and to the opening ceremony of the world's oldest football competition. As the first Finnish team captain in a Cup final team, he was also the first Finn to give the names of his teammates to the Duke of York, in the traditional presentation. The unfortunate thing about the historical moment in Finnish football was that the Finnish football fans did not see the Cup final live. When the final was played in Cardiff, the Finnish national broadcasting company, YLE, who owned the TV rights for the final, showed an ice-hockey match from the World Championships. While hundreds of millions of football fans all over the world witnessed the Finnish team captain's historical moment live, the fans in Voikkaa, Myllykoski and everywhere else in Finland had to wait for the conclusion of an ice-hockey match where Finland didn't even play before they could see their brightest star perform on the pitch in Cardiff. None of this bothered Sami, of course, nor his father Jouko Hyypiä, who was in the stands in Cardiff watching his son play. The moments after the victorious match brought a tear to the corner of the father's eyes. His son's journey from Voikkaa to the FA Cup final had been long and filled with sweet memories.

Sami handled the moment true to form. Not even the royal handshake made the Voikkaa titan get overly excited. 'The Duke did have a firm handshake. Being the team captain didn't make me nervous this time either,' Sami told the media after the final.

'It was only on the evening after the final when I was watching TV that I realised what the FA Cup means to people in Britain. Clearly, this is the highlight of my career so far.'

The British media acclaimed the FA Cup final 2001 as one of the best ever. The biggest star of the match was Michael Owen, but Sami Hyypiä was almost unanimously praised from all sides. Thierry Henry became yet another name on the list of star strikers whom the titanic Finn had disarmed completely during the spring.

Liverpool didn't have any time to celebrate winning the FA Cup, as they travelled to Dortmund, Germany, for the UEFA Cup final against the

Spanish side Alaves on the following Monday. After the victorious FA Cup final, Gérard Houllier said that the time for celebrations would come later.

'We had a talk with the players before the FA Cup final and we all agreed that we would keep our minds on Alaves and the UEFA Cup final regardless of the result in the FA Cup final. I know some teams have celebrated their titles right afterwards and then lost an important match three days later,' Houllier explained.

Sami confirms that the party after the FA Cup final was quiet. 'We had too much to play for in the final week of the season and there was no chance we would ruin everything by partying too much or in an inappropriate manner,' he says. 'We had a team dinner with our spouses, but we went to bed around ten. Of course, our spirits were high, and we knew that if we could succeed in the remaining fixtures as well, we would have the party of our lives.'

Before the UEFA Cup final, Sami received valuable feedback from his defensive partner, Stéphane Henchoz. The Swiss international was profuse in his praise for Sami in a pre-match press conference. 'He is the best defender I've played with. At Blackburn, I played with Colin Hendry, among others, and he is a really good centre-back, too, but Sami is clearly the best defensive partner I've ever had. I think he is absolutely one of the best defenders in Europe,' Henchoz enthused.

Neither Sami nor Henchoz were at their best in the UEFA Cup final against Alaves. Both teams were scoring from almost every other chance and the final will always be remembered as one of the most exciting and eventful in European football history. Sami was once again the captain of the Liverpool side as the team, who were clear favourites in the match, were after a rare treble. Liverpool were strong early on in the match and took the lead as early as the third minute through a goal scored by Markus Babbel. Steven Gerrard made the score 2–0 in the 15th minute before Ivan scored the first goal for Alaves, then Gary McAllister made the score 3–1 at half-time from the penalty spot. Despite Liverpool's strong lead at half-time, the Spaniards did not give in and two goals from Javi Moreno tied the match at 3–3. Robbie Fowler put Liverpool a goal ahead one more time, but a goal by Jordi Cruyff in the final minute took the match into extra-time at 4–4. It seemed like a sure case for a penalty shootout until a free kick from McAllister deflected into the Alaves goal off the head of Geli, an Alaves player. Liverpool won the Treble and Sami Hyypiä was once again invited to raise the trophy as the team captain. This time, Sami asked Robbie Fowler to join him and the two together raised the UEFA Cup trophy in the air.

'OK, so our defence didn't work out in our usual way in this match, but so what?' asked Sami after the match. 'We won an exceptionally entertaining match 5–4 and I bet no one left the stadium because the match was boring or because neither team defended particularly well.

'This is a tremendous achievement, but the most important match of the week is still ahead. We still don't have any time to celebrate,' the captain assured.

Finally, on Saturday, 19 May, Liverpool played their last league match of the season against Charlton in London. Before the final Premiership fixtures, Liverpool had played 62 official matches in the season. Sami had played 57 out of the 62, and the full 90 minutes in each one of them, and in order to achieve Liverpool's main goal of the season, he had to play 90 more minutes with success.

> I have to admit that the bitter results of the previous season's last rounds did come to my mind before the Charlton match. It was then that I decided that nothing like that could happen this season. We hadn't had any time to celebrate the Cup titles we had won in the past week, and we didn't want to spoil anything in this fine season. In the end I was confident that we would win on Saturday and take what's ours.

Sami was right. Liverpool beat Charlton, who had nothing to play for, 4–0, with two goals by Robbie Fowler and a goal apiece from Danny Murphy and Michael Owen – the hero of the spring. The victory guaranteed Liverpool third place in the Premiership and admission to the qualifying rounds of the Champions League.

Finally, it was time for the celebrations. The Reds' party began right after the match in London and continued back home in Liverpool. On Sunday, the fans got to see their heroes in a Liverpool FC parade, where the three Cup title trophies were on display with the manager Houllier and the team captains. Approximately half a million people crowded the city streets and cheered for the players, who had worked persistently throughout the long season. The players received their cheers wearing sunglasses, an accessory that seems to be worn by all successful teams in the world these days. Sami grins as he says:

> The atmosphere was absolutely unbelievable, and I must admit that the sunglasses were needed then. The sunshine was particularly bright on that day.

Seriously, the parade on Sunday will always remain in my mind as one of the most wonderful moments in my life. We had done an enormous amount of hard work, played one of the busiest schedules ever and experienced so much together. Each one of us deserved to be in that parade, and our fans deserved to be part of it all and experience the tremendous festive atmosphere. They supported us both home and away and, for example, in the FA Cup final they practically cheered us to victory during the last ten minutes of the match. I believe that 20 May was an unforgettable day for our fans. To us players, it was exactly that, too.

One of the highlights of the gala dinner later in the evening was Markus Babbel's choice of attire. He had promised a surprise for the players if they won the UEFA Cup, and the German defender kept his word. Sami says:

Markus was a little late for dinner, but I understand completely why. He wore a complete Bavarian outfit, with the lederhosen and everything. He wanted a reception worthy of his attire and waited for the right moment. Markus Babbel is a tremendous player and also a terrific person. I have much respect for him.

I think our success this season was based on our tremendous team spirit and humour. We had promised to commit ourselves to our goals, and we did exactly that. Sunday, 20 May, was a perfect day for reminiscing about the season with the lads in the team and with our good friends, and about half a million people in the city of Liverpool were celebrating with us. I've had many wonderful moments in my life, but that day was indisputably one of the best.

Even though Liverpool's season had come to an end, several of its players, including Sami Hyypiä and Jari Litmanen, could not start their summer holidays just yet. Early June was a time for important international fixtures, more particularly the World Cup qualifiers. In a match that practically destroyed Finland's chances for qualifying for the World Cup, once again Finland drew against Germany in front of a capacity crowd at the Helsinki Olympic Stadium. It seemed as if the Finns were going to get a historic win after Mikael Forssell scored two goals, but the colossal German striker Carsten Jancker ruined the party for the Finnish fans. First, he dived in a battle with Hannu Tihinen, earning a penalty kick for his side. Michael Ballack scored from the spot and only moments later Jancker himself blasted a brilliant volley from long range past Antti

Niemi, the Finland keeper, who really had no chance with either German goal.

SEVEN UNFORGETTABLE MATCHES
28 October 1995, the Helsinki Olympic Stadium
The Finnish Cup final, MyPa 1 FC Jazz 0
'It was my last match in Finland and I scored the winner. The feeling was great and it was a perfect way to bring my career at MyPa to a conclusion.'

11 October 1997, the Helsinki Olympic Stadium
World Cup qualifying match, Finland 1 Hungary 1
'The result was particularly disappointing and it really was a bitter pill to swallow because we didn't make it to the play-offs for the World Cup. The crowd support during the match was unprecedented in Finland.'

14 October 1998, Ali Sami Yen Stadium in Istanbul, Turkey
European Championships qualifying match, Turkey 1 Finland 3
'An incredible win in a true devil's pit. I have never experienced anything like that before or since.'

16 May 1999, Cambuur
Penultimate Dutch League match for Sami, Cambuur 0 Willem II 2
'This was the match where we secured our second place in the league and admission to the Champions League next season. I had already signed with Liverpool. I got the shivers after the match; the others were going to play in the Champions League next year and I was about to leave. I cried, even though we won.'

14 August 1999, Anfield Road
Sami's first match in front of his new home crowd,
Liverpool FC 0 Watford 1
'I will never forget the feeling when I appeared in front of the Anfield fans for the first time. Unfortunately, the defeat we suffered in the match blemishes the memory a little.'

12 May 2001, Millennium Stadium in Cardiff
FA Cup final, Arsenal 1 Liverpool 2
We came back from a one-goal defeat and won the title. I played a solid match. Getting back into the match after Arsenal had taken the lead felt

really difficult at first, but we had an amazing last ten minutes. After our second goal, I was sure we would win the Cup, no matter what.'

16 May 2001, Westfalen Stadium in Dortmund
UEFA Cup final Liverpool 5 Alaves 4
'In principle, you cannot be happy as a defender if your team concedes four goals in a match, but we did win the title and I'm sure the fans thought it was an entertaining match. Not many players get to win the UEFA Cup during their careers.'

A SHORT SUMMER HOLIDAY

A week before the World Cup qualifier, Sami had held his only press conference for the summer. The room at the Helsinki Radisson SAS Hotel was packed with reporters who were thirsty for a comment from the hottest name in Finnish football. The conference took the whole day, as Sami gave dozens of interviews and posed for photographers in the hotel courtyard. People everywhere would see pictures of a smiling Sami sitting in a luxurious convertible BMW. The car wasn't actually Sami's, but the brand was right regardless. Sami's own, more elegant car waited for him in his garage in England.

Sami started his short summer holiday immediately after the match against Germany. He wanted to spend the summer relaxing and enjoying his leisure time. He kept his public appearances to a minimum, but made sure he would also visit a few youth football camps as he had done in previous years. Sami had taken a coaching course during his national service and he has always enjoyed spending his time with young players. Sami looks back over that summer:

> Of course it's great if I can bring joy to someone's day by paying a visit to a football camp. I enjoy signing a few autographs and doing things with the kids. It also gives me a good idea of what the youth players can do these days. When I was watching some youth players bouncing the ball and playing in the summer of 2001, it really made me wonder if I could do things like that when I was their age. I think it's surprising how skilful the youth players are today.

Most of Sami's holiday was spent with friends, or fishing at his summer place. He usually goes fishing with his father, Jouko, and their most common ways of luring fish are angling and trolling.

Our catches vary a lot . . . sometimes you do feel rather forlorn out there, trolling on your own at a lake when it's pouring rain and you don't catch any fish. My character won't let me give in, though. My dad always tells stories about how he's caught pike and salmon there, but I've never seen a single one of them. He's probably caught them with a net.

Another place where people may have spotted Sami's tall figure in the summer was the AC/DC concert in Helsinki. According to Sami, the fresh-spirited rock'n'roll of the veteran Australian band is a perfect counterbalance to the peace of fishing beside a lakeside. Sami says his taste for music is very diverse, but his preference is for the harder side of rock.

As for all footballers, the summer holiday was short but sweet, and after about a month relaxing in Finland, Sami had to report back to duty with his club. This time, however, the return to Liverpool was different than in the previous year. Sami and Niina had decided that they would go on with their lives separately and follow their own paths for now. Niina stayed in Finland and Sami returned to his home in Liverpool. The couple, who had been in a relationship since the summer of 1994, now needed some space from one another.

'At the moment, we both have our own lives. Of course, nobody knows what will happen in the future, but as for now, my life is in Liverpool and Niina's life is in Finland. We have decided, together, that we'll see how things develop and consider our feelings for each other,' Sami explained in the autumn of 2001.

Sami didn't have much time to adapt to single life after many years in a relationship, as Liverpool's pre-season started out at full speed on 1 July. After arriving at Liverpool, Sami experienced another change before the new season as the Number 4 jersey was now available – Rigobert Song had transferred elsewhere. Sami got back his old jersey number and gave up the Number 12 jersey he had been wearing in his first two seasons with Liverpool. Otherwise, the Reds hadn't experienced many changes during the summer. Christian Ziege had transferred to Tottenham and the club had signed a young Norwegian, John Arne Riise, from AC Monaco in France.

Because Liverpool were now in the third qualifying round of the Champions League, the season started earlier than before, and there were tough matches even before the opening round in the Premiership fixtures. Liverpool spent part of their pre-season in Thailand and Singapore, where they were introduced to an unbelievably fanatical group of Liverpool supporters. Originally, part of the trip to Asia was meant to be spent in hard training, but the hot and humid climate allowed for no hard physical workouts. Otherwise, the experience was very rewarding for the team, as there were masses of Liverpool fans among the local people.

> It was quite unbelievable. The local people were really excited about us being there. If any of our players had gone out on their own, I'm sure the fans would have torn their clothes off. Even though the timing of the trip turned out to be poor in terms of our training schedule, meeting the local fans was a tremendous experience.

After a glorious spring, a relaxing summer and a pre-season of hard work, Sami and the rest of the squad were ready to kick off the 2001–02 season. Although winning the title in the English Premiership was the club's main goal for the season, expectations were also high for the Reds' Champions League campaign.

8

New Challenges

THE NEW SEASON AND THE REAL MATCHES STARTED IN AUGUST WITH the third qualifying round of the Champions League. Interestingly for the Finnish football fans, Liverpool were drawn to play FC Haka from Valkeakoski, the side that had won the Finnish Premier League three years in a row. The Finnish team had lost to the Israeli side Maccabi Haifa in the previous round, but because the Israeli team had played an unauthorised player in the second leg, Haka advanced to the next round against Liverpool. The Israeli team had protested and, because of the duration of the proceedings, Haka had to arrange the home leg against Liverpool at short notice. Nevertheless, the Finns' excitement about Liverpool was well proven, as 33,217 tickets were sold for the match at the Helsinki Olympic Stadium in only a few days. Considering that the population of Valkeakoski is approximately 20,000, it is clear that the match was attended by a respectable number of Finnish Liverpool fans as well. Even though the Finnish opponents were quite a mystery to the Reds' players, qualifying for the group stage of the Champions League was such a major incentive for the whole squad that everyone in the side approached the match with a professional attitude. Sami had reminded his curious teammates that FC Haka were not a team to be taken lightly if Liverpool wanted to advance to the next stage of the competition.

'I said it already before the draw that I would love to play against Haka. After all, it was a unique opportunity for Jari and I to play at the Helsinki Olympic Stadium wearing Liverpool red. Of course, it felt quite odd walking into the visitors' dressing-room as I am used to changing in the home team dressing-room with the full Finland squad,' Sami says of the match.

Liverpool manager Gérard Houllier demonstrated his brilliant understanding of the nature of the event and had both Sami Hyypiä and Jari Litmanen in the team. Both Finns received loud cheers and applause as they walked on to the pitch, but so did the other world-class players in the Reds' jerseys. Red was the colour both in the crowd and on the pitch and Haka offered no true challenge to Liverpool. The first half ended with a moderate score of 0–1, but the Reds picked up their form in the second half and blasted past the Finnish side. The final score was 0–5 to Liverpool. Michael Owen scored a hat-trick while Emile Heskey and Sami Hyypiä got a goal apiece to complete the scoring. As expected, the Finnish crowd went wild when Sami scored. Sami recalls:

> I scored after a corner, from a nice pass from Michael . . . In fact, it was almost a mishit by Michael and the ball fell straight to my feet. I scored with my left foot, 'the wooden leg', if you will, and keeping in mind that I mostly score from headers, scoring with my left foot is extremely rare. It did feel good, scoring at the Helsinki Olympic Stadium.
>
> We knew that Haka wouldn't last the whole match at our speed, so we kept the tempo high and started to rack up the goals towards the end. After the final whistle, with 0–5 on the scoreboard, I felt that we had at least one foot in the Champions League already. If nothing else, the away result certainly gave us a good basis to work from in the home leg.

Only four days after the match in Helsinki, Liverpool played Manchester United in the Charity Shield. The final score, 2–1 to Liverpool, meant that the club had won their fourth title of the year. The Liverpool goals were scored by Gary McAllister in the first minute and Michael Owen after 15 minutes, while Manchester United's sensational new signing, Ruud van Nistelrooy, scored their consolation goal. Sami explains:

> We took the match very seriously and prepared well for it. The match was even more important to the fans and also to us players because it was against Manchester United. It is always fun to play against them and, of course, it feels great beating them. They have been very successful in the past few years so, in a way, you always play Manchester United as an underdog. So when we won the match 2–1 and got to raise the shield, we got a boost of confidence for the coming season.
>
> The first half was a particularly solid performance from us and

we managed to score twice, but Manchester United came on for the second half with intensive and determined play. We were struggling at times during the second half but managed to keep them a goal behind, securing our victory and yet another title for the club's trophy room.

Sami had no time to celebrate the win, however, as Finland would play against Belgium in an international friendly in only a few days. As agreed, Sami played only the first half in a match where Finland treated its home fans to a crushing victory, beating the Belgians 4–1. The second leg of the Champions League qualifying round match was a mere formality and Liverpool defeated Haka 4–1. Finally, one of Liverpool's main goals for the year had been achieved and the Reds were in the most prestigious cup competition in Europe for the first time ever. Before the Champions League, however, Liverpool had to play another tough international match in the European Supercup. In the match between the Champions League winner and the UEFA Cup winner from the previous season, Liverpool met the German giants Bayern Munich in Monaco, France.

'It was the first time I had been to Monaco and the hotel was top class. It was on a mountainside, so that the city of Monaco was right down below, spread wide on the coast. The view was stunning when you drew the curtains open in the morning,' Sami says of his first trip to the principality.

The match, which was also televised live in Finland, showed a worldwide audience that, without question, Sami Hyypiä from the tiny town of Voikkaa in Finland had risen to the elite of the planet's football players. To the delight of the football fans in Finland and, of course, the Liverpool supporters throughout the world, Sami led Liverpool to a magnificent 3–2 victory as the team captain. The Liverpool goals were scored by John Arne Riise, their latest acquisition, Michael Owen and Emile Heskey, while Hasan Salihamidzic and Carsten Jancker scored for the Germans. Michael Owen, who scored the match-winner, was awarded Man of the Match in the exciting final, but the jury – formed of significant European football people, among them Michel Platini, Sven-Göran Eriksson and Rinus Michels – made a special note that making a choice between Michael Owen and Sami Hyypiä had been an extremely difficult task. At the award ceremony, the three Liverpool captains – Redknapp, Fowler and Hyypiä – raised the club's fifth trophy in an unforgettable football year.

Bayern Munich had won the Champions League title in the spring, and it felt terrific beating the reigning European club champions. We played well early on in the match, but then lost our edge a bit and had to pick up our level towards the end. The European Supercup title may not be the most highly valued title in football, but, nevertheless, it was the fifth trophy we won in 2001.

As for his own performance in the match, Sami said: 'Of course it is nice if some jury appreciates what I do on the pitch, but it is more important that I am satisfied with my performance myself. Other people's opinions don't mean as much to me.'

Winning the European Supercup took Liverpool to the higher echelons of the FIFA ranking of world football clubs. Simultaneously, Sami Hyypiä's rise to the ranks of the world's top players was sealed as well. For a long time, Liverpool had searched for a defensive leader and with the solid Finnish centre-back they had finally found one. His role as the team captain highlighted Sami's status as one of the key players. The achievements of this product of PaPe in small-town Voikkaa in Finland were recognised worldwide when CNN selected Sami for its All Star team in the summer of 2001. Big Sami was in the impressive company of world stars – and now he had to be counted as one of them.

CNN ALL STAR TEAM IN 2001
Goalkeeper: Oliver Kahn (Bayern Munich, Germany)
Defenders: Bixente Lizarazu (Bayern Munich, France), Alessandro Nesta (Lazio/Italy), Sami Hyypiä (Liverpool/Finland), Lilian Thuram (Parma/France)
Midfielders: Mehmet Scholl (Bayern Munich, Germany), Patrick Vieira (Arsenal/France), Luis Figo (Real Madrid/Portugal), Zinedine Zidane (Juventus/France)
Strikers: Romario (Vasco da Gama/Brazil), Andrei Shevtshenko (AS Milan/the Ukraine)

Sami had got used to his key role in the full Finland team as well. In the remaining World Cup qualifiers of the year – against Albania, Greece and Germany – the Finland defence, led by Sami Hyypiä, was rock solid. The Finland team were productive in attack as well, and the results in the three final qualifying matches were two wins and a draw, with a 7–1 goal difference. The performance of the national side was quite impressive: the demolition of Greece 5–1 at home displayed rare productivity from the

Finland internationals, and a 2–0 win in Albania and a goalless draw away in Germany were other great results. The draw against Germany also meant that England won the group and went straight to the World Cup, while the Germans were forced into the play-offs. For obvious reasons, the Finnish players in England suddenly had many new friends.

There was an interesting little incident during the away fixture against Albania. When the Finland international squad were preparing for their journey home, the personnel at Tirana airport in Albania refused to refuel the airplane unless the fuel was paid for in cash. Moreover, they would only accept US dollars. Needless to say, the pilots and crew didn't have the required amount of cash with them, so the money had to be collected from the players and other passengers on the plane. Somehow, the Finland team managed to collect enough US dollars to pay for the fuel, and the plane departed for Finland soon after. Sami smiles as he recalls the incident:

> I have to say that it was a very bizarre experience – an airline collecting money from the passengers to get enough fuel to fly back! I'm sure the money would have been easier to collect if they had asked for British pounds, but fortunately some of us had enough US dollars to get us out of Albania. I'm sure we would have felt a bit forlorn if we had had to stay there, especially because we were going to play Greece in Helsinki in only a few days. How strange would that have been – arriving at our home fixture late because the airline didn't have enough money to buy fuel for the return flight.

The development of the full Finland squad during the reign of the current coach, Antti Muurinen, has been astounding. Unlike in the past, the Finns now play the ball on the ground even against the toughest opponents, and they never resort to playing overly defensive tactics either. At the same time, the structure of the full international squad has changed: now almost all the players in the squad come from professional teams in Europe. 'We have found a very good system. We now have many good players, and Muurinen encourages everyone to use their skills. It has been fun playing with these lads,' Sami says of the success of the Finland team.

SUCCESS AND HARDSHIP
Liverpool started the new season in the Premiership with high

expectations, aiming to improve on their third place in the league from the previous campaign. However, the season kicked off to a lowly tune: the team did manage to come away with a narrow victory from the opening fixture against West Ham on 18 August, but it was followed by a bitter loss to Bolton. Sami remembers the Bolton game particularly well.

In the final minutes of the match, a Bolton striker took a shot from long range, and it went a bit easily past Sander Westerweld and into the net. Unfortunately, it turned out to be Sander's last match for us. It was not easy seeing a good friend being left out of the side and eventually transferring elsewhere.

Sander and I arrived at Liverpool at the same time, and we had a similar background. We had both played in Holland and we spoke Dutch with each other. He had also helped me settle in at Liverpool. It is always a shame seeing something like that happening, but then again you just have to be prepared for it. Everything can change overnight in the world of football.

In the next league match, it was Aston Villa's turn to beat Liverpool. Two defeats in a row was extremely rare for the team, but there is also something else about the match itself that lingers in Sami's mind. Liverpool had just signed two new keepers, the Poland international Jerzy Dudek from Feyenoord and Chris Kirkland, a young talent from Coventry.

I remember the Aston Villa game particularly well for two reasons: it was Jerzy Dudek's debut for the Reds, and my performance in that match was not the best possible.

I knew Jerzy from my years in Holland and he has proven his skills as a keeper. He is also a good friend and we have been friends from the first day he got here. We both speak Dutch and Jerzy's English wasn't that strong when he came here, so in that sense, I think I have helped him settle in here as well. And I think our cooperation on the pitch has been quite smooth, too. Sander's departure and Jerzy's arrival were simply matters that had to be coped with.

The next defeat Liverpool experienced in the league didn't come until December. In September, Liverpool beat Everton, Tottenham and Newcastle in the Premiership, and in September and October the Reds marched into the second round of the Champions League undefeated. As early as the first match, the Champions League showed that it was a competition worth its reputation.

> The atmosphere in the first Champions League match was fantastic. I don't think we had many players who had played there before – Jari, of course, and I think Markus, Didi and Jerzy as well.
>
> Our first match was against the Portuguese side Boavista, and we wanted a good start for our campaign in the Champions League. We were a bit asleep in the beginning and the opponents managed to score before we got our engines running. Fortunately, Michael equalised in the first half, and the final score was 1–1. Nevertheless, the atmosphere was great, just like in all Champions League matches. The home crowd supported us throughout and the atmosphere was different than in the Premier League matches.

In addition to Boavista, Liverpool faced the German side Borussia Dortmund and the Ukrainians Dynamo Kiev in the Champions League in September. The trip to Germany resulted in a goalless draw, but the home fixture against Dynamo Kiev ended in an historic victory – the first one for the club in their brief history in the competition. The only goal of the match was scored by Jari Litmanen, one of the all-time top scorers in Champions League. In October, the Reds played in three different competitions, the Worthington Cup, Champions League and the English Premier League. The holder's quest in the Worthington Cup, however, was cut short almost before it had started, when Grimsby knocked Liverpool out of the competition. The final score in the cup fixture at Anfield was 1–2 to the First Division side. In the Premiership, the first opponents Liverpool faced were Leeds, on 13 October. The final score in the match was 1–1, but there was an unfortunate, dramatic aspect to the otherwise normal league match.

During the first half, Gérard Houllier started to feel unwell and was taken to a hospital early on in the second half. Examinations showed that Houllier had a heart problem and the boss required immediate surgery. The surgery was performed successfully, but the manager had to take a long break from his work. Even though the team kept their form going under the leadership of Phil Thompson, Houllier's situation shocked the whole club. The pressure on the manager of a successful team in England is immense and the serious illness of their 54-year-old manager gave the players much to reflect upon. After all, there are other things in life besides football and winning titles. Sami talks about what happened:

At half-time, the boss was still there and we didn't know anything about what had happened during the second half. It was quite a shock for all of us when we found out what had happened after the match.

When you think about the last season as a whole, finishing second in the league even though the manager was out for six months is a really good achievement. Of course, Phil Thompson did an excellent job while Houllier was gone. He didn't change anything and everything worked in the same way as before, the manager just wasn't there. I think the club made a wise decision when they didn't bring in anyone else to replace Houllier. After all, Phil knew the way we'd worked before and the routines stayed the same, with the exceptions that we were missing one important figure in training and on match days. As we kept our form throughout the manager's recovery period, I think we demonstrated strong mental capacity and tremendous team spirit. We kept playing well and I think it may have been helpful to the manager's recovery as well.

In their next match, only three days after the dramatic Saturday, the Reds showed their tremendous work ethic and paid their respects to their manager by defeating Dynamo Kiev 2–1 in a Champions League away fixture. The Reds' next Premier League match was also victorious, as they beat Leicester at Filbert Street. The final score was 4–1 and Sami scored his first league goal of the season in the match.

'I think it was off a McAllister free kick – I headed the ball in from only a few yards from the goal line. When you don't score that often, you remember each goal rather clearly. The other three goals for us in the match were all scored by Robbie Fowler,' Sami recalls.

After the league match against Leicester, the Reds travelled to another away fixture in the Champions League. This time, they headed for Portugal to play Boavista. The Reds' undefeated streak remained untouched as they came away from the match with a valuable 1–1 draw in their pockets. Even though Sami Hyypiä was the only Finn who played in the match, he was not the only Finn on the pitch: the other linesman in the match was Markku Tiensuu from Finland. After only six minutes of play, Mr Tiensuu had the sole responsibility of representing Finland at the stadium: Sami hurt his hamstring early on and walked off only six minutes into the match. Sami says of his injury:

I prepared for the match in the same way as I prepare for every match, but I felt something odd in my hamstring after only a couple of minutes' playing. I've never really had muscle injuries like that, so I tried to keep playing, but I soon realised it wasn't going to work. I felt that it was not worth it to try to play and risk making the injury worse.

I felt terrible walking off the field. I felt that I had let down my teammates. It felt particularly bad because I haven't experienced injuries like that that often. I think I was in the dressing-room for the remainder of the first half, but then came out to watch the second half after all. Sometimes you just get injured and there isn't anything you can do about it.

Because of his injury, Sami had to sit out the Reds' next two matches, against Charlton and Borussia Dortmund, but the team performed strongly even without their defensive leader. Both matches ended with a final score of 2–0. The match against Dortmund brought to an end the first round of the Champions League and the win sealed Liverpool FC's progress to the second stage of the competition. The group in which Liverpool were drawn for the second stage was extremely challenging: they would face Barcelona, Galatasaray and AS Roma.

November 2001 could not have taken off with a more fiery battle, when Liverpool hosted their arch rivals, Manchester United, at Anfield. Sami recovered from his injury quickly and he was back in excellent form for the 4 November league match. Liverpool won the match 3–1 and Manchester United's much-dreaded Dutch striker, Ruud van Nistelrooy, had no chance against Sami. After the match, Sir Alex Ferguson regretted his tactical decisions. He told the media that he had made the tactics for the match based on the assumption that Sami wouldn't play. According to Sir Alex, had he known that Sami would play he would have structured Manchester United's attacking style differently. This is yet another example of the status Sami enjoys in England. Sir Alex Ferguson is known as an uncompromising manager whose teams play in the style of his choice regardless of conditions, the importance of the match, or the opinions of supporters or experts. Still, all it took to mess up the legendary manager's tactics was one Finnish centre-back. Sami remembers the win – the Red's fourth in a row over Manchester United:

It was great to be back in shape for the Manchester United game. It was still a bit unsure if my leg would be completely recovered to

SAMI HYYPIÄ

play the full 90 minutes and I heard that the people in Manchester
didn't really think that I would be able to play, but I knew it all
along. Well, everything went well for us in that match, and we
pulled out yet another win against Manchester United.

After the brilliant win over Manchester United, Liverpool played a
satisfactory draw against Blackburn at Ewood Park, but then the team
were brought back down to earth. In spring 2001, Liverpool had knocked
Barcelona out of the UEFA Cup and the opening fixture of the second stage
in the Champions League offered the Spanish side a chance to settle the
score. Barcelona outplayed the Reds at Anfield and travelled home with an
impressive 3–1 win, despite the fact that Michael Owen was the first
player to get his name on the scoresheet that day. Pondering, Sami shakes
his head and says:

> In a way, the match was pretty even until they scored their second
> goal, which made the score 2–1. We could have been 2–0 or 2–1 up,
> but instead they were in total control. They were passing the ball
> around and we were chasing them. They taught us a good lesson
> on how to play football. At their best, Barcelona can play really
> entertaining football. Particularly before their third goal, I think
> they passed the ball to each other at least 30 times without any of
> us touching it, and then they played a through ball to Overmars,
> who scored the final goal of the evening. I don't think any other
> team has ever had as many successful passes in a row before
> scoring a goal.

Despite the unusual defeat against Barcelona, Liverpool ended the month
of November on a positive note and beat Sunderland in a Premier League
fixture at home. November also sealed Sami's final breakthrough to
international stardom, as he was named among the top 50 football players
who were candidates for the European Footballer of the Year award. As
always, the list of nominated players was impressive, with names like
Beckham, Figo, Raúl, Rivaldo, Totti, Zidane . . . as well as Michael Owen
and Steven Gerrard, Sami's teammates. The majority of the players
nominated for the award, also known as the Golden Ball, are traditionally
strikers and midfielders, and the same was true this time around. In
addition to Sami, the only central defenders on the list were Rio Ferdinand
of Leeds, Marcel Desailly of Chelsea, Alessandro Nesta of Lazio and
Sammy Kuffour of Bayern Munich, who often plays as a full-back, too.

158

SAMI HYYPIÄ

The central defenders of many top football nations were not included on the list, and as for the players from other Nordic countries besides Finland, only Henrik Larsson of Glasgow Celtic and Ebbe Sand of Schalke 04 made it to the list.

The European Footballer of the Year has been selected since 1956 on the basis of a poll arranged by the magazine *France Football*. Three players, Johan Cruyff, Michel Platini and Marco van Basten have won the Golden Ball three times. The only other Finnish player who has been nominated for the award is Jari Litmanen, who finished third in the poll in 1995. Today, the winner of the Golden Ball doesn't necessarily have to be of European nationality, but all players who play in the various European leagues are eligible. Therefore, the award is really for the best player in the world, and Sami Hyypiä is one of the best in the world. As it was Sami's teammate, Michael Owen, who won the honours for the Golden Ball that year, it had also become clear that Liverpool were again recognised as one of the planet's top clubs.

GÉRARD HOULLIER: 'THE BEST IS YET TO COME'
In 1998, Liverpool FC manager Gérard Houllier initiated a five-year plan to build a new, title-winning squad and, although it was not originally planned so, Sami Hyypiä has become an essential part in the Reds' rebuilding process and their climb back to the top. Looking back a few years on an August evening at the Melwood training centre, Houllier still remembers the fortunate signing of Sami in 1999:

> It was a fairy tale. When I came to the club in the summer of 1998, we were looking for a centre-back. In November, I was still looking for a centre-back and I travelled everywhere around Europe. One day, Peter Robinson told me of somebody he knew who was working for TV and filming a lot of games had said that the best centre-back he had seen was playing for a small club in Holland. He said the player was Finnish, but he couldn't remember his name.
>
> At the time – I must be very honest – I did not pay a lot of attention to that. But after travelling three months and still not finding the type of player I wanted, I asked Peter if he could talk to this TV guy and ask a bit more about that player. Peter came back to me and said he was in Willem II. At first, someone went there, saw him play and liked what he saw. So I travelled there too,

twice, actually, before finally going there with Peter. At that time, Sami was not playing as a defender, but in front of the defence. Peter may have thought that I would not sign him because of that, but in fact I signed him exactly because of that: if they played him in front of the defence, it means he could pass the ball properly. And I think that everything starts from the back.

The last time Houllier saw Sami play for Willem II he had also arranged a meeting with the prospective player before flying back to Liverpool. The first meeting between the two left Houllier confident that the personality of the tall Finn matched his needs. With a smile the Reds' boss says:

On that occasion, I had a chat with him in a small bar/restaurant and I liked the boy immediately. I liked the look in his eyes and the determination showing through it. And don't forget that he could have played Champions League football in Willem, but he made a choice of a career. I told him we were not in Europe, but we were buying him because I tthought he could do the job to get Liverpool back to the top. I told him more or less about what I wanted from him and so on. That's how it all started.

I knew he would do the job, because technically he was good, both with his right and left foot. Moreover, despite his size he is quicker than you think sometimes and he reads the game well. And, of course, he is commanding in the air. Sometimes there are big players who are not good in the air because they don't use their size in the right way, but Sami is not that way – he uses his size to his advantage. Defensively, it is not only that he is commanding in the air which makes him such a good defender. He is a good defender and he likes to defend. I like centre-backs who like to defend.

So, soon after the meeting with Houllier in Tilburg, Sami travelled to Liverpool and signed a contract with Liverpool FC. The rest is history: his entrance to the English Premiership was strikingly successful, but an even bigger surprise in Sami's first season in the Premiership was the fact that he was named the captain of the squad after being in the club for only a couple of months. For Houllier, however, Sami was a natural choice for team captain.

We named him captain very quickly because we thought he could do the job. As soon as he came here, in the first one or two trainings, I knew he was the player I had been looking for. Already in the training camp, some of the players also came to me and said, 'Ooh, what a defender he is.' He is a commanding figure. He has won the players' respect both by the quality of his play and by the quality of his person.

He is unanimously appreciated by his teammates, the fans, the staff – all the people in the club. He is a good lad, and players like to go out with him. As a captain, he has helped new players to settle in and integrate into the team. He does a good job with that and he knows I believe in him.

According to Houllier, Sami is very professional and reliable and on the pitch he sets an example for the others in the way a good captain should. 'You can always rely on him. Every time we've had a match and he has been about not to play because of a flu or something, he has decided to play and he has been very good. He is very brave, he's got courage and he does it for the team. He is a team player. He can sacrifice himself for the team,' Houllier emphasises.

The 2002–03 campaign is the first season that Sami Hyypiä has started as the official captain of Liverpool FC and Gérard Houllier has great expectations for his trusted man. 'We have a bit of a challenge ahead, because I want Sami to be the first foreign captain at Liverpool to lift the supreme title.'

Houllier does not hesitate to list the qualities that make Sami such a good football player:

He is a very focused and intense player. Some players are shallow and superficial, but Sami is never like that. He is a very deep and intense person, he has a good mentality and a good attitude. I am a great believer in that when the attitude is right, everything else follows.

I personally think he has the qualities of a top-class player. He came from a small club and he has proved that he can rank among the best. This is due to his work, commitment and attitude. He doesn't like to lose. In every training session he seems to put in 100 per cent and play to the full. And this is how you improve: you play to the full every time and push the boundaries to the edge. His success is also due to his personality. He is a winner, he gets really upset when he loses. He is a team player, but a winner.

> I think the best is yet to come. He could be really outstanding,
> and it seems that he steps up his game every year.

When asked about Sami's possible weaknesses, Houllier is not as candid as when praising his captain. 'I am not going to talk about his weaknesses because I don't want our opponents to know about them . . . I don't think he has a lot of them, anyway, but instead, there are definitely some areas of the game where he is very good and one of the best in Europe.'

After a while, the manager does say something slightly critical of Sami's character. 'Sometimes Sami can be gloomy or negative in his thoughts. It's not a negative approach, but a negative spell. But we are all like that. He may have his moments of doubt about himself, which is also good, I think,' Houllier concludes.

Nevertheless, there have been no signs of these momentary doubts or any other insecurities in Sami's game during the years he has been at Liverpool FC. Since Sami joined the club, the Reds' defence has been rock solid. Even in 1999–2000, when Sami and Stéphane Henchoz played their first season together, the Reds' defensive record was the best in the Premiership. In 2000–01, Sami's second season at the club, the Reds' defensive record was second best in the league, and last season, Liverpool FC had the best defensive record in the Premiership again, with the towering Finnish–Swiss duo pairing up in the middle on most occasions. For Houllier as a manager, forming this kind of solid pairing on the pitch is a very important element in his team, and it can be seen in both Sami's and Henchoz's playing time.

> It's a partnership. Stéphane is more like a half-libero, although I
> don't play with a libero. It's a partnership that works, and that's the
> main thing for me. They have a very good mutual understanding,
> and that is why I don't want to change my defence. When we rotate
> players, it is these two players I don't want to rotate. Particularly in
> the defence, it is important to know where your teammates are.

Although Sami Hyypiä has received many personal awards during the last couple of years, Gérard Houllier, surprisingly, does not agree with the notion that Sami has reached the top. Houllier says:

> I don't think he is at the top. First, because for a defender the top
> is around age 31 or 32 if he keeps himself fit. There are some areas
> in which Sami can still improve.

Second, the top also means that you win things at the very top level, which Sami hasn't done so far. And I don't think he is at the top because he is still hungry. When you are at the top, the only thing that can happen is either to stay there or go down. Sami is on his way to the top – which is totally different to me. He is climbing up to the top and I personally think that in two or three years' time we'll have an even better Sami with us.

As for the rebuilding process Houllier started back in 1998, he feels that the current team is close to where he wants it to be. Particularly, the backbone of the team – the vertical column in the middle – is in good form. The Reds have good goalkeepers and centre-backs, and in addition to Sami and Stéphane Henchoz, Jamie Carragher, Djimi Traore and Markus Babbel can also play in the centre if needed. The Liverpool FC squad also has good players in front of the defence, and the age composition of the team will be even better in the future. Houllier summarises:

We have a good base. Steven Gerrard, Michael Owen, John Arne Riise, El-Hadji Diouf and Djimi Traore are all only 22 years old. Almost half of the team is about 22, and they are all going to get better with time. That's also why I think that the experience of Sami and Stéphane is important in the back. And they are not that old either – they are a good age for their position.

Even though things are looking really good for the club right now, Houllier does not want to say that Liverpool is now back at the top for good. 'In sports, you cannot programme success, you can only prepare for it,' the boss explains. 'And this is what we are doing. We may be ahead of our schedule because we have already won some trophies and finished in the top positions of the league, but we are always preparing and the team seems to have improved year in, year out.'

PREMIERSHIP TITLE ESCAPES FROM THE REDS' HANDS

Towards the end of the year, it seemed that Liverpool were going to keep their tremendous form through December as well. They were in the top position in the English Premier League and they started the month's fixtures with an away win against Derby, a goalless draw against AS Roma in Rome and a home win against Middlesbrough. After those three matches, however, the Reds' form dropped significantly. The draw against Fulham at home wasn't that bad a result, but in the next two matches, Liverpool were humbled by two consecutive losses: Chelsea humiliated Liverpool with a 4–0 win at Stamford Bridge, and a few days later, Arsenal visited Anfield and took the three points with a comfortable 2–1 win. Although the Reds did beat Aston Villa with away goals from Litmanen and Smicer right after the two losses, the result from the last match of the year – a draw against West Ham – continued the side's poor run of performances in December. One thing in common for those five matches was the absence of Dietmar Hamann. The German midfielder was suspended due to his red card against Sunderland and Liverpool were not the same team without him. According to Sami, Hamann's absence might have been one significant reason why the Reds lost their edge at the turn of the year. Sami reflects on the value of his teammate:

> Didi Hamann is extremely important to our team's defence. He does a lot of hard work in front of the defenders, and in a way, he is our protector. He interrupts the opponent's passes really well and tackles effectively, too. Furthermore, he reads the game really well, and as he knows where to position himself, he is very effective in interfering with the opponent's passes and attacking. He makes our job a lot easier and I really like playing with him. We have found an understanding and we know each other's game well. He brings a vital balance to our game.

In January, Liverpool continued to perform poorly in the Premiership: first they drew with Bolton at home and then they were beaten by Southampton. A draw against Arsenal at Highbury gave a little hope for the better, but the next fixture brought along yet another disappointing result as the Reds drew with Southampton, this time at Anfield. In the FA Cup, Liverpool advanced to the second round by beating Birmingham, their opponents in the Worthington Cup final the year before, with a comfortable scoreline of 3–0. However, the team were knocked out of the Cup in the next round when Arsenal avenged their loss in the previous FA Cup final. As Liverpool left Highbury after a 1–0 defeat, their hopes of repeating the titles from the last year had been ruined in both domestic cup competitions well before the date of the final. This, of course, allowed the team to focus completely on the English Premier League and the Champions League, although it seemed that league championship had already slipped out of their hands.

SAMI HYYPIÄ

Our performances in the Premiership were solid throughout the autumn, but the holiday season brought along a weak phase for us. I remember that the Chelsea game was particularly bad, and I think it was the substandard phase in December and January that cost us the league title. Even though a lot of people said that we lost our chance to the title in the Tottenham game, the match before the last two rounds in the league last May, I think we lost our grasp of the title a lot earlier. We didn't get enough points from our fixtures around Christmas and in January, and it was a tough time for us, which really tested our mental strength.

In December, the Liverpool squad experienced some changes. After long speculation, the club's long-time goalscorer and vice-captain Robbie Fowler transferred to Leeds. The England international was unsatisfied with the amount of playing time he was getting in the first-team rotation system and decided to seek his fortune elsewhere. Around the same time, the Reds loaned the controversial French striker Nicolas Anelka from Paris Saint German and signed the Czech striking talent Milan Baros, whose transfer had been put off due to a work-permit application process. Sami looks back at the events of December 2001:

In a way, Robbie's transfer was a surprise for everyone, and it was a particularly hard blow for the fans. After all, he had been the fans' favourite for a long time. However, the manager has to think about the big picture, and at that point both the boss and club management thought it best to let Robbie go.

I would think that it was a kind of a fresh start for Robbie himself as well. He had been injured on a few occasions and he hadn't regained the same form as before. At Leeds, everything was new to him and he got more playing time there, too, so I think transferring to Leeds was a smart career move for Robbie. Of course, it is always a shame losing a consistent goalscorer like Robbie, but you never know what can happen in the world of football. At that time, it was simply a change in the squad that we had to live with.

In Finland, December 2001 brought significant recognition for Sami. As expected, he was again selected the Finnish FA Player of the Year, but an even more spectacular achievement was his selection as the Athlete of the Year in Finland. Sami was the winner in both the people's ballot and the

165

media ballot, even though Finnish people have always rated individual athletes higher than team players.

> In terms of individual honours, getting selected the Finnish FA Player of the Year and Athlete of the Year in Finland is the most you can achieve in Finland. It feels great that people value team-sport athletes so highly. It is not often that a team-sport athlete is selected Athlete of the Year in Finland – I think Jari Litmanen was the only one before me.
>
> The selection was a tremendous honour, but I would like to remind everyone that football is a team sport and that no individual can succeed without a strong team. That is why I want to extend my thanks for the award to my teammates, coaches and club management, too.

THE NEW RISE

The poor form of the Reds in mid-winter was quickly put behind them. The schedule in January was extremely tight with eight matches and the team ended the busy month with two 1–0 victories. First, Liverpool beat Manchester United at Old Trafford and then it was Leicester's turn to visit Anfield and leave with no points. The win against Manchester United was the fifth time the Reds had beaten the giants of English football in as many matches. The winner was scored by Danny Murphy.

> I think it could be fair to say that Manchester United dominated most of the match, but we weren't completely disarmed either. It is difficult to go to Old Trafford and dominate the match, and I think any good result starts with solid defending.
>
> Danny scored a neat goal, and the win brought our run of poor performances to an end. Beating Manchester United at Old Trafford does give you an extra boost of faith and confidence, and of course beating Manchester United is always nice for our fans. I think the matches against Manchester United are perhaps the most important matches in the season for the fans.

Liverpool FC's excellent form continued in February. The first side they faced in the short month were Leeds, whom the Reds beat with an impressive 4–0 win at Elland Road. It was Rio Ferdinand who got his name on the scoresheet first, but to his misfortune, he did it in his own end and into his own net. In the second half, Emile Heskey scored twice in a row before Michael Owen sealed the result in the closing minutes of the match. In addition to the three points in the league table, the match had an extra charge:

> It was an interesting match because it was the first time we played against Robbie Fowler. Playing against Robbie gave us an additional boost of motivation because, usually, when someone transfers from a club to another, he scores in the next meeting between his former and current clubs. We talked about it before the match and assured each other that we wouldn't let Robbie score, and he didn't.
>
> Leeds did have their chances in the match, and they were in fact a bit unlucky. The final score doesn't tell the whole truth about the match, but nevertheless, we were able to keep Leeds and Robbie scoreless.

Liverpool's next opponents were Ipswich and the fireworks show that what began at Elland Road continued at Portman Road: the final score in the match was 6–0 to Liverpool. Abel Xavier, the Portuguese defender whom Liverpool had acquired at the end of January, made his debut for the Reds in that match and scored the first goal of the day. Sami also scored at Portman Road, his second goal of the season. Sami notes:

> It was yet another header from a corner. I think that, as a whole, the match was the best we played during that season. We passed the ball around well and really enjoyed playing. Of course, Ipswich were obviously not in their best form that night, but on the other hand, you have to play well if you want to beat a team 6–0 away.
>
> We also had some old scores to settle with them, because Ipswich hadn't agreed to postpone our match in the previous season when we had an extremely tight schedule because of our European duties. I think we all remembered it and got fired up because of it. The result speaks for itself.

At the end of the month, the Reds played Galatasaray twice in a week in the Champions League and faced local rivals Everton at Anfield in between. All three matches ended as draws. In March, Liverpool played seven matches with an impressive record: six wins and a draw. In the Premiership, Liverpool marched to victories against Fulham, Newcastle,

Middlesbrough, Chelsea and Charlton. In particular, beating Chelsea soothed some of the wounds received in the December fixture between the two clubs. In the Champions League, Liverpool played with their backs against the wall. Until March, the Reds had only got three points from three draws in the second group stage. The group was extremely even, and Liverpool needed more points in order to go through to the next round. The first match the Reds played in the Champions League in March was away against Barcelona, and the last Champions League match of the month was at home against AS Roma. At the Nou Camp, Liverpool showed that they had learned their lesson from the last match against the Catalonian giants and didn't allow them to dominate the match like they had done in the previous encounter between the two teams at Anfield. As a result, Liverpool travelled home with a valuable away draw in their pockets, and the last match against AS Roma had become an even more thrilling prospect. With a 2–0 win, Liverpool would qualify regardless of the scoreline in the other match. Sami clearly remembers the incidents in March:

> As for qualifying to the next round, we had everything in our own hands in the AS Roma game. The group was wide open until the last fixtures and any two teams could have qualified on the basis of the last matches. We got an excellent start for the match when Jari scored from the spot. Then, when Emile made it 2–0 in the second half, we knew we would qualify for sure.
>
> I think that the atmosphere in that particular match was the best we had last season. The crowd really lived the match with us, and I'm sure the early goal helped them get inspired. Everyone believed that we would advance. Perhaps it was not the most typical Liverpool style of play we played that day, and I'm sure many fans will remember the match for a long time. I know I will. The atmosphere was great and the spirits were high before the match, and when we sealed our victory and advanced to the next round, the feeling was just unbelievable.

The next fixtures in the Champions League were in April and Liverpool were drawn to play Bayer Leverkusen in the quarter-finals. Until the third round, the German side had played convincing football, but the boys at Liverpool were ready to fight hard to qualify for the semi-finals. After an exciting and even first leg at Anfield, Liverpool were to travel to the away leg with a 1–0 lead. Sami remembers the match particularly well and laughs when he talks about his first goal in the Champions League:

> I scored the winner – again with my left foot. I was so close to the goal that no one would have shot the ball over the bar from that range – although the ball did rise towards the roof of the goal. All I had to do was hit the ball cleanly, I was standing in a good place and I even had time to react, too. So it was completely intentional – I kicked the ball into the net, it didn't just deflect off my foot.

A week from the home leg, Liverpool travelled to Leverkusen. The expectations were high and the match was an unforgettable one but, unfortunately, for the wrong reasons. With the away-goal rule used in all European cup competitions, the team were already in a position to qualify for a place in the semi-final as Jari Litmanen, who had come on as a sub, had made the scoreline 3–2 in the 78th minute. However, a dark cloud soon overshadowed the Liverpool sky as Lucio, Leverkusen's Brazilian defender, made it 4–2 only six minutes from time.

> The win at home gave us a good result to work from in the away leg. I'm sure the spectators thought it was a very interesting and entertaining match as the team looking to qualify for the next round changed back and forth. After Jari scored the 3–2 goal I was sure that we would play in the semi-final. It was such a huge disappointment then when Lucio scored the final goal. The thought that the Leverkusen player who scored the winner [Lucio] would be a world champion in a few more months did not occur to me then.
>
> I do have to admit that Leverkusen were good. We didn't lose to a weak team: they beat Manchester United in the semi-final and could have won the whole competition.

The Reds' Premiership campaign continued victoriously in April. First, Liverpool beat Sunderland away and then Derby visited Anfield and went home defeated. With only three more matches to play, Liverpool still had a slim chance of winning the title, but the dream was finally ruined when Tottenham beat Liverpool at White Hart Lane at the end of April. Despite this, however, finishing second in the league and qualifying automatically for the Champions League were within the Reds' reach in May, and Liverpool were looking for good results from the last two matches. The first of the two remaining fixtures was against Blackburn at Anfield. It turned out to be good entertainment – the teams were taking turns to score until Liverpool finally secured their win with a late goal from Emile Heskey. The final score was 4–3 to Liverpool. Sami scored the third goal of the match and it was his third goal in the Premiership that season. At the same time, Arsenal sealed the championship title by beating Manchester United. This meant that Liverpool would finish second in the league if they beat Ipswich in the last match of the season. As we know now, Liverpool left nothing to chance and beat Ipswich at Anfield with a comfortable 5–0 margin. Even though Liverpool were not able to repeat the flood of trophies from the previous season, they had once again improved their league standing by one position and earned more points than ever before. Second place in the league was the club's best achievement in the top division for ten years. Still, the magnificent sprint the Reds took in the closing fixtures of the season was still not enough to catch Arsenal. Sami is complimentary about the Gunners:

> Arsenal had earned enough points already a few rounds before the end, and at the end of the day, if you don't lose a single away match in the whole season, I think it is quite an achievement in this league because the margins between the clubs are so narrow. I think they deserved to win the title, they left no room for excuses. At least in my eyes, Arsenal were the best team in the league last season.
>
> In a way, Arsenal helped us finish second by beating Manchester United. It was in our hands in the end – by beating Ipswich we would finish second and get automatic admission to the first group stage of the Champions League. And it was quite a good performance from us, after all. We played Ipswich twice during the season, with a goal difference of 11–0.

The 2001–02 season also brought along a change for both Sami and the club. Jamie Redknapp, the team captain who had played for Liverpool since 1991 but had sat out most of the past few years due to injuries, had transferred to Tottenham in mid-April, leaving the club without an official team captain. Redknapp and Robbie Fowler had been the club's first choices for team captain, but now they had both left Anfield. It was hardly a surprise when Sami Hyypiä was named as the official captain of Liverpool FC. The long history of the traditional club does not record many occasions when this honour has been bestowed on a foreign player, but Sami thinks that being a foreigner is not necessarily a problem for the team captain. On the contrary, because of his background, being the team captain might be easier for Sami than for British players. The Liverpool captain considers his role:

> As I am a foreigner myself and thus know how difficult it is arriving in a new country, culture and club, I always try to do my best to help the new lads settle in and teach them how things work here. When you make an effort to make their adjustment as smooth as possible, working together as a team becomes easier for all of us.

FACING THE NEW SEASON WITH A NEW LOOK

After the Premiership season had ended, Sami had a summer holiday that was longer than in the previous years. The Finland international squad did play one more friendly against Latvia at home in May, but there were no qualifying matches because of the World Cup in Japan and South Korea. The match against Latvia ended in a narrow 2–1 victory for Finland, after a hard-fought battle at the Helsinki Olympic Stadium. After the match, Sami was finally able to relax and recharge his batteries for Liverpool's upcoming season. In the 2001–02 campaign he had once again played the most matches for the Reds, a total of 57 appearances. Sami played in 37 league matches, the same number as Stéphane Henchoz, his partner in the Reds' central defence. Only John Arne Riise, who had a tremendous first season with Liverpool, played in all 38 league matches.

Although Sami did have a summer holiday, it didn't mean that he spent his summer without football. In June, Sami worked at the youth camp bearing his name – and the World Cup matches on TV also formed a regular part of Sami's daily programme. It was a summer of mixed emotions:

> I was disappointed that Finland were not involved in the World Cup finals in Japan and Korea, but on the other hand I was able to enjoy quite a long holiday. I had a good rest and really looked forward to putting in some hard work in preparation for the new season.
>
> I watched many World Cup games and took a particular interest in those matches involving my Anfield teammates. I wondered what it would be like to play in the World Cup final some day. It was nice to see Didi Hamann achieve that dream, stepping out to

play against the Brazilians. As I watched the game it struck me that I had been on holiday for five weeks at that point. Meanwhile, Didi had been constantly involved in a string of tiring but highly eventful international matches. It was a strange feeling and I would have swapped all my holidays for a chance to be involved in the game's biggest football final.

During the summer, Sami Hyypiä became an even more familiar face to the Finnish people when his picture was used in a couple of advertising campaigns. The billboards with Sami's picture on them caught everyone's attention in the early summer and Sami also appeared in a few TV commercials. Combined with his success on the football pitch, his increased profile reinforced Sami's position as an A-list Finnish celebrity.

It was a new experience and I just had to get used to it. It did feel a little odd, seeing your own face around every other corner when I was driving in Helsinki. Of course, I wouldn't have to do any of those things if I didn't want to, but I knew what I was doing, so it didn't cause me any stress at all.

There were times when I wondered if I had been a fool to get involved with this kind of stuff. It is not necessarily characteristic of me to be so visible all the time. But I'm sure people had gotten used to seeing me anyway.

In July, Sami reported back with Liverpool FC. The squad had gone through a few changes in the summer. The only first-team players who had left the squad were Nicolas Anelka, who had played for the Reds on a loan contract in the spring, the veteran Gary McAllister and Nick Barmby, who never really managed to establish himself in the Liverpool first team. As expected, Liverpool had acquired some new players to replace those who left the squad. Of the new acquisitions, Senegalese players El-Hadji Diouf and Salif Diao, who had made a name for themselves in the World Cup, aroused the most interest, and the expectations for the Frenchman Bruno Cheyrou were also high. There were no new acquisitions to the Liverpool defence, but Djimi Traore returned to the squad after spending the previous season on loan. Another player to return to the squad was Markus Babbel, who had missed the whole of the previous season due to a serious viral infection. Babbel's return was a pleasant piece of news for both the club and the fans. Sami also welcomed Babbel's return with great pleasure and relief, for he had been really worried about the illness of his good friend. At its worst, Babbel's condition had been extremely severe and the German defender was not even able to walk at times. Throughout the season, the Liverpool players all worried about their teammate, who was being treated in Germany. Sami says:

> I called Markus regularly during his illness, but unfortunately I had no time to visit him in Germany. If I had had a little more free time at any point, I would definitely have paid him a visit. Nevertheless, as we kept in touch over the phone, it was great to hear that he was getting better and better.
>
> It is great to have a good friend back in the squad and doing what he wants to do. Hearing about Markus's illness and seeing how his weight dropped and muscles atrophied was quite a shock for us. Later I saw him in a wheelchair on TV, and it really made me think how fortunate you are when you remain healthy. I wouldn't want anyone to experience what Markus had to go through. Fortunately, he was strong and fought his way back. Now he's back in form.

Over the previous three seasons, the Liverpool defence had been the toughest in the league: the Reds had twice conceded the least goals in the Premiership and in one season there was only one team with less goals against them in the Premiership. With the addition of Babbel and Traore to the toughest defence in the Premiership, Liverpool's solid defence looked guaranteed for years to come, despite losing Stephen Wright to Sunderland right before the season. Sami Hyypiä and Stéphane Henchoz still formed the backbone of the Reds' defence. Sami's appreciation for his partner at the back is extremely high and he hopes that the public will also recognise the Swiss defender's importance to the team:

> Stéphane is a tremendous player and we found a common tune immediately in my first season here. We never really spoke about the things we do on the pitch either. Of course, if we make mistakes at the back we talk them through and think about the ways in which to improve our game. I think we have worked well together from the start. We are very much alike as players and the way we think about the game is very similar. Altogether, I have really enjoyed playing with him and at times it has annoyed me a little that Stéphane hasn't gotten the appreciation he deserves.

173

He is rather quiet off the field, and perhaps on the field, too, but he does his job in style. I don't think there is any need for him to change at all, we are all different and the ways in which we work are also different. Just as long as you do your share on the pitch, everyone is happy.

While praising the work of his fellow defenders, Sami also wants to underline that the success of the Liverpool defence is a result from the seamless cooperation of the whole team. Football is a team sport. Sami praises his teammates:

In principle, the defensive records we have accomplished make us defenders look good, but I want to stress the fact that defending is not only done by the defenders and the goalkeeper. The whole team deserves credit for doing the work that a successful defence requires and we have done the work well as a team. It has been easy to play in the back when the forwards and midfielders have taken care of their defensive duties conscientiously.

The week before the start of the Premiership, Liverpool played at the Millennium Stadium in the Community Shield against Arsenal, a game which saw Markus Babbel return to the squad and Arsenal win by a solitary goal. Then it was on to the opening game of the Premiership, away at Aston Villa, the game that Sky had chosen to open their season. Liverpool won 1–0 through a John Arne Riise goal. Sami said:

It was pleasing to get the season off to a positive start. We created a lot of chances and could have won by two or three goals. Their keeper, Peter Enckelman, played very well. Villa has him to thank that the score wasn't more than 1–0.

Liverpool started the season well, going unbeaten in their first 12 Premiership fixtures. One of those games was away to Bolton, a game that Liverpool won 3–2 and which saw Milan Baros, a young Czech international, score two of the goals. Sami knows about the pressures young players have to cope with to succeed.

It's always satisfying when a player comes into the team and makes an immediate impact. Milan had worked very hard in pre-season and had looked sharp. He is a perfect example of what can be

SAMI HYYPIÄ

achieved through determination and desire. He is also an example
of the calibre of player we have in our squad. We have people on
the bench – some don't even make it there – who are of real quality,
who we can call on any time, and who will do a good job. Of
course, it can sometimes be difficult if you haven't played for a
while and you are suddenly thrust into the starting line-up. You
only have 90 minutes to show you are up for it. That's a big test,
but Milan passed his so well. Having said that, it's important to
remember that Milan is still young and that he can't be expected to
score two goals every time he plays.

Liverpool's Champions League campaign meanwhile had not got off to the
best of starts with a defeat in Valencia followed by a 1–1 draw at home to
the Swiss team FC Basel. The result against FC Basel was the most
disappointing, with Liverpool dominating the game and having 15
attempts on goal in each half whilst the Swiss team had two attempts in
the whole game! The next two games were against Spartak Moscow, where
Liverpool won both games convincingly, the home win bringing Sami's
first goal of the season for Liverpool, whilst the away win saw Michael
Owen score his second hat-trick of the season.

The qualifying campaign for Euro 2004 got underway and Finland's
first game was at home in Helsinki against Wales. The result went to Wales
with a 2–0 victory. This was followed with a 3–0 win against Azerbaijan,
with Sami scoring his second international goal. Then, disappointingly, a
2–0 defeat in Serbia and Montenegro (formerly Yugoslavia) left Finland
with a lot to do to qualify for the finals in Portugal.

In late October, Liverpool were leading the Premiership. With ten
games played, the Reds were a point in front of Arsenal and five in front
of third-placed Spurs, who were at Anfield on 26 October. It was a special
day as it brought back to the club for the first time an old Anfield
favourite, Jamie Redknapp. Sami had enjoyed Jamie's company and he was
a great help when he first joined the club. Sami reflects:

Jamie was at Liverpool for a long time and he was loved here. I
know everybody respected and admired what he did for this club.
The reception he received from the fans was tremendous. Jamie
was a great help not just to me but to all the players who arrived at
the club. He did a lot of work as captain in helping us to settle. It
was hard to see him leave at the end of the season, but football can
be like that sometimes. However, I am happy for him that he has

shaken off his injuries and that he is doing what he loves to do – which is playing football.

The game saw Liverpool win 2–1 and maintain their position at the top as they went in to November. In the Champions League, a defeat at home to Valencia meant Liverpool had to win in Basel to go through to the second stage.

November saw Sami win the Player of the Year in Finland, an honour which he felt very proud to receive. Whilst a League victory against West Ham and Worthington Cup success against Southampton kept the excellent start going, all this was about to change. The Reds were about to embark on a run that would not see them winning in the Premiership for the next 11 games. Not only this, but early in the game with Basel, Liverpool were 3–0 down. They showed tremendous character to bring the game back to 3–3, but time was the villain as Liverpool looked like they could have gone on to win the game if there had been five minutes more. A very disappointed Sami said:

> I never like losing. In fact, I don't know a player who does. But there are various degrees of pain associated with each defeat. This was one of the worst. Everyone knows that achieving a good run in the Champions League was one of our targets for the season. Nobody said we'd go all the way and win it, but after reaching the quarter-finals last season, we certainly believed that we should have gone further than the first round this time. The manner in which we went out of the tournament hurt as much as the elimination itself. At half-time in Basel most people probably thought we had no chance, so to respond so well in the second half and go so close to getting a winner was agonising – especially as this result came on the back of our defeat against Middlesbrough.
>
> I can't explain why we played so poorly in that opening 30 minutes in Switzerland. We certainly did not underestimate Basel and we approached the game with a positive attitude. However, there is no doubt that their first goal rocked us, and it automatically altered our game plan. Looking back, all three goals could have been avoided, which is especially disappointing. If we had managed to score just once before half-time, or if we'd had just five minutes longer, then I think we could have pulled off an amazing comeback.
>
> The positive thing to come out of Tuesday's match is that

nobody can doubt the character of the team. I can't think of many sides who, after going three goals down, would have genuinely believed they could score four times without reply in 45 minutes. Of course we left Switzerland with regrets. But in my view it wasn't the game over there which put us out, it was the one against Basel at Anfield. If we'd had a bit more luck that night we would have won instead of drawn, and so we would have just required a point. That said, we had six matches to try and qualify for the second round. If we couldn't finish in the top two in our group then I suppose we have to be honest and admit that we probably didn't deserve to go through.

The next game saw Liverpool draw 0–0 at home to Sunderland, a match where Liverpool had more than 20 attempts on goal and the visitors not a single one. A defeat at Fulham followed by a win in the first leg of the UEFA Cup match against Vitesse Arnhem put an end to a disappointing November.

The tasty fixture of Liverpool v. Manchester United was the first game of a very busy period, with the Reds playing nine games in December. Sami scored his first Premiership goal of the season, but any personal joy he felt was replaced with disappointment over the result – a 2–1 defeat – but also feelings of support for his friend and goalkeeper Jerzy Dudek whose mistake let United take the lead in a very tight contest. Gérard Houillier knew the best way for Jerzy to move forward was to play him in the very next game against Ipswich in the Worthington Cup. With the world's press watching and expecting young England prospect Chris Kirkland to play, Jerzy was named on the teamsheet. The Liverpool fans gave Jerzy a tremendous reception and Jerzy certainly knew what wonderful support he had, from the fans, teammates and staff. Sami knows how much the fans play their part and the support for Jerzy was fantastic.

I was so impressed with the support shown by the fans towards Jerzy. It was very nice to see that the fans were right behind the team and behind Jerzy when things aren't going right. They are tremendous fans, they have the energy and the willingness to support the team whatever happens.

Liverpool moved into the quarter-final of the Worthington Cup with a 5–4 win on penalties against Ipswich. The month continued with cup success in both the UEFA and Worthington, but three draws and a defeat saw Liverpool move down the table.

In January the cups were again a heavy part of the schedule, with the Worthington semi-final and the third round of the FA Cup. A 1–0 win at Maine Road in the FA Cup was followed by a tough trip to Bramall Lane, where Sheffield United took a 2–1 first-leg lead, Liverpool's goal being scored by Neil Mellor, a player brought through the Liverpool Academy.

Liverpool had come in for some criticism from the press as their poor League form continued with defeat at Newcastle and draws against Aston Villa and Arsenal. Sami recalls:

> As far as I am concerned, the papers can say what they want about us. There is no denying that we had been through a bad period, but things change. Confidence is the most important factor. When it's not going your way, your confidence goes down and you start to fear everything is against you. When you get the results we were having, it affects everybody. You have to be mentally capable of dealing with those kinds of things and grow as a club and be stronger for it. The expectations at Liverpool are that you win every game and be at the top of the League.
>
> The manager helped us. He took the stick when we were not performing, but he is not out on the pitch. The players are there to do that and we had to take responsibility. The boss cares about everyone in the squad. He took some of the pressure off us and that helped us to perform. We kept believing in ourselves because if you have doubts about yourselves as a team they can build in your mind. But if your mind is free and you have vision, you can get there.

Sami then went on to give his thoughts on Liverpool newcomer Neil Mellor:

> One of the most pleasing things at that time was the presence and performance of Neil Mellor. He had earned his chance, shown in training that he could score goals and that's exactly what he did. Neil is an example of how, if he is good enough, a young player will always be given his chance. The English game has changed along with European Union regulations. As a result, a lot of foreign players have come over here. But it's very important for English football that young talent is developed.

The semi-final return leg at Anfield proved to be a great cup-tie, with thousands coming over the Pennines from Sheffield to ensure a cracking atmosphere. Liverpool won 2–0, with goals from Diouf and Owen. A March final against their great rivals Manchester United was to take place at the Millennium Stadium, Cardiff, with the winners receiving the first UEFA Cup place. The month ended with a win at Southampton, Liverpool's first League win since West Ham in early November.

February started well with a 3–0 win at West Ham, but then disappointment followed with the shock Cup exit, Crystal Palace coming to Anfield and winning 2–0 to send the Reds crashing out of the FA Cup. A 1–1 draw with Middlesbrough maintained the frustrations of what could be a season without achieving any of the goals set at the start.

The UEFA Cup was next up and Liverpool comfortably saw off Auxerre with wins home and away. Sami had enjoyed the rarity of two winning goals in two consecutive games, with a goal for Finland in the friendly against Northern Ireland and the winner in Auxerre. The pressure continued with a defeat away at Birmingham, a game which saw Sami reach an impressive milestone – his 200th game for the Reds, an amazing record considering he was still in his fourth season.

With the run-in about to start, Sami could look forward to the Worthington Cup final, a Battle of Britain tie against Celtic and some progress in the League. The final was a fantastic game and saw Liverpool take their revenge with a 2–0 win, Sami keeping the impressive Van Nistelrooy at bay and going on to lift the trophy, also ensuring Liverpool a place in next season's UEFA Cup.

Victories followed in the League, with the Reds beating Bolton, Spurs and Leeds. The only disappointment came in the UEFA Cup. A 1–1 draw at Celtic Park meant Liverpool either had to win or secure a goalless draw to see them through to the semi-final. Celtic, however, won 2–0 at Anfield and they would progress to the final. A disappointed Sami said:

> I didn't feel we did ourselves justice in the game at Anfield. We had put a lot of hard work into the first leg in Glasgow to give ourselves a favourable position for the home leg, but we didn't play to our normal level and we were sloppy at times. This result didn't just end our UEFA Cup ambitions: it also ended the continuity we had established from recent results. Going through would have been a big boost. Conceding the first goal just before half-time hurt us, but at half-time we were still confident we could turn things around. But for all our efforts there was no way through, and John Hartson's good goal near the end killed things off.

In March, the Finnish national team had an Euro 2004 qualifier in Italy, a game in which they had to get a result. Italy won 2–0. With four games to play Finland were fourth in the group on three points.

In April, Sami experienced a first at Liverpool. With three minutes gone in the game at Old Trafford, he was adjudged to have brought Van Nistelrooy down. A penalty was awarded and a red card received as he had stopped an opponent when having a clear run on goal. Game over. Liverpool lost 4–0. Sami then missed the win in the local derby against Everton at Goodison.

The season moved to a dramatic climax, with Liverpool still in contention for the fourth Champions League spot. Arsenal, Manchester United and Newcastle had by now stretched away from the chasing pack. With four games to go, it was becoming a race between the Reds and Chelsea. Liverpool won their next two games against Charlton – Sami scoring his fourth of the season – and West Brom, a game which saw Michael Owen score his 100th Premiership goal.

Liverpool now moved into the final two games of the season. Unfortunately, the next brought a defeat at home to Manchester City, with Nicolas Anelka scoring both City goals late on. Liverpool would then have to head to London to face Chelsea knowing that only a win would be good enough to put them through to the lucrative Champions League. Any other result would see Chelsea head into a contest of Europe's finest. Not long into the first half, Sami was free in the area and his glancing header took Liverpool into a 1–0 lead – a typical captain's effort and a tremendous start at a highly charged Stamford Bridge. Again Liverpool didn't hold on to the lead and within minutes Marcel Desailly had equalised, quickly followed up by a Jesper Gronkjaer winner just before half-time. Chelsea was in the Champions League. Liverpool's season had ended.

Sami ended the season top of the OPTA stats for defenders, but he was disappointed as he headed back to Finland to pick himself up for the forthcoming Euro 2004 qualifiers.

A defeat in Norway was not the best preparation. In Helsinki, the national team added to their points tally with a convincing 3–0 win over Serbia and Montenegro, with Sami scoring his eighth goal of the season. The win had put them back in the frame for Portugal, but a 2–0 defeat at home to Italy the following Wednesday made the dream of Portugal a distant one.

2002–03 was a season of few highs, but Sami believes the experience will make the Liverpool side stronger. Looking back at the season he said:

We are a young team and I'm confident that we can win the League during my time at Liverpool. Nobody can build a highly successful team in just a couple of years. We enjoyed the Treble two seasons ago and I'm happy we did it but maybe it came a bit too early. Because of that Treble our expectations are much higher than they were two years ago. Winning the Worthington Cup this season does not mean it has been a successful one. We have high standards and we want to improve year in and year out. The last season has been disappointing, but we will get stronger. Building a successful team is a long process, but we will get there in the end.

Epilogue: Sami Hyypiä the Person

SAMI'S CHANGE FROM A QUIET YOUTH FROM VOIKKAA INTO A professional who can deal with the media smoothly and naturally is probably not as big as it may appear. The qualities that helped him make his way to the elite group of football players in the world – determination and persistence – characterised him even when he was a youth. His modesty also developed during his youth years. He never particularly aimed for the limelight, but this is not to say that he was never assertive or ambitious. His will to shun unnecessary headlines and publicity isn't a sign of retreat or defeatism.

> Already at school, I was always more in the background of things than up front, making myself important. I think I still have it in me. I don't want to be the first in line, but I don't want to be the last either.
>
> Another trait that characterises me is that I do everything with the fullest commitment. If I set out to do something, I don't want to leave it undone or finish it carelessly: I want to finish it in the best possible way. This showed particularly at school and in the army, and I think this is also why I've sometimes lost my temper.
>
> I never even thought about not finishing the upper secondary school and taking the final exams. During the upper secondary, I was also considering the different alternatives in higher education. After all, you can never know how your football career will turn out. That is one good reason to take care of your school work properly. If, for some reason, you don't make a living out of football, you can always study and get yourself a profession. I was never afraid that I would have nothing if my football career ended.

I feel that I'm smart enough to study my way into another profession after my football career anyway.

School is also important because you never know when your passion for football will come to an end. It is only when you're a little older that you'll know what it is that really interests you. I think you should always have a back-up plan. Your football career may end abruptly, too, because you never know about the human body.

Sami also thinks that football shouldn't be too serious at a young age: 'I think that, as a youth, the most important thing about football is to enjoy it and have fun. Of course, it is always useful to have a winner's attitude – I couldn't stand losing as a youth either.'

People need dreams, but they shouldn't control your life. Even Sami has had to give up some of the things he liked as a youth player, although it is certainly not to the detriment of world football or Sami himself that little Sami didn't grow up to be a prolific goalscorer like his favourite player.

When I was young I followed Ian Rush quite a bit. Liverpool were my favourite team and, at that time, Rush was their best goalscorer. I think it is quite natural that you watch the strikers more as a youth, but as the years have gone by, I've obviously learnt to respect and admire the defenders, too. At Kumu and MyPa, being able to watch Esa Pekonen from close range surely had a tremendous influence on me. That's how things tend to change.

In any case, hard work is the key to success in football, just like in everything else, too. You can get to a certain point with pure talent, but in order to succeed you have to refine the talent and work hard to make the most out of it. There is no short-cut to success. As for myself, I can honestly say that I would not trade the days I've spent with football for anything else.

As a person, Sami is an interesting mix of a calm, ordinary lad and fiery fighter:

As for my nature, perhaps the first thing that comes to my mind is that I'm balanced and peaceful. Ambition and a winning attitude are the characteristics that show up more on the pitch, but then again, I'm like that off the pitch, too. No matter what the game – whether it be cards, board games, *Trivial Pursuit* or *Who Wants to*

Be a Millionaire? – I always want to win and it really irritates me
and I may lose my temper if I lose. Some may think it is bad if you
can't put up with losing, but that's just the way I am. I want to win.
Besides, I think that everyone should have at least a little ambition
in their lives.

Other than that, I don't really stress out about life. Being a
professional football player puts enough pressure on my shoulders
and outside of the game I try to live my life in a little more relaxed
way. However, it is quite difficult to keep the job out of mind in
my free time. I know it would be better if I could keep work and
free time apart from each other, but I do bring my mood from
training and matches home with me. Of course, things that happen
in training and matches should be taken care of there, but I'm not
really good at it. My mood at home is more dependent on how
things are going at work. If there have been troubles or something
troubles me, you can easily see that at home. I snap at little things
and my face is sour even though it shouldn't be. After all, nothing
should be wrong at home. This is probably one of the flaws in my
character.

Still, Sami is by no means a solemn person with no sense of humour.
Instead, it is quite certain that people who've met him are more likely to
remember his wide, cheerful smile. 'I do know how to laugh, for example
at good jokes or funny movies,' explains a smiling Sami. 'And of course,
the referees' calls sometimes make me laugh, too. They are sometimes so
unbelievable that the only thing you can do is laugh at them – you can't
lose your temper about them.'

The smile remains on his face when he starts to talk about the movies
he likes. The Finnish comic character Uuno Turhapuro and the number of
films created around him are particular favourites:

I have all the Turhapuro movies on tape. I had taped them from TV
despite the rather poor quality of TV recordings, but as soon as
they released them on video, I bought them all. They are a form of
Finnish entertainment that is fun to watch abroad. Besides, I think
Finns are the only people who would understand the humour in
them anyway. In addition to the Turhapuro movies, I enjoy
watching action movies.

All this is not to say that there isn't a sensitive side to my
character, too. There have been times that I've cried for a reason

other than being substituted for a girl . . . Even at an older age, there have been some moments in my life that have made me cry. Even an emotional scene at the end of a movie has brought a teardrop to the corner of my eye, and really, I'm not ashamed of it.

Winning titles and other great achievements have never made Sami cry, though, not even when he has raised the trophies as a team captain, or even at the recent Finnish FA award ceremony, for example.

Of course I appreciate all the titles and achievements a great deal, but perhaps the final matches haven't had the sort of emotional charge that would have made me cry for joy. I have always tried to concentrate on the match as if it were any other match in the schedule that I want to win. It doesn't make it any different if it's a cup final, you have to focus on the job no matter what the match. The difference is, of course, that after the final it is fun to raise the trophy in the air and it feels good to have made so many fans happy. That's when you are all smiles.

I have cried after losses, however. There are actually quite a few times, so it is rather hard to separate them from each other. One of the last times was probably near the end of the 2000–01 season, after the match against Leicester. I had a terrible cold then and I felt really sick. Before the match, I almost told the boss that I was unable to play. At half-time, Houllier told me that I was good to go on, and I was exhausted during the second half – I was barely fit to run at all. In the end, Leicester made the score 2–0 and they won the match. I cried after the match, and I think one of the reasons for the emotional reaction besides the defeat was the cold and sick feeling I had. The match was also very important for us, because we were still fighting for admission to the Champions League.

CARRYING THE RESPONSIBILITY

Sami's account of his feelings after the Leicester match remind me of the things the people interviewed for this book said about his self-criticism and sense of responsibility. A cold and feeling sick will not make Sami sit out a match, and yet such an illness, he feels, is no excuse for a substandard performance on the pitch. I tell Sami that his father, Jouko Hyypiä, for example, thinks that sometimes the weight Sami wants to carry on his shoulders is unreasonably heavy: he shouldn't try to carry the whole team. Sami doesn't agree but he does admit that the speculation about his self-criticism holds some truth.

> I don't think I take too large a responsibility for the team. If I've made a mistake, I can admit it and take full responsibility. I never look for excuses for my mistakes. If I miss the ball, I don't make up excuses and say, for instance, that my shoelaces were undone. I think it is better to put your hands up and admit the mistake. Everyone makes mistakes, in all walks of life.
>
> After a match, if the manager shows me the mistakes I made, I approve of it and won't start explaining that this and that player didn't do their job either. I don't know if this is taking too large a responsibility. Maybe I'm just that type of a player who easily takes the blame, because I never – or very rarely – make a case for defending myself or complaining. I think I can handle justified criticism well, but if the blame is off-base, I won't take it. As for the manager and the coaches, they never criticise me for no reason, but sometimes the press write articles that I simply can't take on board.
>
> Self-criticism, on the other hand, is just a dominant quality in my character that won't go away, and I think it has helped me forward in my career. I think it is good to be critical of oneself. Often after a match, I think about the things I did right and the things I did wrong, and what could have been done otherwise so that I wouldn't have made the mistakes or that I would have played a certain ball better. Sometimes I also watch the matches on tape at home.
>
> Still, I wouldn't say that I'm a perfectionist. I just try to become a better player through self-criticism.

Sometimes self-criticism is not enough. In England, Sami has often noticed that the performances of defenders in particular are continuously under the scrutiny of a critical eye. 'If you make a mistake at the back, the finger of the media points directly at you. It is pretty brutal sometimes, because the way you play is never totally up to your own effort,' Sami reflects. 'It is a team sport and the whole team is responsible for the results. It is hard being a defender but, then again, I guess it is even harder being a keeper.'

The pressure on the goalkeepers in the Premiership was demonstrated early on in the 2001–02 season at Liverpool. Sander Westerveld, the first-team number-one keeper made a few mistakes in a league match against

Bolton and the Reds lost 2–1. Only a few days after that match, Liverpool bought two new keepers. Obviously, the acquisition of new players doesn't always follow such dramatic turns, and perhaps the acquisition of the new keepers at Liverpool just happened to take place at a bad time for Westerveld. In any case, the events demonstrated how heavy the continuous pressure is on the players at the top European clubs. Sami analyses the situation:

> A striker can have ten chances at the goal and fail eight times, and yet he is a hero if he scores twice. If a defender makes one mistake and the opponent scores from it, he is a traitor who lost the match for the team. I am totally aware of this. We're all human and everyone makes mistakes. And if you happen to make one, you just have to learn from it and not make the same mistake again.
>
> Defining a personal mistake is sometimes complicated anyway. If, for example, you lose a header and the opponent gets the second ball and scores, whose fault is it? Is it the fault of the player who lost the ball in the air or the one who was supposed to win the second ball? In a team sport, there are always 11 winners and 11 losers. Everyone has their share of responsibility for the final result.

Before the beginning of the 2001–02 season, Sami gained personal experience of the quick manner in which defenders' mistakes make the headlines. In a friendly pre-season match against Ajax Amsterdam, Sami played worse than usual, and he practically gave away one goal to the opponent when he slipped at a decisive moment. A comment made by Gérard Houllier, saying he wouldn't have signed Sami from Willem if had played the same way at Willem, spread rapidly round the world through the media. The statement didn't bother Sami much:

> I think it was a harmless, humorous comment, and yet I also think that I wouldn't be playing for Liverpool right now if Houllier had seen me play like this for Willem.
>
> I wasn't in the best possible form in that match. We'd had a long and strenuous training camp and I was tired. Houllier didn't say anything special to me after the match, but he didn't go and buy us a new centre-back either. I think he understood that I was tired and it was best if I forgot about the match and concentrated on the next one. We won the next match 3–0 and I scored, and that's the end of it.

Houllier's faith in Sami wasn't even close to decreasing after one weak performance in a pre-season friendly. When the new season started, the Finnish centre-back was the towering pillar in the centre of Liverpool's defence once more. Before the minor injury that sidelined him in October, Sami was the only Liverpool player who had played in all official matches of the season. According to the man himself, he has no intention of taking on any unnecessary pressure in the future either.

> I will always go on to the pitch with the mindset that I will do my best and give everything I have for the team. Maybe some people nowadays expect some wonder performances from me, but I will always focus on taking care of my job as well as possible. I won't try any fancy moves or any marvellous tricks, I'll just do what I've been doing for the past ten years. It's not worth trying something you haven't done before or something you can't do. You have to concentrate on the things you're good at, and that should do it. For me, it has been enough thus far, and I should think it'll do in the future, too.

Even though Sami often talks about only doing his best, I remind him about the silverware he has gathered in his trophy case. At Liverpool, he has actually gained a taste of major victories for the first time in his career, and you would think things like that would mean everything to an ambitious player like Sami. Surprisingly, however, Sami doesn't want to emphasise any achievements individually. It is the overall performance that counts the most.

> Of course, every football player wants to win titles in his career. You have to have ambition and desire for winning, and of course I'm happy that we have won those titles. Not many players get to win the FA Cup or the UEFA Cup in their careers, and yet I could just as well be happy with my career if I didn't win many titles. There are players who have never won titles, and still, you can't think of them as failures. It is a matter of how you view your career and what you want from it. In that sense, my attitude towards my career has always been relaxed in a way, although every match I've played has been very important. The idea is that I go one day at a time. If you have terribly high objectives all the time, you only end up getting disappointed when you don't achieve them. When you proceed one day and match at a time, you save yourself from major

disappointments and you can always look back at your career later
as a continuous entity.

Even during the greatest moments of victory and joy, Sami still has a
humble attitude towards winning. Behind every victory there is a
tremendous amount of work and a team effort and an individual player
should not be given all the credit, he argues. That is also the reason why
Sami has been hesitant in raising the respected cup titles as a team captain:
he wants to honour the hierarchy in the team.

Sami's laid-back attitude to his career and winning does not mean that
he doesn't care fiercely about the game, though. On the pitch, Sami always
takes his job seriously and he expects the same of others – both his
teammates and his opponents. According to Sami, hard but fair is the way
football should be played – seriously, but not over the top. Sami
disapproves of all kinds of dirty tackles and dishonesty on the pitch. This
subject doesn't even bring out that familiar smile on his face. It is evident
that this is an important matter to him:

> I hate fakery, diving and dirty challenges. That's another great
> thing about English football – you don't see much diving or players
> rolling on the ground in pretend agony. Although these, too, have
> increased in the past few years with the increasing number of
> foreign players.
>
> Another thing about diving and faking injuries that really
> irritates me is the fact that referees are human, too, and they make
> mistakes just as we players do. There is no way they can see
> everything on the pitch, and you cannot always blame them for the
> mistakes they make. If, for example, there is a penalty in the match
> as a result of a dive when no one has made contact with the fallen
> player, it is a great injustice. I wish someone would come up with
> the means to fix this problem – it should come to an end.
>
> I have the same kind of attitude towards dishonesty in my life
> outside football, too. If someone lies to me or deceives me, it is a
> bad blow to my trust in him. On the other hand, life on the pitch
> and off the pitch are different in that, even though I aim to play
> hard but fair in football, I've never meant to be particularly hard
> off the field. I've never been in a fight, but I've escaped a few,
> though.

SAMI HYYPIÄ

PEOPLE CLOSE TO SAMI

Once again, our conversation is strongly leaning towards being concerned solely with football, even though the intention was to hear Sami talk about himself as a person. I bring up relationships, but even here football works its way back into the story. Sami starts to tell me about his parents, Irma and Jouko Hyypiä. Sami's mother and father have been close to their son's most important moments – and what can you say when football has played a central role in most of them.

> My parents have supported my career since the beginning. As a youth, of course, my dad was the coach, so I never had a problem with transportation to training. We rode in our car together, and the trip to the pitch was short anyway. Besides, I'm sure Mum and Dad would have driven me to training and back if there was a need for it. They have supported my career throughout.
>
> At times, I think football has taken up too much of our lives. As long as I can remember, much of our conversations have been focused on football, and they still do. Maybe we could have focused on something else at times. There are many other important things in life which you could talk about with your family.

In addition to his parents, Sami reminds me of the support he has received from his former long-term girlfriend, Niina. Unselfishly, she smoothed out the bumps in the sometimes rough road of a professional football player and gave her unconditional support to Sami. It was not always easy – it can be difficult to balance the duties of professional football with normal daily life. As a football player, you have to make room for your matches, training, physical treatment and rest in a selfish way, and the away matches take away much from time spent together as well. Therefore, Sami is truly grateful for Niina's patience even though their relationship came to an end in the summer of 2001.

> Niina's presence made my life abroad a lot easier. For example, if I had been alone when moving to Holland, I'm sure it would have been twice as hard moving there. Niina always supported me in the good and the bad, and I am grateful for that. She also tried to make me think about other things besides football and keep my job away from home. And I think she even had some success in that.

191

When they were living abroad, domestic matters and errands were primarily Niina's responsibility and she let Sami concentrate on football. Sami had moved to Holland and England alone at first, and Niina followed afterwards. Thus, Sami, too, had to make some decisions about the design of his home, but he openly admits that Niina always had the final word. Sami explains:

> It's not that she never liked my purchases, although she did comment on some things. Nevertheless, Niina was usually responsible for the decor in the house. She enjoyed her time abroad, but it must have been hard for her overall. She was never really able to plan her own life, because you never knew where we would go and when we would leave. In that sense, she was dependent on me, and yet I think she did well for herself. She even studied to become a hair stylist in England.

Friends also mean a great deal to Sami. The life of a football player abroad can easily become lonely toil and the ties to old friends make for an important outlet for sharing his troubles. Except for his teammates, Sami really hasn't made any friends in Liverpool. Sami ponders the problems of his new-found fame:

> It is difficult to make new friends here in England. Or, I'm sure I would find friends here easily, but their interests might differ greatly from mine, I should say. At the moment, I'm pretty hesitant with people that I don't know. I don't make friends with people that quickly, because it is hard for me to say whether they want to be friends with me just because I play for Liverpool FC or because of how I am as a person. I'd much rather keep the small circle of friends I have and remain distant to others. In Finland, I don't even have much time to make new friends, because I'm only there for a month in the year. As for my old friends, I haven't seen any change in their behaviour, and I don't think my behaviour in their company has changed either. I think I'm still the same person that I was before I left Finland.
>
> I think it is natural that you don't keep in touch with everyone all the time, but it doesn't mean that they would be out of my mind. I still have quite a few friends from my childhood that I keep in touch with. But perhaps I could try to call them a bit more often.
>
> People move on with their lives. Most of my friends from the

school or from the youth teams already have families and they have settled down, so in that sense our lives are quite different from each other. When I come for a summer holiday in Finland and ask my friends to come along to some place, it doesn't always work that way. They have their families and children they have to look after, and our circle of friends has also changed a little because of that. Nowadays, I probably have less friends who are my age – many are a little older – but I've known them for quite some time, too. I've met a lot of people during my career.

If the lives of some childhood friends have changed in the course of time, Sami's life hasn't remained completely unchanged either. Being a professional football player sets limitations on a person and you have to stick to the rules even at the cost of your social life.

If my friends ask me out and we have training the next day, I have to turn down the offer. So in that sense my work sets restrictions on my life quite a bit. I think that I've changed a little as a person, too, but that's more out of necessity. When I go outside, more and more people come and ask for my autograph and other things, and I don't really get to walk the streets in privacy any more. You have to learn to keep a certain distance. Even with my friends, I can't go anywhere I want, and this, of course, also restricts my social life.

The fact remains that everything I've ever done, I've taken seriously. Right now, football is my job, and I want to take it seriously. Some people even think that I take it too seriously, but that's the way I am and it's not easy to change it. Sometimes I do think that maybe I should have a bit more of a relaxed attitude towards the whole thing, but then again, it might soon show on the pitch, too.

THE JOY AND PAIN OF FAME

As I walk next to Sami in Helsinki, I cannot help but notice that I'm walking with a celebrity. In particular, those who are a bit drunk seem to have the courage to approach the Liverpool star. According to Sami, people left him alone when he was still playing in Finland, and during his years at Willem he was recognised in Kouvola and Tilburg, of course. In England, his publicity struck with force in a country where football is almost a religion, especially when you are successful. The glory of the English stadiums reflects all the way to Finland.

In Finland, many people's attitude towards me changed overnight when I signed with Liverpool. I think it is wrong that when a player transfers from one club to another, people's respect for him changes as well. Signing with Liverpool didn't change anything about me as a person or even as a player. However, the interest the media and the people had in me changed completely. When I was walking the streets in Helsinki during my years in Holland, not many people knew who I was, although I didn't hang around in Helsinki that much back then anyway. Nevertheless, now the people there know me and I still don't spend much time there. Of course, back home it was enough that I was playing at Willem for people to know who I was and whisper to other as I walked by. All that is an inevitable part of the job, though, and you have to live with it.

It is hard for me to say how I've changed as a person in Liverpool. I am certain that some things about a person have to change, because I can't do everything the way people generally do. After all, people live for football in Liverpool. For example, I can't go wherever I want to, and I have to think about where I move about. If I happen to go to the wrong place at the wrong time, there will be quite a mess. I've managed to take care of my shopping and other daily routines rather normally. However, particularly in the afternoon, there are times when the shops are crowded with people, and that is why I'd rather do my shopping early in the morning or late in the evening.

The number of people that come and ask for my autograph has increased and they show up in the most unusual places. It's not always fun if I want to be on my own just like any other private person, but I do understand the way things work and that it is all part of my job. But if I'm having a meal in a restaurant and my mouth is full of food when someone asks for an autograph, I think it is a little inconsiderate. Nevertheless, I am kind – sometimes even a bit too kind – by nature and I always try not to hurt anyone's feelings, and I will sign the autograph even in an unusual situation, most of the time. These days, I've decided not to interrupt my meal for the signature, though, and I'll sign them afterwards. Besides, most people have understood that I won't give my autograph in the middle of my lunch or dinner. And if someone gets angry about it, it's their own fault.

Fame is not always a curse, though – why else would people crucify themselves for it so eagerly?

> Being famous does have its advantages, too, but I don't really need any of that. When I'm reserving a table at a restaurant, for example, I might be able to find one at short notice, but I don't want to use my position that way. When I call up a restaurant and ask for a table, I always ask them to tell me immediately if there isn't one available. I don't want anyone to think that things had to be arranged for me, and that others would suffer from it. It actually makes me a bit uneasy if people do things to please me and make their own work more inconvenient.
>
> Actually, publicity doesn't mean a thing to me. I would like to lead a normal life just like any other person, but publicity is part of my job and I accept that completely. But I don't have to make the headlines or the tabloids every day. Sometimes I just don't understand people who want to make a fuss about themselves. It's not always so easy to be in the limelight.

As a Liverpool player, Sami also gets to meet people that many dream of coming face to face with. Sometimes other celebrities practically cling on to football players.

> All kinds of people come to talk to us, of course, but I don't really know if it's that flattering. Obviously, many of them are people whom I would like to meet just as anyone else would – musicians, actors, etc. They are at the top of their own field, and I have nothing against it if I know a few of them.
>
> If I can help them with something, for example, by arranging tickets for them to our matches, I'm sure they can help me in a similar way, if needed. I know a few, not that many, public figures, and my experiences with them have been quite good. Some of them have given me a lot in the mental aspect of publicity, and perhaps I have been able to offer something in return. It's never a one-way street, and it shouldn't be. And I don't mean to say that you should always try to take advantage of other people. It's just nice if people from different fields know each other.

Sami has learnt to be careful with the people hanging around him. Famous people always attract the company of spongers. 'I'm pretty sure that there are more people in this world who like me because I'm a football player instead of who I am as a person.'

And how could people actually know Sami beyond his public image? Sami's parents told me that many friends of the family have been happy to notice that the boy is his good old self after seeing him on TV. Undoubtedly, Sami's appearance and thick regional dialect create an image of a person who is comfortable with his fame. And working with the media is just another aspect of the modern game. 'The media is part of the football world just like publicity,' says Sami. 'In principle, I have nothing against it, it's part of the job and in a way, a duty, too. You have to talk with the reporters, but because I am a football player, I would like to talk about football with them, not about anything else.'

The line between the public and the private Sami Hyypiä is clear for the man himself:

> I will never let any magazine or other form of media make a story about my home where they will take photographs of every room in the house and introduce them or my car to their readership. I want to keep my privacy. If the media wants to know something about football, I will answer any question with pleasure. However, when you become more popular, the media starts to become more interested in the less relevant matters than the priorities, i.e. the events on the pitch.
>
> Still, I've never had any problems with the media, and I don't think I ever will. Of course, I've sometimes lost my temper because of groundless criticism and I've wanted to fix it somehow. I don't read the papers that much anyway. More often than not, the articles are written by one or two reporters presenting their opinions, and they are not always objective either. Therefore, I'm not that interested in the reviews, whether they be good or bad. The criticism always finds its way to my ears – someone will always read it out.

There is one principle Sami wants to hold on to. Every story that is written about him has to be agreed with him personally and the media has to respect those mutual agreements. 'From my viewpoint, it would a be pretty serious offence if someone wrote a story about my private life behind my back, no matter what the context. I might consider taking some action then.'

In Liverpool, Sami has to work with the media every week, 11 months of the year. In the summer, he holds only one press conference in Finland. 'I want to take some time off from everything, and when I'm on holiday there is no point in anyone coming and asking for an interview,' Sami explains. 'Everything is done during that one day at the beginning of the summer. Besides, the leagues are on a break in the summer, too, so there isn't much to talk about in football, and I don't have much to say about anything else.'

Members of the media are not the only people who want their share of Sami in the summer. The star player from Liverpool FC has been a perfect model for all sorts of advertisements.

> I get all kinds of requests throughout the summer, so much that if I were to make it to all different events, shootings, etc., I would have to divide myself into two or three different people. If I tried to do everything, I wouldn't have a single day off all year and, of course, that's not what I want. For me, the summer holiday is first and foremost for relaxation, taking it easy and recharging my batteries for the next season.
>
> Sometimes some people think that an hour at a youth football camp, for example, in some distant little town, is not much to ask, but you should keep in mind that travelling takes up a surprising amount of time, too. Besides, I purposefully make an attempt to visit different events as much as possible and I like spending time with kids. Visiting the youth football camps and other events has given me much pleasure. It is nice to notice that the kids are enjoying their time and that I can make them happy.

CAREER PLANS

The final meeting with Sami is coming to an end, but there is one more important topic to discuss, and I'm trying my luck. I point out that there is no conversation about modern football without talking about money. Players are bought and sold, price tags are attached to people. For example, Sami cost £2.7 million in May 1999 when he transferred from Willem to Liverpool. Today, his value has gone up considerably. In comparison, Jaap Stam, another centre-back who left Willem for a Premiership club, cost the Italian side Lazio £17 million when Manchester United sold him in autumn 2001. As for their football qualities, Sami and Stam are in the same category, which suggests that Sami's price should be around the same amount as Stam's transfer fee. It feels odd sitting next to a man who is worth almost £20 million. Sami explains:

> Each player has his price in this game. I have never thought about it as the slave trade. The price of a player is up to the clubs who are making the deal, the one who is selling and the other who is buying. No one's value is known before he is sold to another club. The value is where the two clubs meet.
>
> Those figures do sound outrageous. I don't know my own price because I'm not planning on transferring anywhere. Besides, I never think about the value of a player anyway. It becomes an issue only if you transfer somewhere.

The players not only cost a lot for their clubs to buy, but they also make a lot of money in wages. In comparison to common working men, Sami stepped up to a new wage level even when he moved to Holland. In England, the wages increased further. Sami performs a quick calculation.

> In Holland, even an average player makes more money than the top players in Finland. I don't know about the others, but my wage slip in Holland was as many figures as in Finland, but the difference was that the wages were paid in Dutch guilders, which are worth three times more than the Finnish mark. And yet, the difference between Holland and England is dramatic, much greater than between Holland and Finland.

Money has never been a motive for Sami, even though he does admit that you start to think about finances as you get older. He says:

> The older you get, the more money starts to mean to you. After all, no one can play and make money off football for the rest of his life. It all comes to an end between 35 and 40 years of age. It is important that you have some money saved when you quit playing. Like many others, I don't have a profession, which basically means that I have to have enough money at the end of my career to support me while I get myself a new profession. Nevertheless, money was never among the most important reasons for playing football for me. I still enjoy the game, and I am fortunate to have turned my favourite hobby into work. I make my living out of a sport that I've loved since I was a kid.

SAMI HYYPIÄ

At the moment, football as a job is more important to Sami than the money paid for it. He wouldn't leave Liverpool for a lower-level club for more money, at least not for a long time.

> When I'm around 33 or 34, I might consider leaving if I could get a good deal somewhere for a couple of years. You have to keep in mind, however, that your football career doesn't last a lifetime. It may be that you get injured in the next match and you won't play a single match after that. You must keep that in mind.

Although the importance of money for the future is clear to Sami, making a lot of money now also makes some of the practical things in life easier, and has done throughout his active football career.

> If, for example, I want to buy a new TV, I can go ahead and do that without having to think: 'Am I going to be able to pay my rent?' or 'Will I have enough money for food?' So, in a way, money does make your life a bit easier, but it doesn't matter to me right now how much money I have. Just as long as I have enough to make ends meet.

I remind him that many people also dream about being able to retire before turning 40, like professional football players do, and then rest on their laurels for the rest of their lives. This idea is strange to Sami, though. Life goes on after a football career, but where? Sami can't say for sure if he will finish his career abroad or return to Finland.

> I really haven't thought about it. If I'm in such a shape physically that my health is in no immediate danger, it may just as well be that I'll play in Finland for some time after my professional career. I'll see when it is time.
>
> Besides, you can't know in advance how life after football will turn out. I enjoy being in Finland, but, then again, I've also enjoyed living abroad. If there is something abroad that I want to do – if I got a chance to study somewhere or work with football, for example – it might be just as likely that I won't return to Finland. I can't say no, but I can't say yes either.
>
> In any case, returning to school is one serious option. I haven't given this idea any more thought, but I do have to get myself another profession after my football career. I will definitely not

spend the rest of my life doing nothing. Studying does come to my mind as a good option.

No matter where I live, it is always great to come to Finland. Finland will always be Finland, and I have my friends and family here. As time is limited, I never have time to see everyone. You have to make choices.

Sami Hyypiä reports back to duty at Liverpool. He exchanges his stylish black suit for a black leather jacket and trousers. Still, the tall star remains composed and elegant. And the elegance is still there when he dresses up in the Reds' jersey again and walks out of the tunnel in his shorts to face yet another crowd of tens of thousands of people. You can tell from his every gesture that he is a man who knows what he wants and is ready to work hard to achieve his goals. You just have to respect Sami Hyypiä's attitude towards his work and his life.

I have had the chance to follow the life of a world-class football player from an exceptionally close range and I'm slowly beginning to understand why Finnish football is gradually making progress. Our youth players now have home-grown idols, of whom we could only dream ten years ago. Smart, confident and determined world-class players, the Finnish internationals, led by the example of Sami Hyypiä and Jari Litmanen, have shown that the road from the frozen gravel pitch to the world arenas, with the likes of Rivaldo, Michael Owen and Luis Figo, is not that long after all. The prototype of a successful Finnish athlete doesn't have to be a hermit toiling in a swamp to achieve fortune and fame in cross-country skiing – Finland can produce stars equipped for the most popular team sport in the world.

Finnish football no longer has to suffer from a lack of confidence, we no longer have to complain about the quality of our domestic league. We have future stars here, we just have to find them and make them shine. Training, hard work and humble attitude can make a Finnish football player a world-class player. Every week, one of them is a head above everyone else in the English Premiership. Right now, it is Sami Hyypiä. Who's next?

Appendix: Statistics and Career Records

Date and place of birth: 7 October 1973, Porvoo
Height/weight: 196 cm/89 kg

Clubs:

Youth level:
Pallo-Peikot (PaPe), Voikkaa
Kumu, Kuusankoski

First team:
Kumu, Kuusankoski
Myllykosken Pallo -47 (MyPa), Anjalankoski
Willem II, Tilburg (Holland)
Liverpool FC (England)

Head Coaches and Managers:

Club teams:

Kumu	Keijo Voutilainen (1991)
MyPa	Harri Kampman (1992–95)
Willem II	Theo de Jong (1996)
	Jimmy Calderwood (SCO, 1996–97)
	Co Adriaanse (1997–99)
Liverpool FC	Gérard Houllier (FRA, 1999–)

Finnish National Team:

	Jukka Vakkila (1992)
	Jukka Ikäläinen (1994–96)
	Richard Møller-Nielsen (DEN, 1996–99)
	Antti Muurinen (2000–)

SAMI HYYPIÄ

Achievements:

League titles/finishes:
Runner-up, English Premier League, Liverpool FC 2002
Third place, English Premier League, Liverpool FC 2001
Runner-up, Dutch Premier League, Willem II 1999
Three times runner-up in Finnish Premier League with MyPa, in 1993, 1994, 1995

Cup titles:
UEFA Supercup champion 2001 (captain of Liverpool FC in the final)
UEFA Cup champion 2001 (captain of Liverpool FC in the final)
FA Cup champion 2001 (captain of Liverpool FC in the final)
FA Charity Shield winner 2001 (captain of Liverpool FC in the final)
Worthington Cup champion 2001, 2003
Finnish Cup champion, MyPa 1992, 1995

Recognitions/Awards:
Athlete of the Year in Finland 2001
Finnish FA Player of the Year 1999, 2001, 2002
Football Player of the Year 1999, 2000, 2001, 2002 in Finland (selected by the Finnish media)
UEFA Player of the Year, 18th place, 2001
Nominated candidate for UEFA Defenceman of the Year 2002
Finnish FA Most Talented Player of the Year 1991
Finnish FA Best Player of the Under-21 National Team 1994, 1995
English Premier League Player of the Month award November 1999
Willem II, First-team captain, 1998–99 (most of the season)
Liverpool FC, First-team captain, 1999–2000 (most of the season)
Liverpool FC, First-team captain, 2000–01 (part of the season)
Liverpool FC, First-team captain, 2001–02 (most of the season)
Liverpool FC, First-team captain, 2002–03 (official nomination)
Member of the English Premier League All-Star team in 2000, 2001, 2002
Norway's *Tipsbladet* magazine's Player of the Year in the English Premier League 1999–2000
Nominated candidate for English Premier League Player of the Year Award in 1999–2000
Member of the *News of the World* All-star team 2000–01
Finland's *Veikkaaja* magazine's Best Defender in the English Premier League in 2000–01
Liverpool FC Player of the Year (selected by Liverpool FC's supporters' clubs) 1999–2000, 2000–01, 2001–02
Member of the CNN All-star team 2001
FourFourTwo magazine's Best Defender of the Premier League award 2000–01
Member of *L'Equipe*'s All-star team 2000–01
UEFA Champions League's Most Valued Player 2001–02 (voted by www.uefa.com readers)
UEFA Champions League's Best Defender 2001–02 (voted by www.uefa.com readers)
Member of the UEFA All-star team 2001–02

SAMI HYYPIÄ

Appearances and goals – domestic leagues and cup competitions (end of 2002–03 season):

Finland:

Finnish *Veikkausliiga*	4 seasons, 96 appearances, 8 goals
Finnish first division	1 season, 19 appearances
Finnish Cup	4 seasons
Finnish League Cup	2 seasons
TOTAL	5 seasons, 115 appearances, 8 goals

(No official records could be obtained for the Finnish Cup and the Finnish League Cup)

Holland:

Dutch *Eredivisie*	4 seasons, 100 appearances, 3 goals
KNVB-Beker Cup	4 seasons

(No official records could be obtained for the Dutch Cup)

England:

FA Carling Premiership	4 seasons, 146 appearances, 11 goals
FA Cup	4 seasons, 13 appearances
Worthington Cup	4 seasons, 13 appearances, 1 goal
FA Charity/ Community Shield	2 seasons, 2 appearances
TOTAL	4 seasons, 174 appearances, 12 goals

European cups:

UEFA Champions League	2 seasons, 19 appearances, 2 goals
UEFA Champions League qualifying round	1 season, 2 appearances, 1 goal
Cup-Winners' Cup	1 season, 1 appearance
UEFA Cup	5 seasons, 29 appearances, 1 goal
European Supercup	1 season, 1 appearance
TOTAL	7 seasons, 52 appearances, 4 goals

Appearances and goals – international (up to 1.8.2003):

The full international squad	9 seasons, 55 appearances, 4 goals
Under-21 national team	4 seasons, 26 appearances, 8 goals
Under-19 national team	2 seasons, 5 appearances, 1 goal
Under-18 national team	1 season, 9 appearances, 2 goals
TOTAL	11 seasons, 95 appearances, 15 goals

OVERALL TOTAL	11 seasons, 536 appearances, 42 goals

(Not including the Finnish Cup, the Finnish League Cup and the Dutch Cup)

SAMI HYYPIÄ

Career in years:
(N = neutral, H = home fixture, A = away fixture)
(ECQ = European Championships Qualifier, WCQ = World Cup Qualifier, NCT = Nordic Championship Tournament)

Youth years:
1980–89 PaPe (Under-9–Under-19)
1990–91 Kumu (Under-21)

First-team career:
1991

Kumu First division	19 appearances, 5th place
Finnish Cup	Quarter-final Kuusysi v. Kumu 4–1
Finland Under-18 appearances	Yugoslavia N 0–0 90 min.
	USA N 1–2 90 min.
	Holland (ECQ) A 3–0 90 min.
	Austria (ECQ) H 0–3 90 min.
	Poland H 0–0 90 min.
	Poland H 3–0 90 min. 1 goal
	Norway (ECQ) A 1–0 90 min.
	Austria A 2–0 90 min. 1 goal
	Holland (ECQ) H 2–0 90 min.
TOTAL	9 appearances, 2 goals
Finland Under-19 appearance	Denmark H 4–1 90 min. 1 goal

Awards/Recognitions: Finnish FA Most Talented Player of the Year

1992

MyPa *Veikkausliiga*	33 appearances, 4th place
Finnish Cup final	MyPa v. Jaro 2–0
Finland full international squad appearance	Tunisia A 1–1 9 min.
Finland Under-21 appearances	Poland A 1–1 90 min.
	Bulgaria (ECQ) H 0–0 90 min.
	Poland H 2–0 90 min.
	Sweden (ECQ) H 1–0 90 min.
	France (ECQ) A 2–1 90 min.
TOTAL	5 appearances
Finland Under-19 appearances	Holland N 2–0 90 min.
	Italy A 0–0 90 min.
	France N 3–2 90 min.
	Spain N 2–0 90 min.
TOTAL	4 appearances

Achievements: Finnish Cup title
MyPa starting 11: Mihail Birjukov, Sami Hyypiä, Janne Mäkelä, Esa Pekonen (1 goal), Mika Viljanen, Yrjö Happonen (72. Tomi Kinnunen), Janne Lindberg, Jari Litmanen (1 goal), Jukka Koskinen, Jukka Turunen, Mauri Keskitalo (84. Sipi Savolainen)

1993

MyPa *Veikkausliiga*	12 appearances, 2nd place
Finnish Cup	Quarter-final MyPa v. HJK 0–1
Cup-Winners' Cup	Qualifying round MyPa v. Valur A 1–3 45 min.
Finland Under-21	
appearances	Bulgaria (ECQ) A 1–3 90 min.
	Austria (ECQ) H 2–0 90 min. 1 goal
	Israel (ECQ) H 1–0 90 min.
	Austria (ECQ) A 2–2 90 min.
	France (ECQ) H 0–1 90 min.
	Sweden (ECQ) A 0–4 90 min.
	Israel (ECQ) A 1–2 90 min. 1 goal
TOTAL	7 appearances, 2 goals

Achievements: 2nd place in the Finnish Premier League
MyPa squad: Mihail Birjukov, Juha Hasu, Yrjö Happonen, Ilpo Hellsten, Toni Huttunen, Sami Hyypiä, Mauri Keskitalo, Tomi Kinnunen, Jukka Koskinen, Saku Laaksonen, Janne Lindberg, Janne Mäkelä, Esa Pekonen, Marko Rajamäki, Anders Roth, Jukka Turunen, Mika Viljanen, James Beattie, Darrell Duffy, Marko Helkala, Jarkko Koskinen, Sergej Nejman, Santos

1994

MyPa *Veikkausliiga*	25 appearances, 5 goals, 2nd place
Finnish Cup	Sixth round MP v. MyPa 7–6 on penalties (2–2)
Finnish League Cup	Semi-final MyPa v. HJK 2–3
UEFA Cup qualifying	
round	Inter Bratislava A 3–0 90 min.
	Inter Bratislava H 0–1 90 min.
UEFA Cup first round	Boavista A 1–2 90 min.
	Boavista H 1–1 90 min.
TOTAL	4 appearances
Finland full international	
squad appearances	Estonia A 7–0 90 min.
	Spain A 0–2 90 min.
TOTAL	2 appearances
Finland Under-21	
appearances	Zambia N 1–1 90 min.
	India A 4–1 90 min.
	Iran N 1–2 90 min.
	Sweden H 1–4 90 min.
	Scotland (ECQ) H 1–0 90 min.
	Greece (ECQ) A 4–3 90 min. 1 goal
	Germany A 1–2 90 min. 1 goal
	San Marino (ECQ) H 4–0 90 min. 1 goal
TOTAL	8 appearances, 3 goals

Achievements: 2nd place in the Finnish Premier League
MyPa squad: Petri Jakonen, Niclas Grönholm, Toni Huttunen, Sami Hyypiä, Joonas Kolkka, Jukka Koskinen, Saku Laaksonen, Janne Lehtinen, Janne Lindberg, Janne Mäkelä, Marko Rajamäki, Anders Roth, Petri Tiainen, Mika Viljanen, Ilpo Hellsten, Mika Hernesniemi, Mauri Keskitalo, Jarkko Koskinen

SAMI HYYPIÄ

Awards/Recognitions: Finnish FA Best Player of the Under-21 National Team

1995

MyPa *Veikkausliiga*	26 appearances, 3 goals, 2nd place
Finnish Cup final	MyPa v. FC Jazz 1–0

2nd place in group B of the Finnish League Cup

UEFA Cup qualifying round	Motherwell A 3–1 90 min.
	Motherwell H 0–2 90 min.
UEFA Cup first round	PSV Eindhoven H 1–1 90 min.
	PSV Eindhoven A 1–7 90 min.
TOTAL	4 appearances
Finland full international squad appearances	Trinidad & Tobago A 2–2 90 min.
	San Marino (ECQ) A 2–0 8 min.
	Faeroe islands (ECQ) A 4–0 90 min.
	Turkey H 0–0 70 min.
TOTAL	4 appearances
Finland Under-21 appearances	San Marino (ECQ) A 6–0 45 min. 2 goals
	Denmark H 1–0 90 min. 1 goal
	Greece (ECQ) H 1–0 90 min.
	Russia (ECQ) H 1–1 90 min.
	Scotland (ECQ) A 0–5 90 min.
	Russia (ECQ) A 0–3 90 min.
TOTAL	6 appearances, 3 goals

Achievements: Finnish Cup title
MyPa starting 11: Petri Jakonen, Mika Viljanen, Sami Hyypiä (1 goal), Sami Mahlio, Antti Pohja, Petri Tiainen, Anders Roth, Mauri Keskitalo (65. Mika Hernesniemi), Niclas Grönholm, Jukka Koskinen, Toni Huttunen

2nd place in the Finnish Premier League
MyPa squad: Petri Jakonen, Vesa Vuorinen, Tommi Kautonen, Mika Viljanen, Sami Hyypiä, Jarkko Koskinen, Sami Mahlio, Antti Pohja, Petri Tiainen, Anders Roth, Mauri Keskitalo, Niclas Grönholm, Jukka Koskinen, Mika Hernesniemi, Toni Huttunen, Joonas Kolkka, Ilpo Hellsten, Jukka Lindström

Awards/Recognitions: Finnish FA Best Player of the Under-21 National Team

1995–96

Willem II *Eredivisie*	14 appearances, 12th place

1996

Finland full international squad appearances	France A 0–2 90 min.
	Turkey H 1–2 76 min.
	Latvia A 0–0 90 min.
	Hungary (WCQ) A 0–1 90 min.
	Switzerland (WCQ) H 2–3 9 min.
TOTAL	5 appearances

SAMI HYYPIÄ

1996–97

Willem II *Eredivisie*	30 appearances, 1 goal, 15th place
Dutch Cup	Semi-final Roda JC v. Willem II 1–0

1997

Finland full international

squad appearances	Azerbaijan (WCQ) A 2–1 90 min.
	Norway (WCQ) A 1–1 3 min.
	Azerbaijan (WCQ) H 3–0 90 min.
	Hungary (WCQ) H 1–1 90 min.
TOTAL	4 appearances

1997–98

Willem II *Eredivisie*	30 appearances, 0 goals, 5th place
Dutch cup	Third round FC Twente v. Willem II 1–0

1998

Finland full international

squad appearances	Scotland A 1–1 90 min.
	Germany H 0–0 90 min.
	France H 0–1 90 min.
	Slovakia A 0–0 90 min.
	Moldova (ECQ) H 3–2 90 min.
	Northern Ireland (ECQ) A 0–1 90 min.
	Turkey (ECQ) A 3–1 90 min.
TOTAL	7 appearances

1998–99

Willem II *Eredivisie*	26 appearances, 2 goals, 2nd place
Dutch Cup	Second round Willem II v. FC Zwolle 0–2
UEFA Cup first round	Dinamo Tbilisi H 3–0 90 min.
	Dinamo Tbilisi A 3–0 90 min.
UEFA Cup second round	Real Betis H 1–1 70 min.
	Real Betis A 0–3 90 min.
TOTAL	4 appearances

Achievements: *Eredivisie*, 2nd place
Willem II squad: Jim van Fessem, Reinder Hendriks, Delamo Hill, Sami Hyypiä, Jukka Koskinen, Frank van Kouwen, Joris Mathijsen, Jos van Nieuwstadt, Geoffrey Prommayon, Mark Schenning, Raymond Victoria, Arno Arts, Tomásh Galashek, Huub Loeffen, István Szekér, Marcel Valk, Yassine Abdellaoui, Mariano Bombarda, Jatto Ceesay, Marco Heering, Erwin Hermes, Marino Promes, Adil Ramzi, Ousmane Sanou, Dennis Schulp

1999

Finland full international

squad appearances	Poland N 1–1 90 min.
	Germany A 0–2 90 min.
	Slovenia A 1–1 45 min.
	Turkey (ECQ) H 2–4 90 min.
	Moldova (ECQ) A 0–0 90 min.
	Germany (ECQ) H 1–2 90 min.

SAMI HYYPIÄ

TOTAL   7 appearances, 1 goal

Awards/Recognitions: Finnish FA Player of the Year
Football Player of the Year (selected by the Finnish media)

1999–2000
Liverpool FC FA Carling
   Premiership   38 appearances, 2 goals, 4th place
FA Cup   Fourth round Liverpool FC v. Blackburn 0–1
Worthington Cup   Third round Southampton v. Liverpool FC 2–1

2000
Finland full international
   squad appearances   Wales A 2–1 90 min.
                     Latvia A 0–1 90 min.
                     Norway (NCT) H 3–1 90 min.
                     Albania (WCQ) H 2–1 90 min.
                     Greece (WCQ) A 0–1 90 min.
                     England (WCQ) H 0–0 90 min.
TOTAL   6 appearances

Awards/Recognitions: Football Player of the Year (selected by the Finnish media)

2000–01
Liverpool FC FA
   Premiership   35 appearances, 3 goals, 3rd place
FA Cup final   Liverpool FC v. Arsenal 2–1
Worthington Cup final   Liverpool FC v. Birmingham 5–4 on penalties (1–1)
UEFA Cup first round   Rapid Bucuresti H 0–0 90 min.
UEFA Cup second round   Slovan Liberec A 3–2 90 min.
UEFA Cup third round   Olympiakos A 2–2 90 min.
                        Olympiakos H 2–0 90 min.
UEFA Cup fourth round   Roma A 2–0 90 min.
                        Roma H 0–1 90 min.
UEFA Cup quarter-final FC Porto A 0–0 90 min.
                        FC Porto H 2–0 90 min.
UEFA Cup semi-final   Barcelona A 0–0 90 min.
                        Barcelona H 1–0 90 min.
UEFA Cup final   Liverpool FC v. Alaves N 5–4 (overtime) 116 min.
TOTAL   11 appearances

Achievements: UEFA Cup title
Liverpool FC starting 11: Sander Westerveld, Markus Babbel (1 goal), Jamie
Carragher, Dietmar Hamann, Stéphane Henchoz (56. Vladimir Smicer), Sami
Hyypiä, Steven Gerrard (1 goal), Gary McAllister (1 goal), Emile Heskey (65.
Robbie Fowler, 1 goal), Michael Owen (79. Patrik Berger), Danny Murphy

SAMI HYYPIÄ

FA Cup title
Liverpool FC squad: Sander Westerveld, Markus Babbel, Jamie Carragher, Dietmar Hamann (60. Gary McAllister), Stéphane Henchoz, Sami Hyypiä, Danny Murphy (77. Patrik Berger), Steven Gerrard, Emile Heskey, Michael Owen (2 goals), Vladimir Smicer (77. Robbie Fowler)

Worthington Cup title
Liverpool FC squad: Sander Westerveld, Markus Babbel, Jamie Carragher, Dietmar Hamann, Stéphane Henchoz, Sami Hyypiä, Steven Gerrard (75. Gary McAllister), Vladimir Smicer (82. Nick Barmby), Emile Heskey, Robbie Fowler (1 goal), Igor Biscan (95. Christian Ziege)

2001
Finland full international

squad appearances	Luxemburg A 1–0 45 min.
	England (WCQ) A 1–2 90 min.
	Germany (WCQ) H 2–2 90 min.
	Belgium H 4–1 45 min.
	Albania (WCQ) A 2–0 90 min.
	Greece (WCQ) K 5–1 90 min.
	Germany (WCQ) A 0–0 90 min.
TOTAL	7 appearances

Awards/Recognitions: Finnish FA Player of the Year
Football Player of the Year (selected by the Finnish media)

2001–02

Liverpool FC FA Premiership	37 appearances, 3 goals, 2nd place
FA Charity Shield	Manchester United v. Liverpool FC 1–2
Worthington Cup	Third round Liverpool FC v. Grimsby 1–2
FA Cup	Fourth round Arsenal v. Liverpool FC 0–1
European Supercup	Liverpool FC v. FC Bayern Munich 3–2
UEFA Champions League, 3rd qualifying round	FC Haka A 5–0 90 min. 1 goal
	FC Haka H 4–1 90 min.
TOTAL	2 appearances, 1 goal
UEFA Champions League, First group stage	Boavista H 1–1 90 min.
	Borussia Dortmund A 0–0 90 min.
	Dynamo Kiev H 1–0 90 min.
	Dynamo Kiev A 2–1 90 min.
	Boavista A 1–1 6 min.
Second group stage	Barcelona H 1–3 90 min
	AS Roma V 0–0 90 min.
	Galatasaray H 0–0 90 min.
	Galatasaray V 1–1 90 min.
	Barcelona V 0–0 90 min.
	AS Roma H 2–0 90 min.
Quarter-finals	Bayer Leverkusen H 1–0 90 min. 1 goal
	Bayer Leverkusen A 2–4 90 min.
TOTAL	13 appearances, 1 goal

SAMI HYYPIÄ

Achievements: European Supercup title
Liverpool FC squad: Sander Westerveld, Markus Babbel, Jamie Carragher, Steven Gerrard (66. Igor Biscan), Dietmar Hamann, Stéphane Henchoz, Emile Heskey (1 goal), Sami Hyypiä, Gary McAllister, Michael Owen (1 goal, 83. Robbie Fowler), John Arne Riise (1 goal, 70. Danny Murphy)

FA Charity Shield win
Liverpool FC squad: Sander Westerveld, Markus Babbel, Nick Barmby (72. Igor Biscan), Dietmar Hamann, Stéphane Henchoz, Emile Heskey, Sami Hyypiä, Gary McAllister (1 goal), Danny Murphy (72. Patrik Berger), Michael Owen (1 goal), John Arne Riise (83. Jamie Carragher)

2002–03
Liverpool FC FA

Premiership	36 appearances, 3 goals, 5th place
FA Community Shield	Arsenal v. Liverpool FC 1–0
Worthington Cup final	Liverpool FC v. Manchester United 2–0
FA Cup	Fourth round Liverpool FC v. Crystal Palace 0–2
UEFA Champions League,	
First group stage	Valencia A 0–2 90 min.
	Basel H 1–1 90 min.
	Spartak Moscow H 5–0 90 min. 1 goal
	Spartak Moscow A 3–1 90 min.
	Valencia H 0–1 90 min.
	Basel A 3–3 90 min.
TOTAL	6 appearances, 1 goal
UEFA Cup third round	Vitesse Arnhem A 1–0 90 min.
	Vitesse Arnhem H 1–0 90 min.
UEFA Cup fourth round	Auxerre A 1–0 90 min. 1 goal
	Auxerre H 1–0 90 min.
UEFA Cup fifth round	Celtic A 1–1 90 min.
	Celtic H 0–2 90 min.
TOTAL	6 appearances, 1 goal

Achievements: Worthington Cup title
Liverpool FC squad: Jamie Carragher, El-Hadji Diouf (90. Igor Biscan), Jerzy Dudek, Steven Gerrard (1 goal), Dietmar Hamann, Stephane Henchoz, Emile Heskey (60. Milan Baros; 88. Vladimir Smicer), Sami Hyypiä, Danny Murphy, Michael Owen (1 goal), John Arne Riise

2002
Finland full international

squad appearances	Portugal A 4–1 45 min.
	Latvia H 2–1 90 min.
	Ireland H 0–3 45 min.
	Wales H 0–2 90 min.
	Azerbaijan H 3–0 90 min. 1 goal
	Serbia/Montenegro A 0–2 90 min.
TOTAL	6 appearances, 1 goal

Awards/Recognitions: Finnish Player of the Year
Football Player of the Year (selected by the Finnish media)

SAMI HYYPIÄ

2003
Finland full international
squad appearances   Northern Ireland A 1–0 60 min. 1 goal
                     Italy A 0–2 90 min.
                     Iceland H 3–0 90 min.
                     Norway A 0–2 90 min.
                     Serbia/Montenegro H 3–0 90 min. 1 goal
                     Italy H 0–2 90 min.
TOTAL   6 appearances, 2 goals

Debut matches (league, European cups and national teams):

League debuts:
1st appearance in the Finnish *Veikkausliiga*: 26 April 1992, FC Jazz v. MyPa 0–2
MyPa squad: Mihail Birjukov, Janne Mäkelä, Sami Hyypiä, Esa Pekonen, Jukka
Koskinen, Mika Viljanen, Jari Litmanen, Yrjö Happonen, Janne Lindberg, Sipi
Savolainen (67. Mauri Keskitalo), Jukka Turunen

1st appearance in the Dutch *Eredivisie*: 9 February 1996, Willem II v. Vitesse 0–5
Willem II squad: Jimmy van Fessem, Marc Latupeirissa, John Feskens, Dave
Smits (80. Sami Hyypiä), Adri Bogers, Bert Konterman, Henry van der Vegt, Ron
Vos (46. Marc van Hintum), Jack De Gier, John Lammers, Jatto Ceesay (68. Joonas
Kolkka)

1st appearance in the English Premiership: 7 August 1999, Sheffield Wednesday
v. Liverpool FC 1–2
Liverpool FC squad: Sander Westerveld, Vegard Heggem, Dominic Matteo,
Dietmar Hamann (24. David Thompson), Jamie Carragher, Sami Hyypiä, Jamie
Redknapp, Vladimir Smicer, Robbie Fowler (1 goal), Titi Camara (1 goal, 89. Erik
Meijer), Patrik Berger (81. Steve Staunton)

European cup debuts:
1st appearance in European cup competition: the Cup-Winners' Cup, 18 August
1993, Reykjavik, Iceland – Valur v. MyPa 3–1
MyPa squad: Mihail Birjukov, Janne Mäkelä, Mika Viljanen, Jukka Koskinen, Esa
Pekonen, Janne Lindberg, Saku Laaksonen (71. Tomi Kinnunen), Yrjö Happonen
(46. Sami Hyypiä), Anders Roth, Marko Rajamäki (1 goal), Jukka Turunen

1st UEFA Cup appearance: 10 August 1994, Bratislava, Slovakia – Inter Bratislava
v. MyPa 0–3
MyPa squad: Petri Jakonen, Janne Mäkelä, Mika Viljanen, Sami Hyypiä, Jukka
Koskinen, Janne Lindberg, Toni Huttunen, Anders Roth, Marko Rajamäki (1 goal, 80.
Niclas Grönholm), Joonas Kolkka (2 goals), Janne Lehtinen

1st appearance in the UEFA Champions League qualifying rounds: 8 August 2001,
Helsinki, Finland – FC Haka v. Liverpool FC 0–5
Liverpool FC squad: Pegguy Arphexad, Markus Babbel, Patrik Berger, Jamie
Carragher, Steven Gerrard (64. Danny Murphy), Dietmar Hamann, Stéphane
Henchoz, Emile Heskey (1 goal, 72. Robbie Fowler), Sami Hyypiä (1 goal), Jari
Litmanen (58. Gary McAllister), Michael Owen (3 goals)

SAMI HYYPIÄ

1st appearance in the UEFA Champions League: 11 September 2001, Liverpool FC
v. Boavista 1–1
Liverpool FC squad: Jerzy Dudek, Jamie Carragher, Steven Gerrard, Dietmar
Hamann, Stéphane Henchoz, Emile Heskey, Sami Hyypiä, Gary McAllister, Danny
Murphy (71. John Arne Riise), Michael Owen (1 goal), Grégory Vignal

National team debuts:
1st ever national team appearance: the Finland Under-18 team, 23 March 1991,
Santargancelo – Finland v. Yugoslavia 0–0
Finland squad: Teuvo Moilanen, Janne Laine, Sami Hyypiä, Petri Kokko, Sasu
Iivonen, Kimmo Repo, Teemu Ingi (80. Janne Oinas), Johan Bergström, Tomi
Leivo-Jokimäki, Jani Myllyniemi (75. Jukka Heikkilä), Johan Ekroth (71. Arto
Partanen)

1st Finland Under-19 appearance: 30 October 1991, Vantaa, Finland – Finland v.
Denmark 4–1
Finland squad: Antti Niemi, Ville Nylund (87. Harri Ylönen), Antti Heinola, Sami
Mahlio (79. Marko Helin), Mika Walldén, Sami Hyypiä (1 goal), Mika Nurmela (1
goal, 85. Janne Lehtinen), Juha Karvinen, Sami Ristilä, Rami Nieminen, Jani
Suikkanen (2 goals, 75. Harri Korhonen)

1st Finland Under-21 appearance: 8 April 1992, Mlawa, Poland – Poland v. Finland
1–1
Finland squad: Antti Niemi, Ville Nylund, Antti Heinola, Sami Mahlio (23. Tommi
Kautonen), Mika Walldén, Sami Hyypiä, Jari Sulander (76. Kai Nyyssönen),
Marko Helin, Antti Sumiala (1 goal), Mika Nurmela, Jokke Kangaskorpi

1st appearance with the full international squad: 7 November 1992, Tunis –
Tunisia v. Finland 1–1
Finland squad: Antti Niemi, Jari Kinnunen, Aki Hyryläinen, Markku Kanerva,
Ilkka Remes, Pasi Tauriainen (82. Sami Hyypiä), Jari Litmanen, Ari Hjelm (1
goal), Petri Järvinen, Jari Vanhala (66. Jari Rinne), Antti Sumiala (55. Mika
Nurmela)

First goals (league, European cups and national teams):

League matches:
1st goal in the Finnish *Veikkausliiga:* 8 May 1994, MyPa v. HJK 1–1
MyPa squad: Petri Jakonen, Janne Mäkelä, Mika Viljanen, Sami Hyypiä (1 goal),
Janne Lindberg, Petri Tiainen (62. Anders Roth), Niclas Grönholm, Janne
Lehtinen, Marko Rajamäki, Toni Huttunen, Saku Laaksonen (62. Joonas Kolkka)

1st goal in the Dutch *Eredivisie*: 5 April 1997, Heerenveen v. Willem II 3–1
Willem II squad: Kris Mampaey, Geoffrey Prommayon, Sami Hyypiä (1 goal), John
Feskens, Marc van Hintum, Tomas Galásek, Bert Konterman, Henry van der Vegt
(85. Fernando Derveld), Huub Loeffen (85. Ousmane Sanou), Mark Schenning,
Joonas Kolkka

1st goal in the FA Carling Premiership: 11 September 1999, Liverpool FC v.
Manchester United 2–3

SAMI HYYPIÄ

Liverpool FC squad: Sander Westerveld, Rigobert Song, Dominic Matteo, Jamie Redknapp, Jamie Carragher, Sami Hyypiä (1 goal), Steven Gerrard (64. Vegard Heggem), David Thompson (46. Vladimir Smicer), Robbie Fowler, Titi Camara (64. Michael Owen), Patrik Berger (1 goal)

European cup competition:
1st goal in the UEFA Champions League qualifying round matches: 8 August 2001, Helsinki – FC Haka v. Liverpool FC 0–5

1st goal in the UEFA Champions League: 3 April 2002, Liverpool FC v. Bayer Leverkusen 1–0
Liverpool FC squad: Jerzy Dudek, Jamie Carragher, Sami Hyypiä (1 goal), Stéphane Henchoz, John Arne Riise, Steven Gerrard, Dietmar Hamann, Danny Murphy, Vladimir Smicer (75. Patrik Berger), Emile Heskey, Michael Owen (70. Jari Litmanen)

National teams:
1st goal for Finland, Finland Under-18 national team: 7 August 1991, Riihimäki, Finland – Finland v. Poland 3–0
Finland squad: Tommi Kainulainen (46. Teuvo Moilanen), Lasse Karjalainen (57. Teemu Ingi), Janne Laine, Petri Kokko, Janne Oinas (89. Jukka Heikkilä), Sami Hyypiä (1 goal), Jari Lahtinen (84. Max Peltonen), Jussi Nuorela, Tomi Leivo-Jokimäki, Antti Sumiala (1 goal), Sami Ristilä (1 goal, 76. Kimmo Repo)

1st goal for Finland Under-19 national team: 30 October 1991, Vantaa, Finland – Finland v. Denmark 4–1

1st goal for Finland Under-21 national team: 12 May 1993, Pori, Finland – Finland v. Austria 2–0
Finland squad: Antti Niemi, Marko Helin, Jani Keula, Mika Walldén, Jussi Nuorela, Sami Hyypiä (1 goal), Jari Sulander (79. Kim Lehtonen), Kai Nyyssönen, Antti Sumiala (1 goal), Mika Nurmela, Jokke Kangaskorpi (82. Sami Väisänen)

1st goal for the Finland full international squad: 9 October 1999, Helsinki, Finland – Finland v. Northern Ireland 4–1
Finland squad: Jani Viander, Mika Lehkosuo, Toni Kuivasto, Sami Hyypiä (1 goal), Hannu Tihinen, Jarkko Wiss (86. Simo Valakari), Joonas Kolkka (2 goals), Aki Riihilahti (86. Sami Ylä-Jussila), Mika-Matti Paatelainen, Jari Litmanen, Jonatan Johansson (1 goal)

THE LIVERPOOL WAY
Houllier, Anfield and the New Global Game
John Williams

ISBN 1 84018 709 3
£9.99 (pb)
Now available
156 x 234mm
256pp
Football

In season 2002–03, Liverpool manager Gérard Houllier seemed destined to bring title success back to Anfield after another bout of pre-season spending and an early unbeaten run of form. But doubts soon started to take over as Liverpool's performances at home and in Europe began to crumble. It wasn't long before fans began to question the manager's philosophy and style. Was Houllier a great tactician or a nervous puppet-master? Was his direct way of playing really 'the Liverpool way', mapping a connection right back to Tom Watson's time at the club in the early part of the twentieth century?

The Liverpool Way assesses Houllier's Liverpool and also examines the general state of English football at present. Drawing on exclusive interview material, it charts Houllier's attempt to lead his increasingly global roster of expensive stars to the highest levels of the European game. It concludes by posing serious questions about the future trajectory of European football and the likely role of Houllier and Liverpool FC in the new 'global' era of football.

John Williams has written widely on football and football culture. Previous publications include *Hooligans Abroad, The Roots of Football Hooliganism, Game Without Frontiers, Into the Red* and *Is It All Over: Can Football Survive The Premier League?*

INTO THE RED

Liverpool FC and the Changing Face of English Football

John Williams

ISBN 1 84018 673 9
£7.99 (pb)
Now available
198 x 129mm
240pp
Mainstream Sport

After a decade in the wilderness following the domestic and European glory of the 1970s and '80s, French coach Gérard Houllier has turned around the fortunes of Liverpool FC in the first years of the new millennium. *Into the Red* charts the history of the club, comparing its success under Houllier with that under previous managers, and includes detailed analysis of the triumphs and headline-grabbing events up until the close of season 2001–02. The book features contributions from key members of the current Anfield contingent and, on a broader level, evaluates the state of the contemporary English game and Liverpool FC's place in it.

THE RED REVOLUTION
Liverpool Under Houllier

Conrad Mewton

ISBN 1 84018 627 9
£9.99 (pb)
Now available
234 x 156mm
192pp
Football

Liverpool FC have been reborn under the management of the genial but determined Frenchman, Gérard Houllier. Once more a force to be reckoned with, the Reds won five coveted trophies in 2001 alone.

Each of Houllier's four seasons to date are comprehensively reviewed, examining how he rebuilt the club, bringing renewed glory and silverware, rid it of its 'Spice Boys' image, instilled new disciplines and tactics and fostered home-grown talents such as Michael Owen and Steven Gerrard. Written with the passion and understanding of a genuine football fan, this book provides expert analysis of Houllier and his transformation of Liverpool FC.

Conrad Mewton is a media and sports lawyer and lifelong Liverpool supporter. He is the author of the well-received *Music and the Internet Revolution* and lives in London.

LIVERPOOL'S DREAM TEAM

Stan Hey

ISBN 1 84018 681 X
£7.99 (pb)
Now available
198 x 129mm
192pp
Mainstream Sport

Liverpool's Dream Team is a collection of in-depth interviews with the players involved in taking Liverpool to the pinnacle of the domestic and European game since the 1960s. It encompasses the cream of Bill Shankly's League and Cup-winning side of '64 and '65, the best of the European Cup-winning team of '77, and the legends that led Liverpool to three further European Cup wins, a hat-trick of League titles and four League Cups between 1977 and 1984. There is also analysis of the Anfield stars who have excelled on the pitch in recent years to complete what is a fascinating overview of Liverpool's glory days.

Stan Hey was born in Liverpool and is the author of two novels, *Filling Spaces* and *Sudden Unprovided Death*. He has been a Liverpool supporter since 1960.

NO BALONEY
From Peckham to Las Vegas

Frank Maloney with Kevin Brennan
Introduction by Ricky Gervais

ISBN 1 84018 701 8
£15.99 (hb)
Now available
234 x 156mm
336pp
Biography/Boxing

From the streets of Peckham to the neon-lit strip of Las Vegas, Frank Maloney's life has been a roller-coaster ride that even he finds hard to believe at times. The Cockney-born son of Irish parents, he once harboured thoughts of becoming a priest, but instead went on to manage Lennox Lewis for 12 years and help him become the undisputed heavyweight champion of the world.

In *No Baloney*, Frank lifts the lid on the world of big-time boxing and its household names, and gives a remarkable account of his time with Lewis, revealing stories and offering opinions that can only come from a true insider. He also gives an insight into the way money, sex, drugs, politics, bribery and corruption have played their part in the sport.

But Maloney's story is not just about boxing. It is also about one of life's characters whose colourful past is told with a brand of humour and emotion that makes it compelling reading. Once dubbed a 'Mental Midget' and 'Pugilistic Pigmy' by Don King, he has gone on to have the last laugh over the American promoter and all those who thought he would fail.

BADFELLAS
FIFA Family at War
John Sugden and Alan Tomlinson

ISBN 1 84018 684 4
£7.99 (pb)
Now available
198 x 129mm
288pp
Mainstream Sport

World football's governing body FIFA has claimed
credit for the success of the football World Cup and
the expansion of the world game generally, but
behind the scenes the administration of the world
game is in a shambles. *Badfellas* catalogues FIFA's
expanding fortunes, recurrent crises and internal
rivalries and traces the growth of the World Cup
from its politically driven origins in Uruguay in
1930 to one of the world's most lucrative media
spectacles. It shows how Dr João Havelange and
Sepp Blatter have carved up the riches of the football
bonanza over the last 25 years and details why the
good guys in football's corridors of power find it so
hard to mount any successful challenge to the
badfellas and their legacy.

GOING ORIENTAL
Football after World Cup 2002
Edited by Mark Perryman

ISBN 1 84018 677 1
£7.99 (pb)
Now available
198 x 129mm
208pp
Mainstream Sport

World Cup 2002: there has never been a tournament like it. With an upset arising almost every day, *Going Oriental* explores the event's substantial impact on the world. Has the football world order been changed for good? How will the power struggle in FIFA unfold? And what does the way the English follow their team say about the state of the nation? All of this and more is extensively analysed in a gripping new collection of essays.

Contributors include Simon Kuper, Pete Davis, Jim White, John Williams, Philip Cornwall and Japanese writer Hiroyuki Morita.

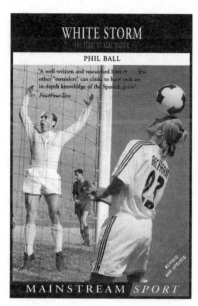

ISBN 1 84018 763 8
£7.99 (pb)
Now available
198 x 129mm
224pp
Mainstream Sport

Barcelona and Manchester United may wish to dispute the observation, but Real Madrid are the world's greatest football club. The team's achievements over the years include twenty-eight League titles, nine European Cups, twelve Spanish Cups, two UEFA Cups and two World Club Championship titles. Their stunning victory in the 2002 Champions League dispelled any lingering doubts as to their supremacy, and set the club up nicely for the century ahead.

The story of Real's first century is, however, much more than the mere sum of its achievements. Behind the shine of the trophies is the darker side of the club's association with fascism, and, more than anything else, almost 30 years after Franco's death Real Madrid still represent the bullish concept of *'Madridismo'* – the idea that nothing really matters outside the solid walls of the Bernabéu.

White Storm charts the history of the club from its foundations to the latest embodiment of *Madridismo* – Raúl, ending with an analysis of the arrival of David Beckham and what it might mean for the future of the club.

PLAYING FOR UNCLE SAM
The Brits' Story of the North American Soccer League
David Tossell

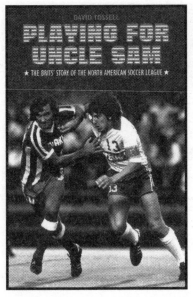

ISBN 1 84018 748 4
£9.99 (pb)
Now available
198 x 129mm
256pp
Football

A coach transported to the field in a hearse as he played dead. An English manager taken at gunpoint to an Argentinian jail after trying to sign that country's World Cup captain. The hero of 1966 who talked his team out of going on strike on the eve of a title decider.

All are part of the British professionals' story of life in the North American Soccer League in the '70s and early '80s, when everyone – from star turn to unsung journeyman – had the chance to play alongside Pelé, Cruyff, Beckenbauer and Eusebio in the greatest galaxy of world stars ever assembled in one league.

To mark the 20th anniversary of the NASL's final season in 1984, *Playing for Uncle Sam* recalls the British players and coaches who were part of an organisation that changed the face of football with its shoot-outs, new offside rule and wacky marketing methods.

Through interviews with many of the British contingent who accepted the offer of the Yankee dollar, including Rodney Marsh and George Best, *Playing For Uncle Sam* recalls one of the most remarkable episodes in football history.

FOOTBALL IN OUR TIME

A Photographic Record of Our National Game

Stuart Clarke

ISBN 1 84018 736 0
£20.00 (hb)
October 2003
250 x 250mm
240pp
Football

Stuart Clarke's photography captures the passion, comedy and beauty that is at the heart of modern British football culture. His work spans the whole of the game, from landmark internationals and the glamour of the Premiership to the sparse dressing-rooms of the lower divisions and the non-league games played to only a handful of supporters. He has been active as a photographer during an era that has seen the sport subject to enormous change, a time when grounds like Burnden Park and The Dell have become memories and the English and Scottish leagues have been flooded with foreign talent.

Football In Our Time brings together 14 years of Clarke's best photography, selected himself from his vast collection. It successfully represents the camaraderie of football, the thrill of the match, the agony of defeat and the special affection that bonds people to their clubs. It is an intimate and thought-provoking collection that will be enjoyed by anyone caught up in the culture of the modern game, as well as people with an interest in art, photography and social documentary.

ATHENS TO ATHENS
The Official History of the Olympic Games and the IOC, 1894–2004

David Miller

ISBN I 84018 587 2
£35.00 (hb)
October 2003
280 x 230mm
528pp
Sport

Athens to Athens is the first full account of the history of the Olympic Games since its inception in 1894. It is the lavishly illustrated, chronological story of the re-creation of the Games by Pierre de Coubertin, of the often tempestuous and controversial fortunes of the governing body, together with the highs and lows of the Games themselves.

It also tells the story of the historic competitors – from Spyridon Louis (the inaugural Marathon winner) and such heroes as Jim Thorpe, Paavo Nurmi, Sonja Henie, Jesse Owens, Fanny Blankers-Koen, Kip Keino, Mark Spitz, Franz Klammer and Carl Lewis, through to Steve Redgrave and Kathy Freeman. Detailed background is provided to the many crises – the Nazi Games of 1936; the terrorist slaughter of Israelis at the 1972 Munich Games; the boycotts; the new commercialism from 1984 onwards; the advent of professionals from 1988; and the ongoing threat of drug abuse.

As the sporting world awaits, with eager expectation, the Games' return in 2004 to the country of their ancient origins, *Athens to Athens* provides the definitive document of one of the world's most famous sporting festivals.